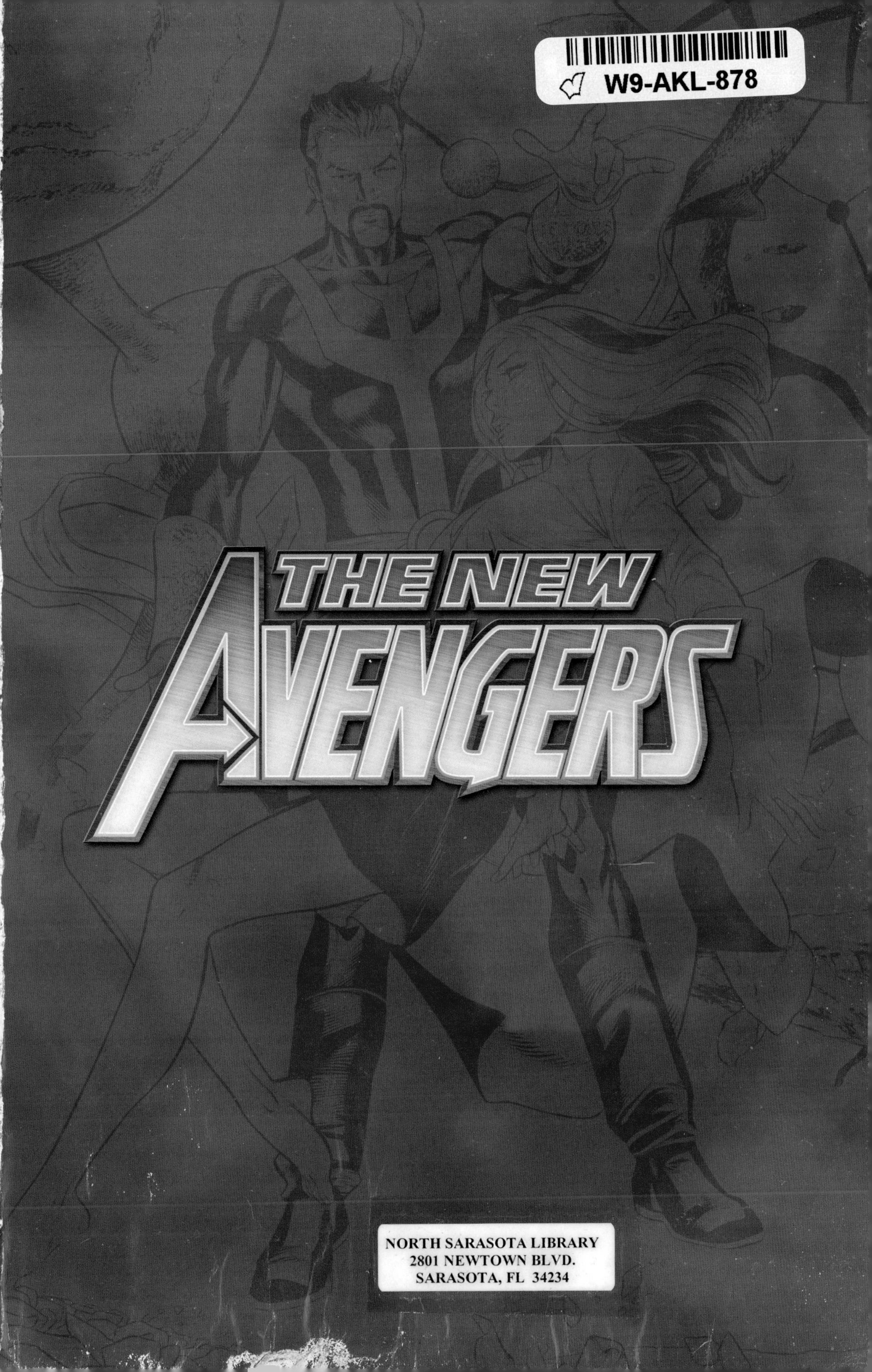
THE NEW
AVENGERS

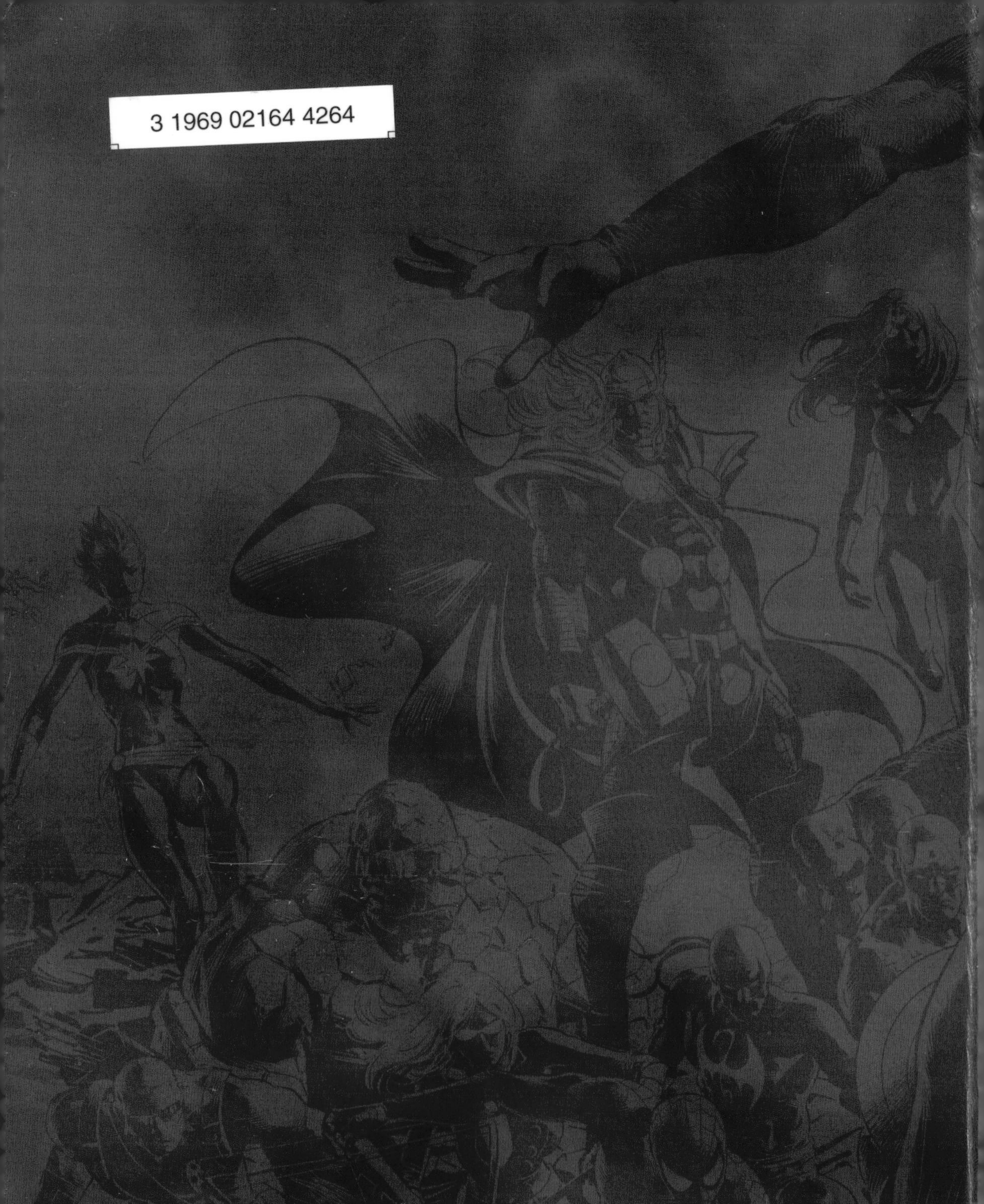

Collection Editor: JENNIFER GRÜNWALD • Assistant Editors: ALEX STARBUCK & NELSON RIBEIRO
Editor, Special Projects: MARK D. BEAZLEY • Senior Editor, Special Projects: JEFF YOUNGQUIST • Senior Vice President of Sales: DAVID GABRIEL
SVP of Brand Planning & Communications: MICHAEL PASCIULLO

Editor in Chief: AXEL ALONSO • Chief Creative Officer: JOE QUESADA • Publisher: DAN BUCKLEY • Executive Producer: ALAN FINE

NEW AVENGERS BY BRIAN MICHAEL BENDIS VOL. 5. Contains material originally published in magazine form as NEW AVENGERS #31-34. First printing 2013. Hardcover ISBN# 978-0-7851-6158-5. Softcover ISBN# 978-0-7851-6159-2. Published by MARVEL WORLDWIDE, INC., a subsidiary of MARVEL ENTERTAINMENT, LLC. OFFICE OF PUBLICATION: 135 West 50th Street, New York, NY 10020. **Printed in the U.S.A.** ALAN FINE, EVP - Office of the President, Marvel Worldwide, Inc. and EVP & CMO Marvel Characters B.V.; DAN BUCKLEY, Publisher & President - Print, Animation & Digital Divisions; JOE QUESADA, Chief Creative Officer; TOM BREVOORT, SVP of Publishing; DAVID BOGART, SVP of Operations & Procurement, Publishing; RUWAN JAYATILLEKE, SVP & Associate Publisher, Publishing; C.B. CEBULSKI, SVP of Creator & Content Development; DAVID GABRIEL, SVP of Publishing Sales & Circulation; MICHAEL PASCIULLO, SVP of Brand Planning & Communications; JIM O'KEEFE, VP of Operations & Logistics; DAN CARR, Executive Director of Publishing Technology; SUSAN CRESPI, Editorial Operations Manager; ALEX MORALES, Publishing Operations Manager; STAN LEE, Chairman Emeritus. For information regarding advertising in Marvel Comics or on Marvel.com, please contact Niza Disla, Director of Marvel Partnerships, at ndisla@marvel.com. For Marvel subscription inquiries, please call 800-217-9158. **Manufactured between 12/24/2012 and 2/11/2013 (hardcover), and 12/24/2012 and 8/5/2013 (softcover), by R.R. DONNELLEY, INC., SALEM, VA, USA.**

10 9 8 7 6 5 4 3 2 1

THE NEW AVENGERS

WRITER
BRIAN MICHAEL BENDIS

ARTIST, #31
MICHAEL GAYDOS
PENCILER, #32
CARLOS PACHECO
INKERS, #32
ROGER MARTINEZ
WITH **CAM SMITH & SCOTT HANNA**
ARTIST, #33
MICHAEL AVON OEMING
ARTIST, #34
MIKE DEODATO
JAM ARTISTS, #34
**CHUCK BB, FAREL DALRYMPLE,
MING DOYLE, LUCY KNISLEY,
BECKY CLOONAN & YVES BIGEREL**
COLOR ARTIST
RAIN BEREDO
LETTERER
VC'S JOE CARAMAGNA
COVER ART
MIKE DEODATO & RAIN BEREDO

ASSISTANT EDITOR
JAKE THOMAS
EDITORS
TOM BREVOORT WITH **LAUREN SANKOVITCH**

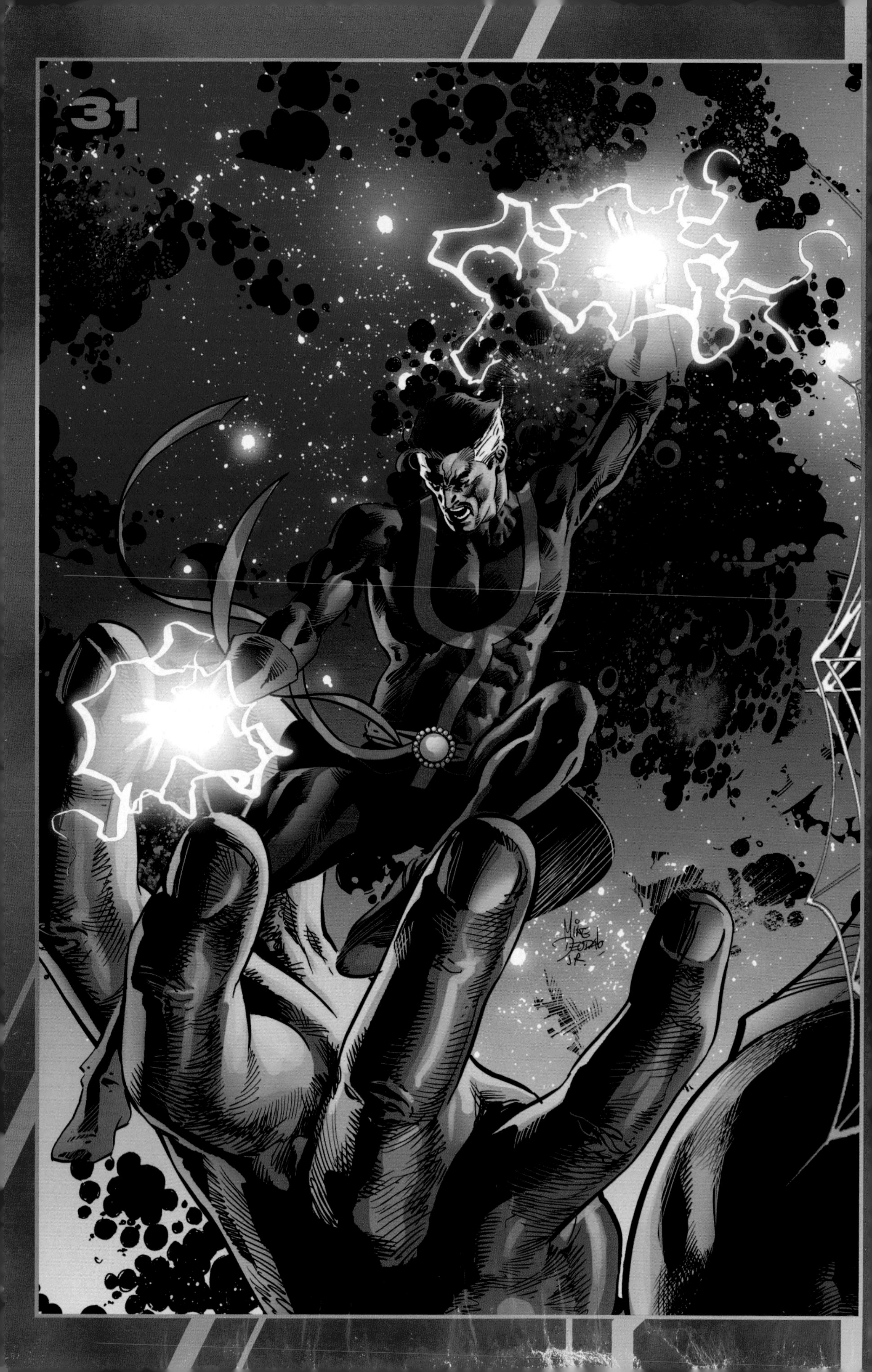
31
MIKE DEODATO JR.

EARTH'S MIGHTIEST HEROES, UNITED AGAINST A COMMON THREAT! ON THAT DAY THE AVENGERS WERE BORN, TO FIGHT FOES THAT NO SINGLE HERO COULD WITHSTAND!

NEW AVENGERS

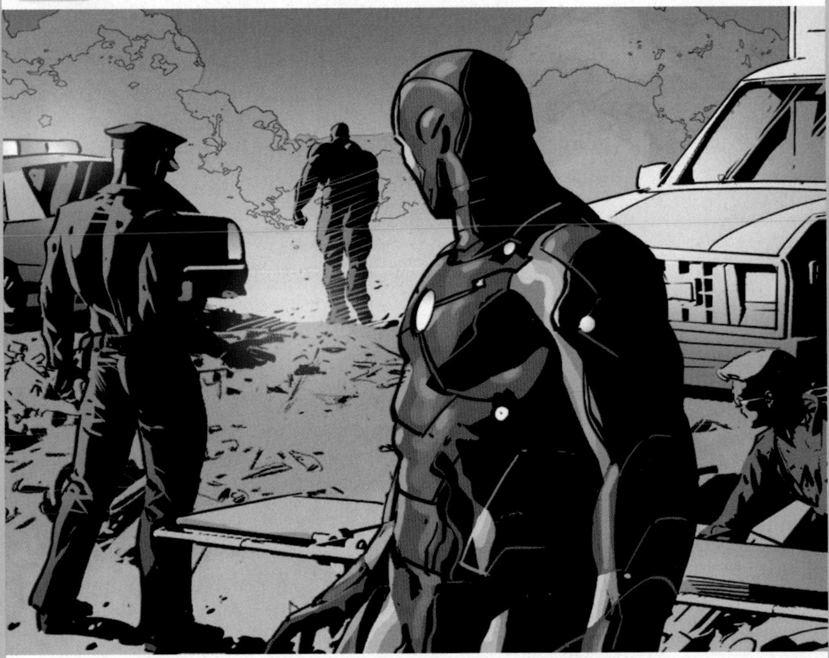

AVENGERS COMMANDER STEVE ROGERS GAVE LUKE CAGE, JESSICA JONES, MS. MARVEL, MOCKINGBIRD, DAREDEVIL, SPIDER-MAN, DR. STRANGE, WOLVERINE, IRON FIST AND THE THING THE KEYS TO AVENGERS MANSION, A LIAISON IN THE CONTROVERSIAL FORM OF VICTORIA HAND, AND FREE REIN TO PROTECT THE WORLD ANY WAY THEY SEE FIT.

THE CATASTROPHIC PHOENIX FORCE RETURNED, EVENTUALLY MANIFESTING FULLY IN THE X-MEN LEADER CYCLOPS, WHO BECAME THE DARK PHOENIX. ALTHOUGH THE AVENGERS ALLIED WITH THE X-MEN TO STOP CYCLOPS AND DISPEL THE PHOENIX FORCE, IT PROVED ONE BRUSH WITH A WORLD-DESTROYING FORCE TOO MANY FOR TEAM LEADER AND NEW FAMILY MAN LUKE CAGE, WHO HAS OPTED TO LEAVE THE TEAM.

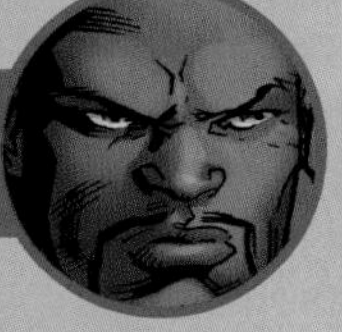
LUKE CAGE

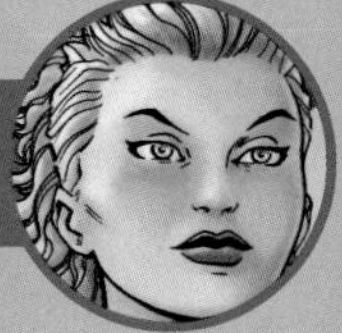
CAPTAIN MARVEL

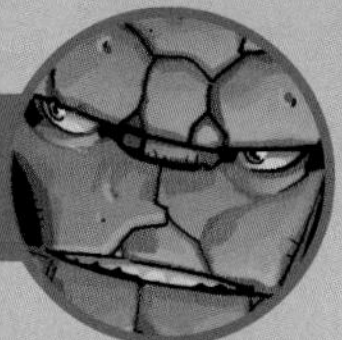
THING

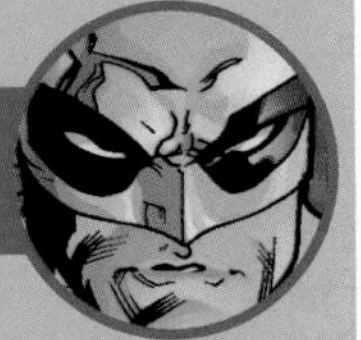
IRON FIST

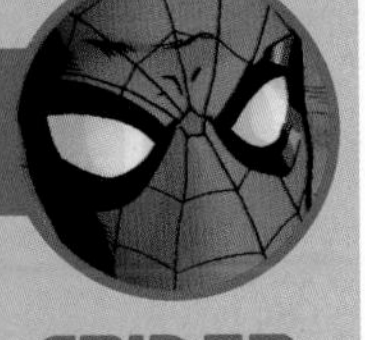
SPIDER-MAN

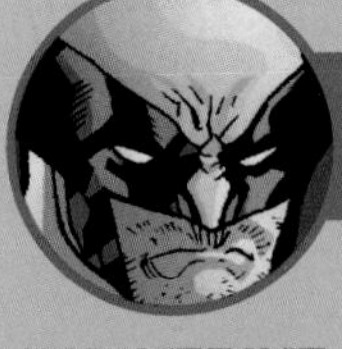
WOLVERINE

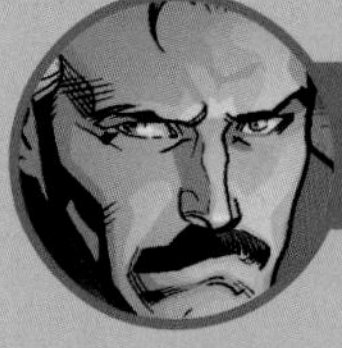
DR. STRANGE

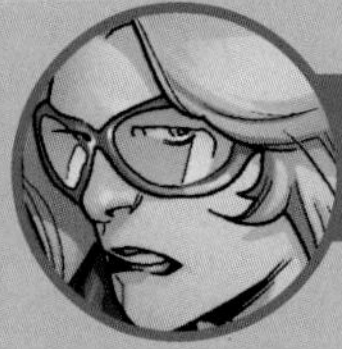
MOCKINGBIRD

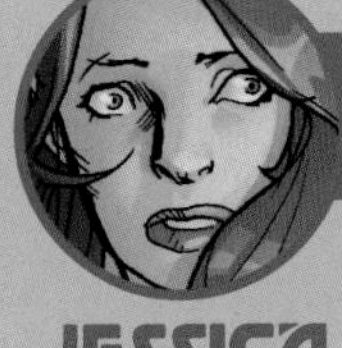
JESSICA JONES

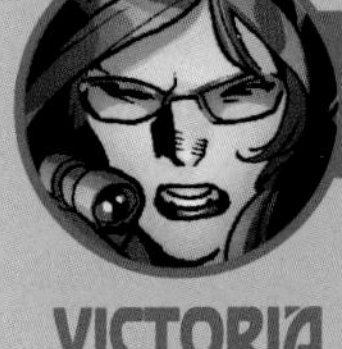
VICTORIA HAND

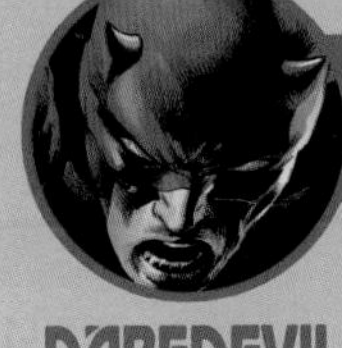
DAREDEVIL

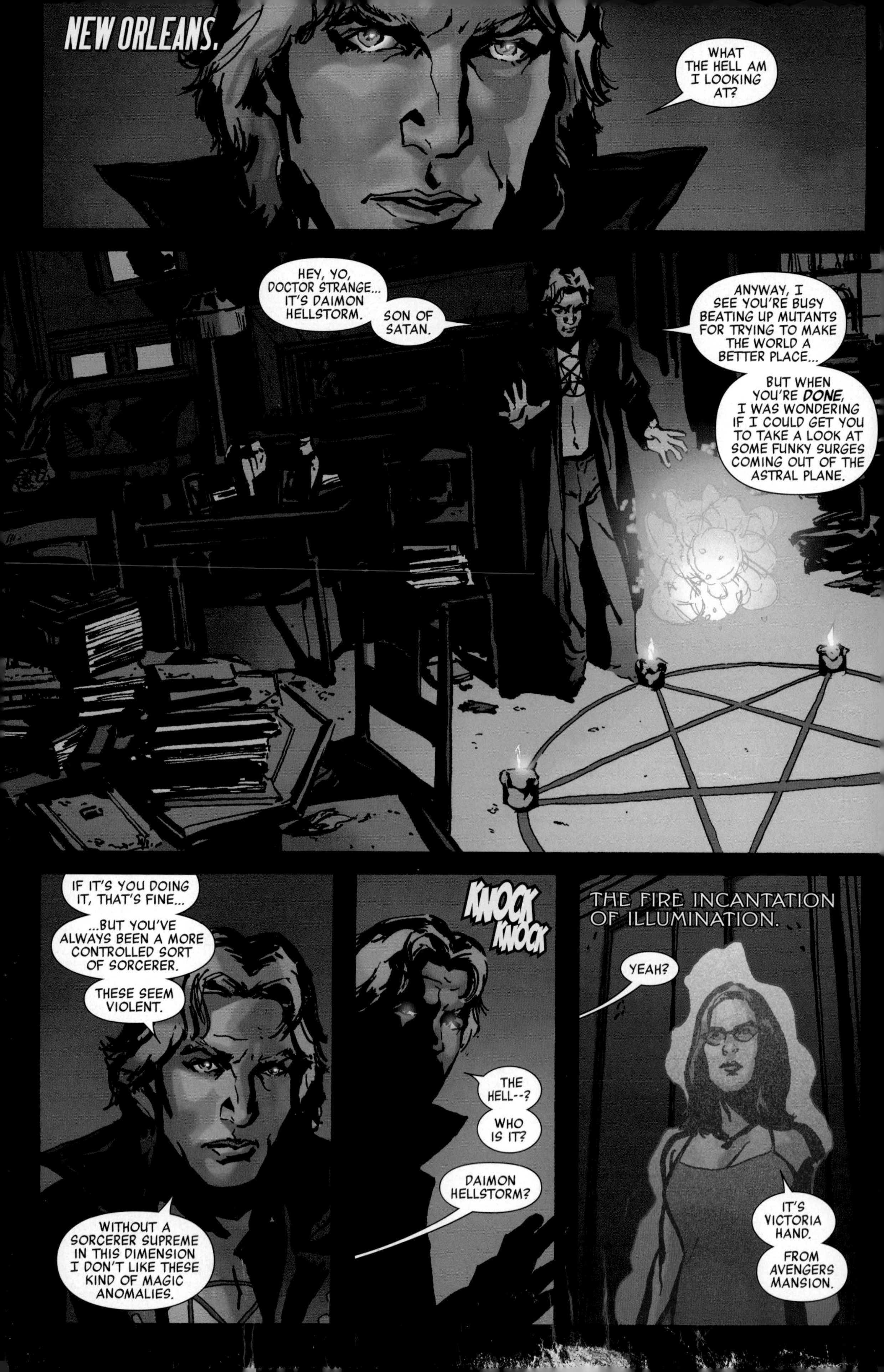
NEW ORLEANS.
WHAT THE HELL AM I LOOKING AT?
HEY, YO, DOCTOR STRANGE... IT'S DAIMON HELLSTORM.
SON OF SATAN.
ANYWAY, I SEE YOU'RE BUSY BEATING UP MUTANTS FOR TRYING TO MAKE THE WORLD A BETTER PLACE...
BUT WHEN YOU'RE DONE, I WAS WONDERING IF I COULD GET YOU TO TAKE A LOOK AT SOME FUNKY SURGES COMING OUT OF THE ASTRAL PLANE.
IF IT'S YOU DOING IT, THAT'S FINE...
...BUT YOU'VE ALWAYS BEEN A MORE CONTROLLED SORT OF SORCERER.
THESE SEEM VIOLENT.
WITHOUT A SORCERER SUPREME IN THIS DIMENSION I DON'T LIKE THESE KIND OF MAGIC ANOMALIES.
KNOCK KNOCK
THE HELL--?
WHO IS IT?
DAIMON HELLSTORM?
THE FIRE INCANTATION OF ILLUMINATION.
YEAH?
IT'S VICTORIA HAND.
FROM AVENGERS MANSION.

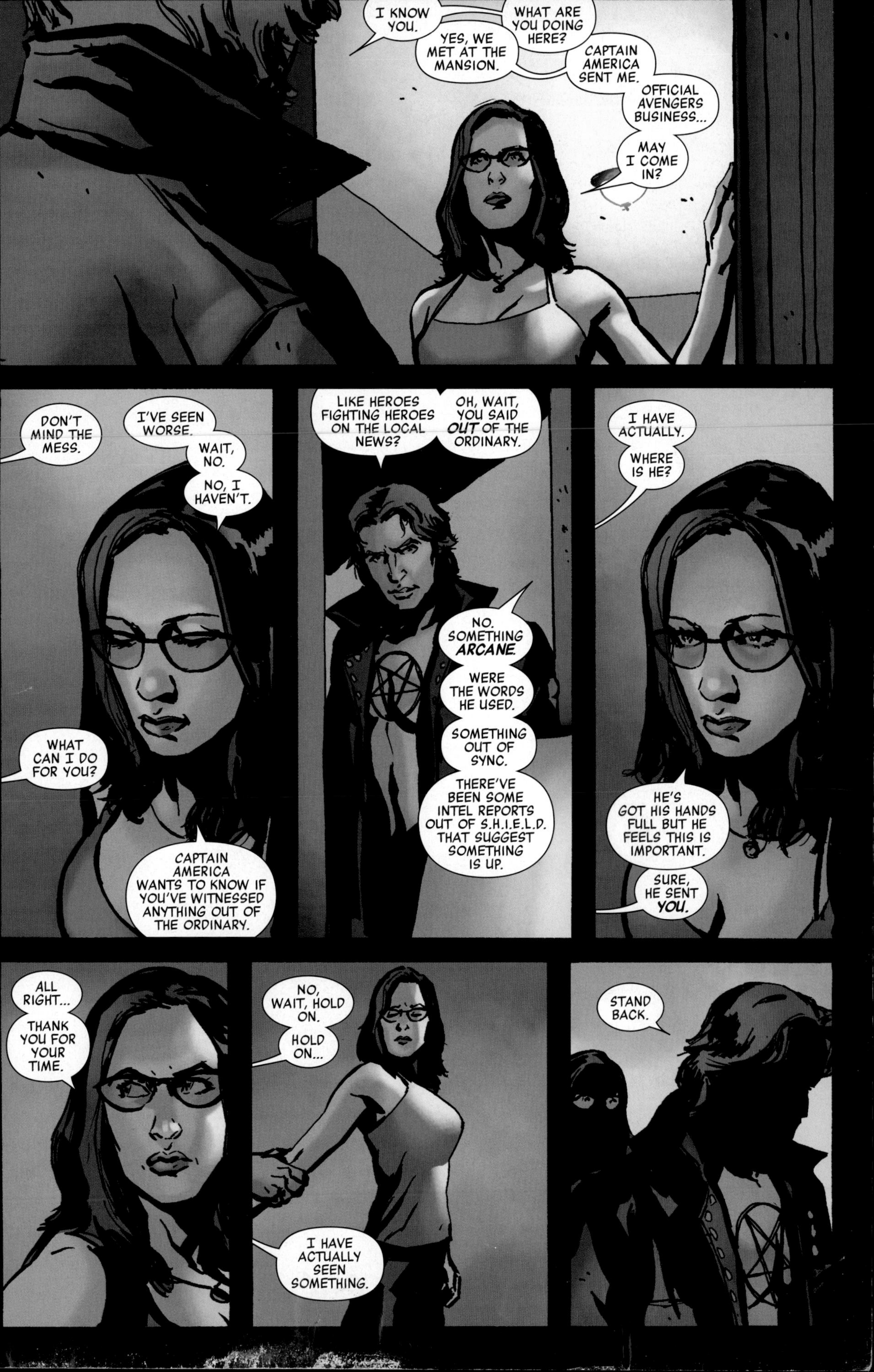
I KNOW YOU.
WHAT ARE YOU DOING HERE?
YES, WE MET AT THE MANSION.
CAPTAIN AMERICA SENT ME.
OFFICIAL AVENGERS BUSINESS...
MAY I COME IN?
DON'T MIND THE MESS.
I'VE SEEN WORSE.
WAIT, NO.
NO, I HAVEN'T.
WHAT CAN I DO FOR YOU?
CAPTAIN AMERICA WANTS TO KNOW IF YOU'VE WITNESSED ANYTHING OUT OF THE ORDINARY.
LIKE HEROES FIGHTING HEROES ON THE LOCAL NEWS?
OH, WAIT, YOU SAID *OUT* OF THE ORDINARY.
NO. SOMETHING ***ARCANE***.
WERE THE WORDS HE USED.
SOMETHING OUT OF SYNC.
THERE'VE BEEN SOME INTEL REPORTS OUT OF S.H.I.E.L.D. THAT SUGGEST SOMETHING IS UP.
I HAVE ACTUALLY.
WHERE IS HE?
HE'S GOT HIS HANDS FULL BUT HE FEELS THIS IS IMPORTANT.
SURE, HE SENT ***YOU***.
ALL RIGHT...
THANK YOU FOR YOUR TIME.
NO, WAIT, HOLD ON.
HOLD ON...
I HAVE ACTUALLY SEEN SOMETHING.
STAND BACK.

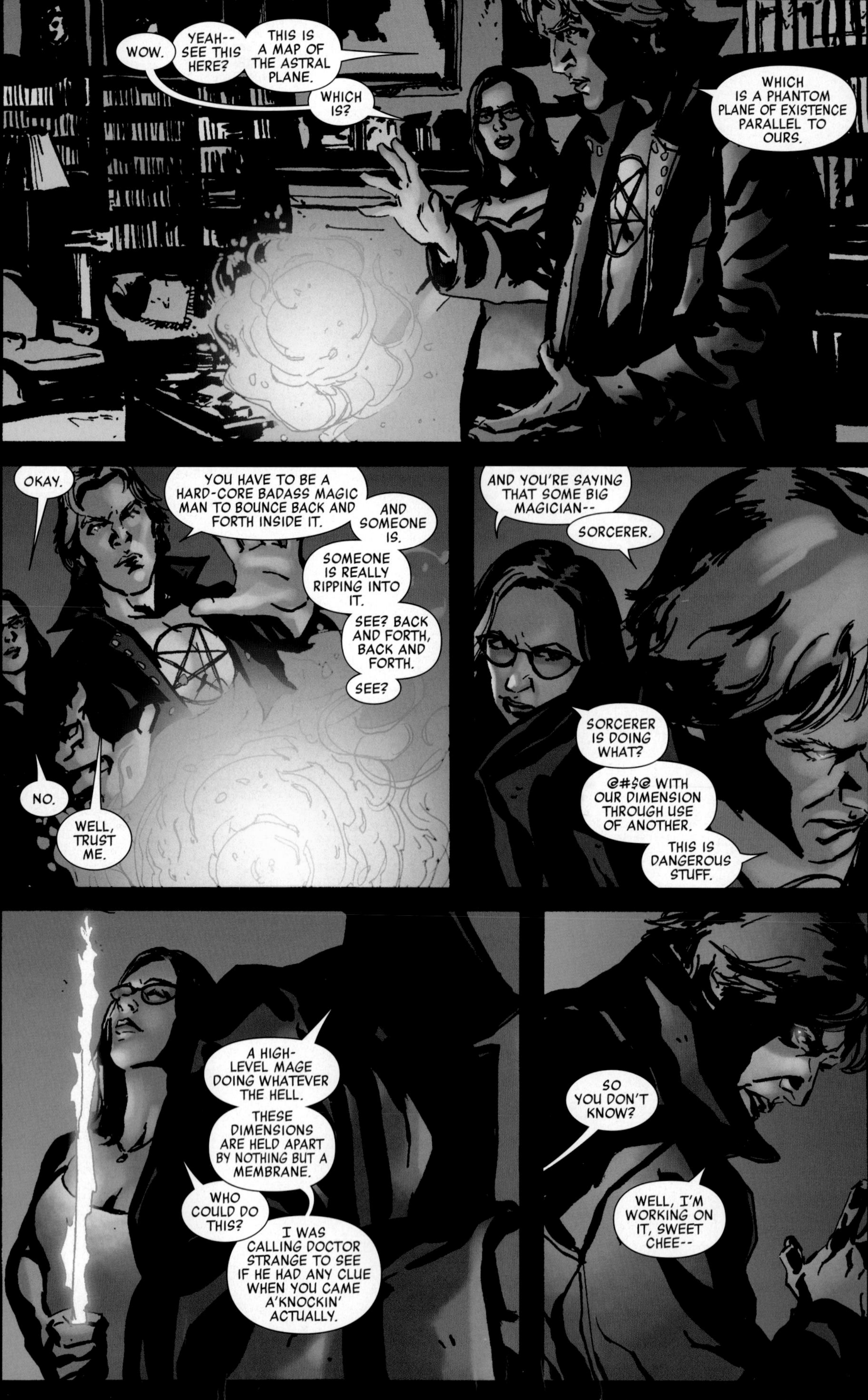
WOW.
YEAH-- SEE THIS HERE?
THIS IS A MAP OF THE ASTRAL PLANE.
WHICH IS?
WHICH IS A PHANTOM PLANE OF EXISTENCE PARALLEL TO OURS.
OKAY.
YOU HAVE TO BE A HARD-CORE BADASS MAGIC MAN TO BOUNCE BACK AND FORTH INSIDE IT.
AND SOMEONE IS.
SOMEONE IS REALLY RIPPING INTO IT.
SEE? BACK AND FORTH, BACK AND FORTH.
SEE?
NO.
WELL, TRUST ME.
AND YOU'RE SAYING THAT SOME BIG MAGICIAN--
SORCERER.
SORCERER IS DOING WHAT?
@#$@ WITH OUR DIMENSION THROUGH USE OF ANOTHER.
THIS IS DANGEROUS STUFF.
A HIGH-LEVEL MAGE DOING WHATEVER THE HELL.
THESE DIMENSIONS ARE HELD APART BY NOTHING BUT A MEMBRANE.
WHO COULD DO THIS?
I WAS CALLING DOCTOR STRANGE TO SEE IF HE HAD ANY CLUE WHEN YOU CAME A'KNOCKIN' ACTUALLY.
SO YOU DON'T KNOW?
WELL, I'M WORKING ON IT, SWEET CHEE--

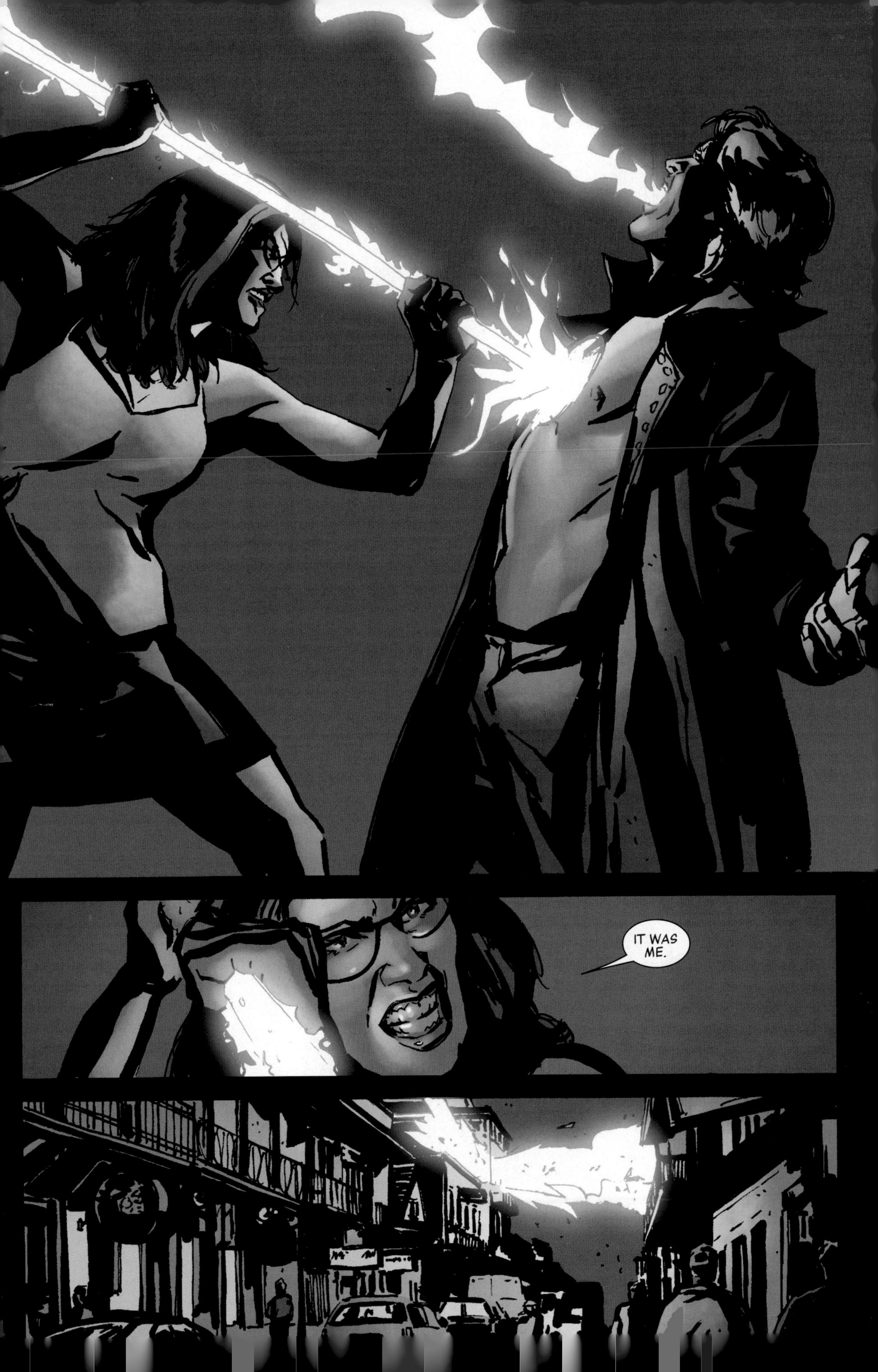
IT WAS ME.

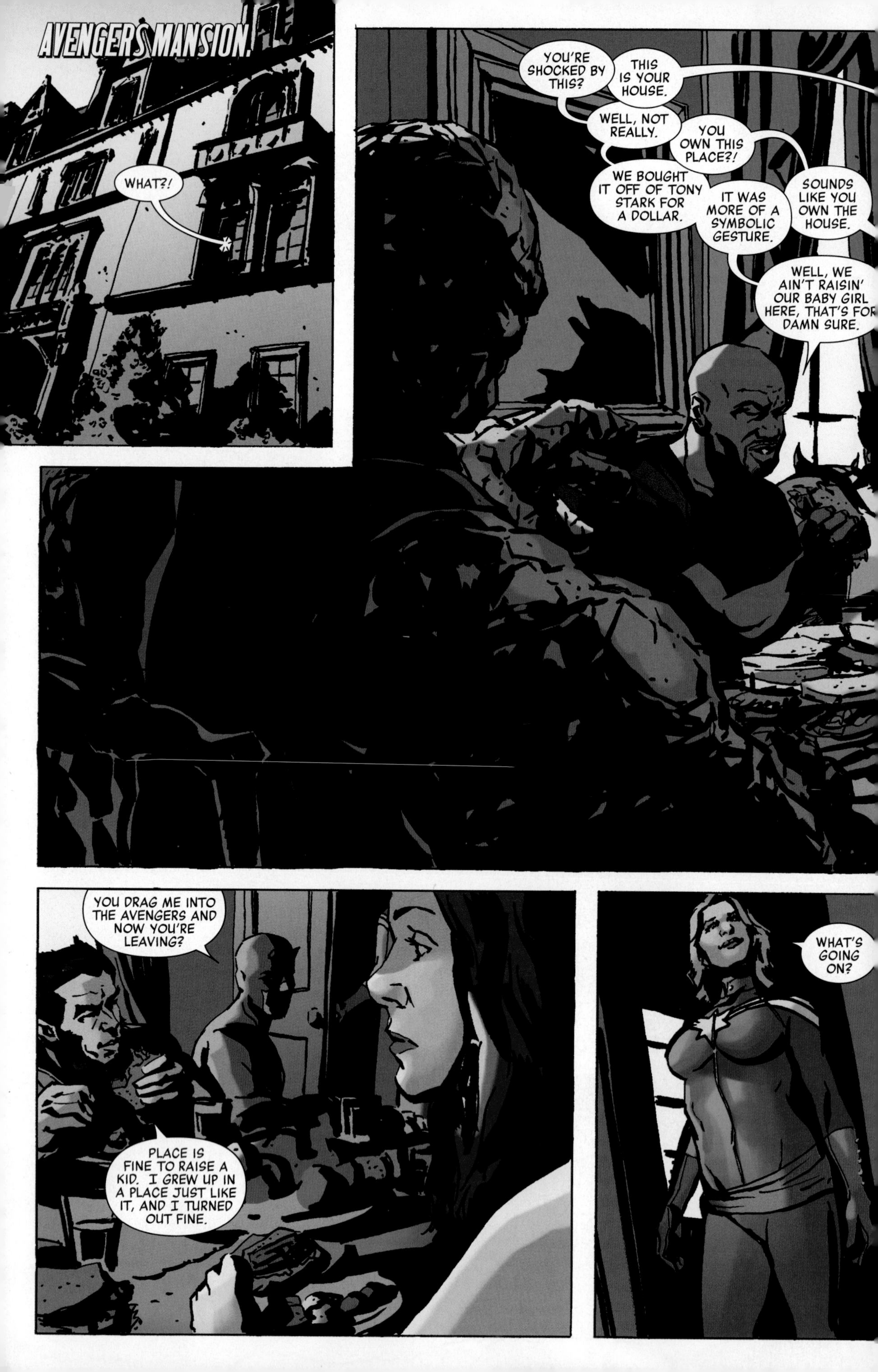
AVENGERS MANSION.
WHAT?!
YOU'RE SHOCKED BY THIS?
THIS IS YOUR HOUSE.
WELL, NOT REALLY.
YOU OWN THIS PLACE?!
WE BOUGHT IT OFF OF TONY STARK FOR A DOLLAR.
IT WAS MORE OF A SYMBOLIC GESTURE.
SOUNDS LIKE YOU OWN THE HOUSE.
WELL, WE AIN'T RAISIN' OUR BABY GIRL HERE, THAT'S FOR DAMN SURE.
YOU DRAG ME INTO THE AVENGERS AND NOW YOU'RE LEAVING?
PLACE IS FINE TO RAISE A KID. I GREW UP IN A PLACE JUST LIKE IT, AND I TURNED OUT FINE.
WHAT'S GOING ON?

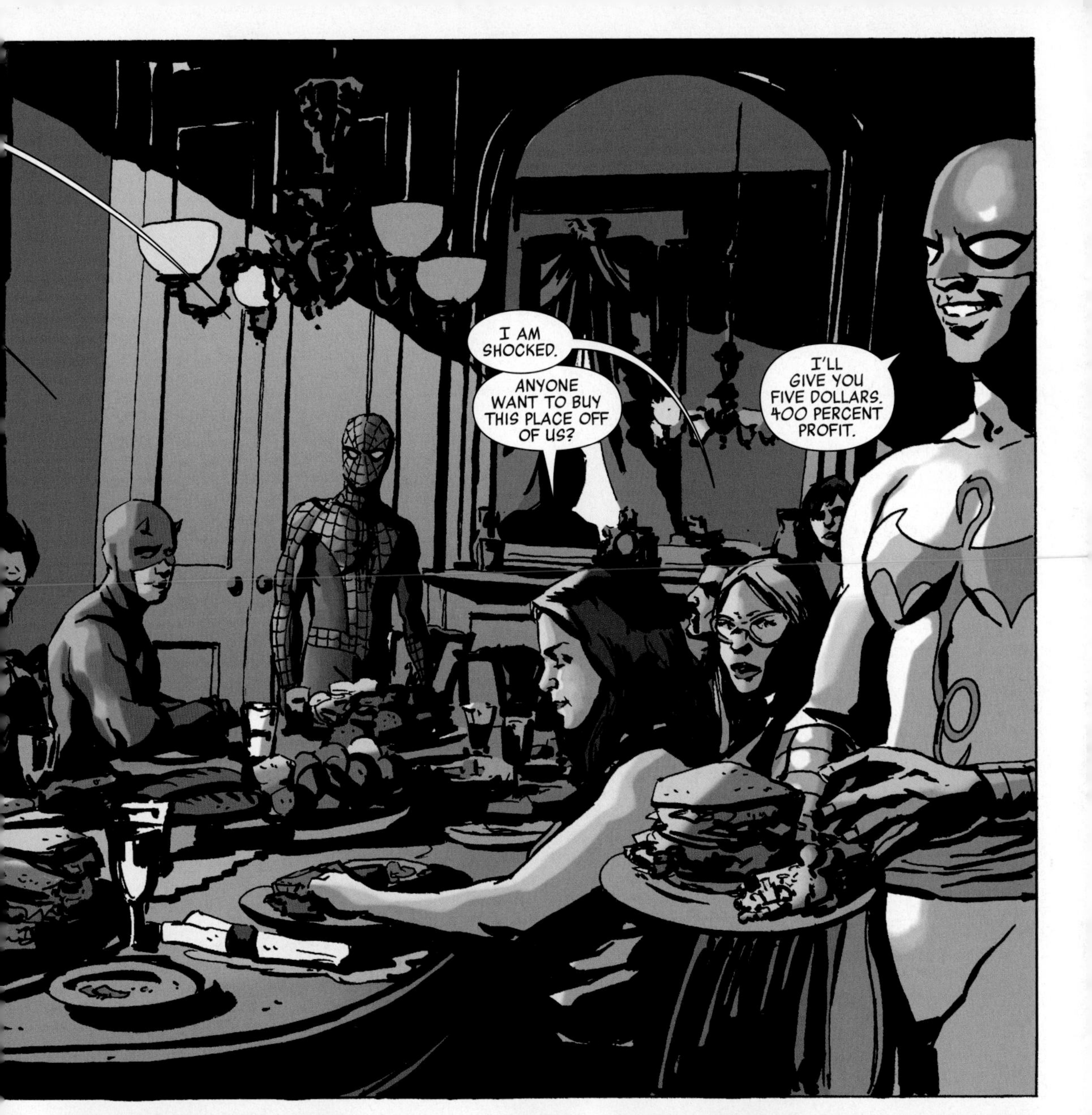
I AM SHOCKED.
ANYONE WANT TO BUY THIS PLACE OFF OF US?
I'LL GIVE YOU FIVE DOLLARS. 400 PERCENT PROFIT.

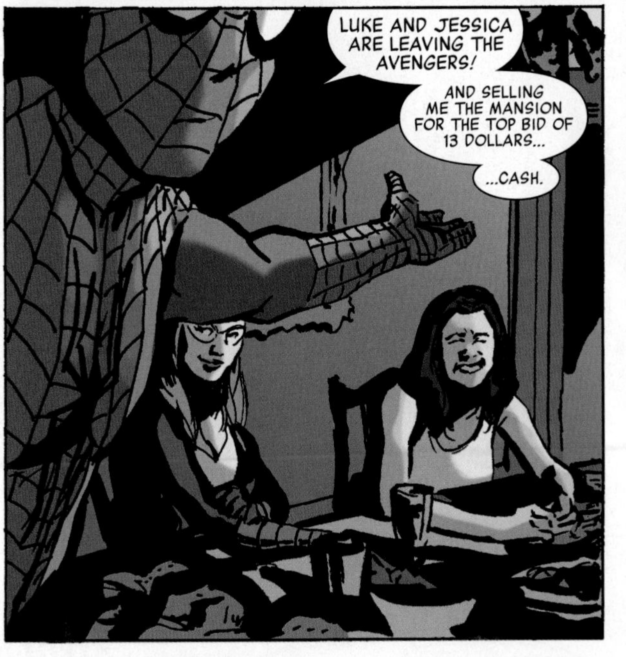
LUKE AND JESSICA ARE LEAVING THE AVENGERS!
AND SELLING ME THE MANSION FOR THE TOP BID OF 13 DOLLARS...
...CASH.

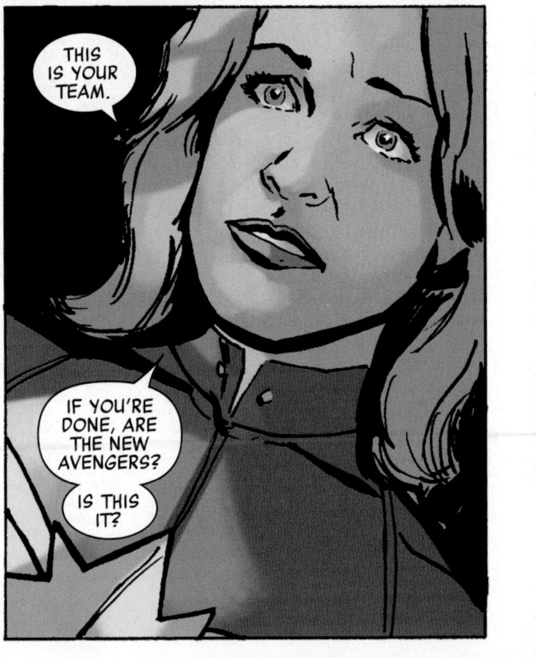
THIS IS YOUR TEAM.
IF YOU'RE DONE, ARE THE NEW AVENGERS?
IS THIS IT?

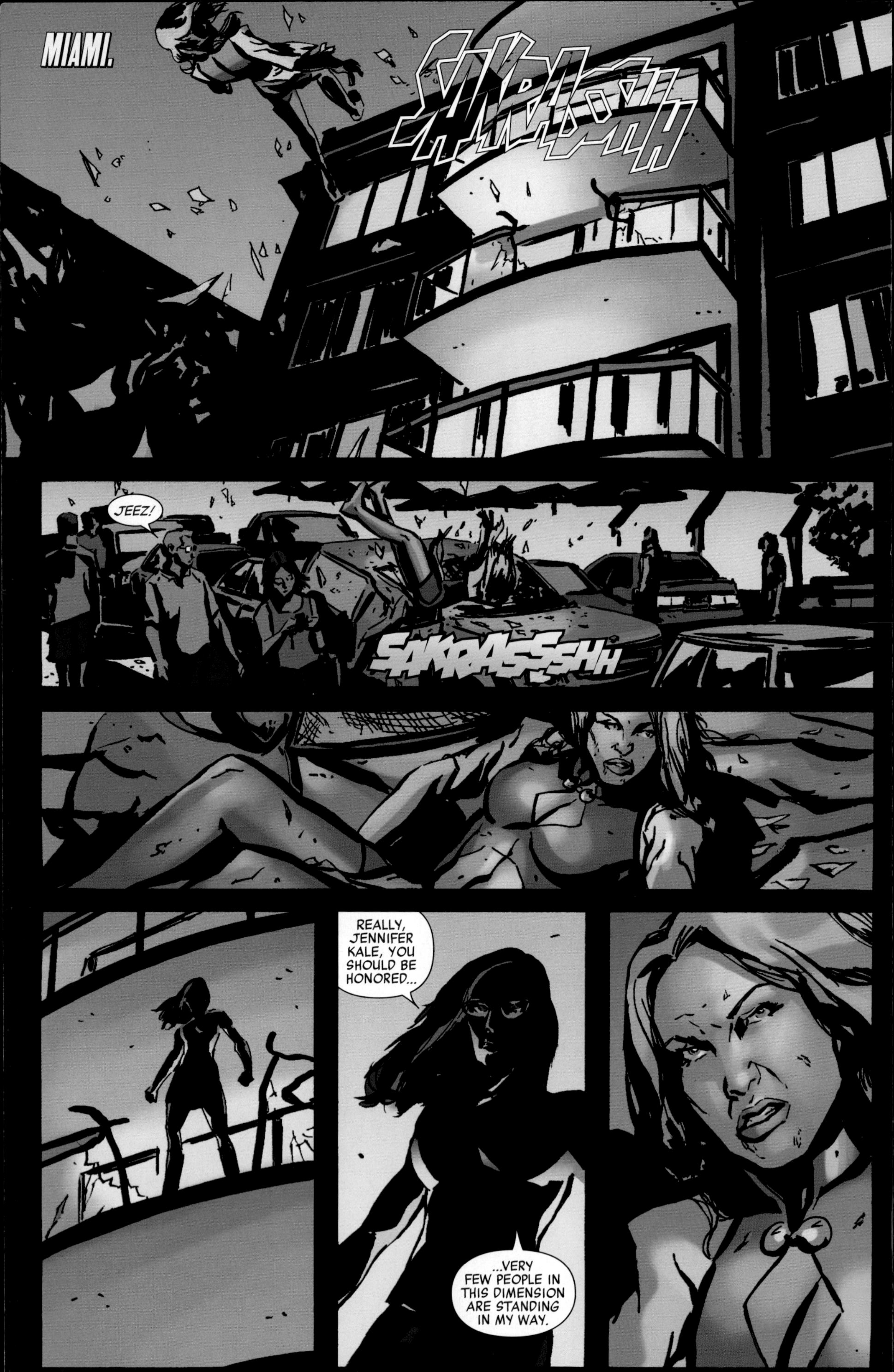
MIAMI.
JEEZ!
SAKRASSSHH
REALLY, JENNIFER KALE, YOU SHOULD BE HONORED...
...VERY FEW PEOPLE IN THIS DIMENSION ARE STANDING IN MY WAY.

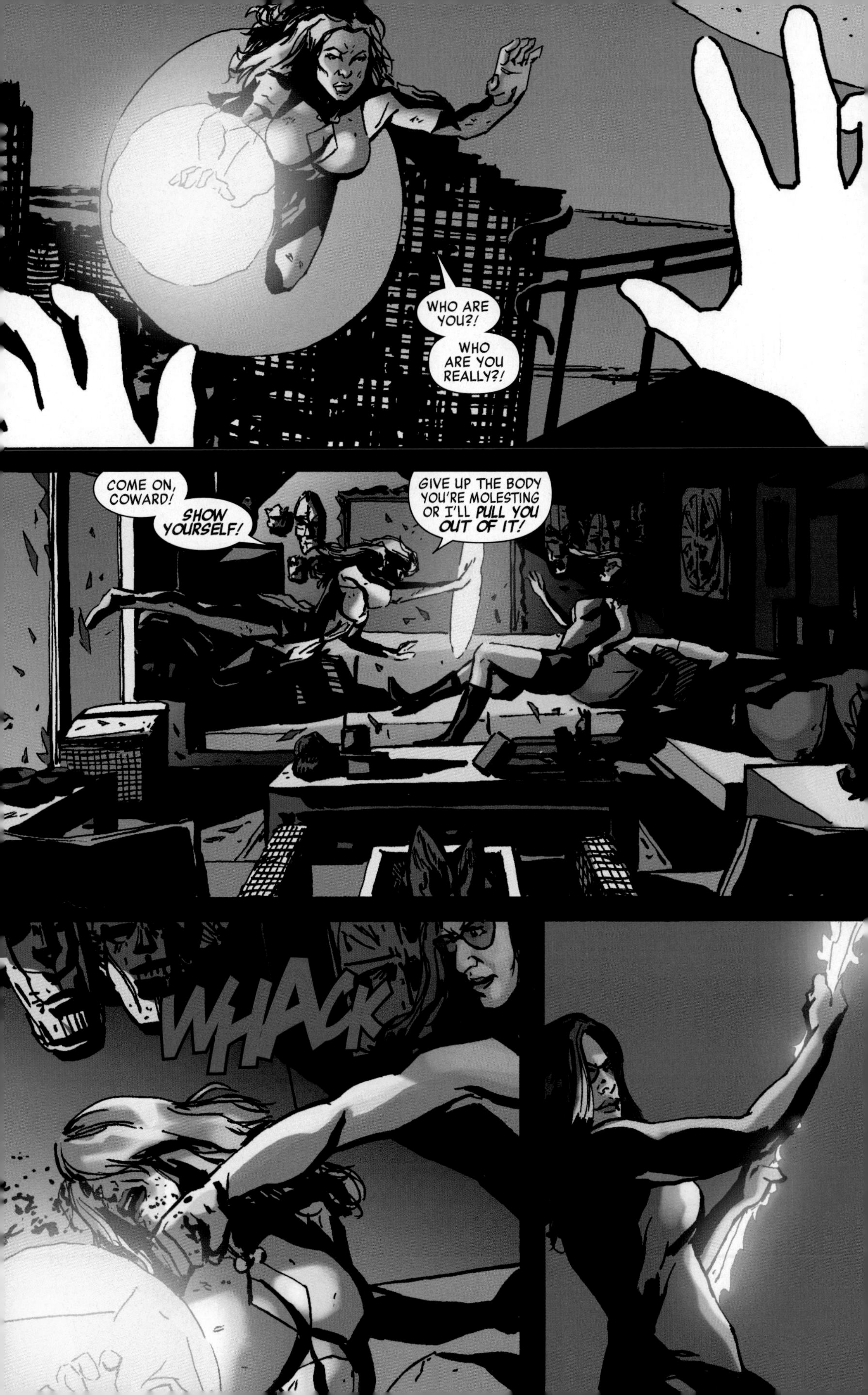
WHO ARE YOU?!
WHO ARE YOU REALLY?!
COME ON, COWARD! SHOW YOURSELF!
GIVE UP THE BODY YOU'RE MOLESTING OR I'LL PULL YOU OUT OF IT!
WHACK

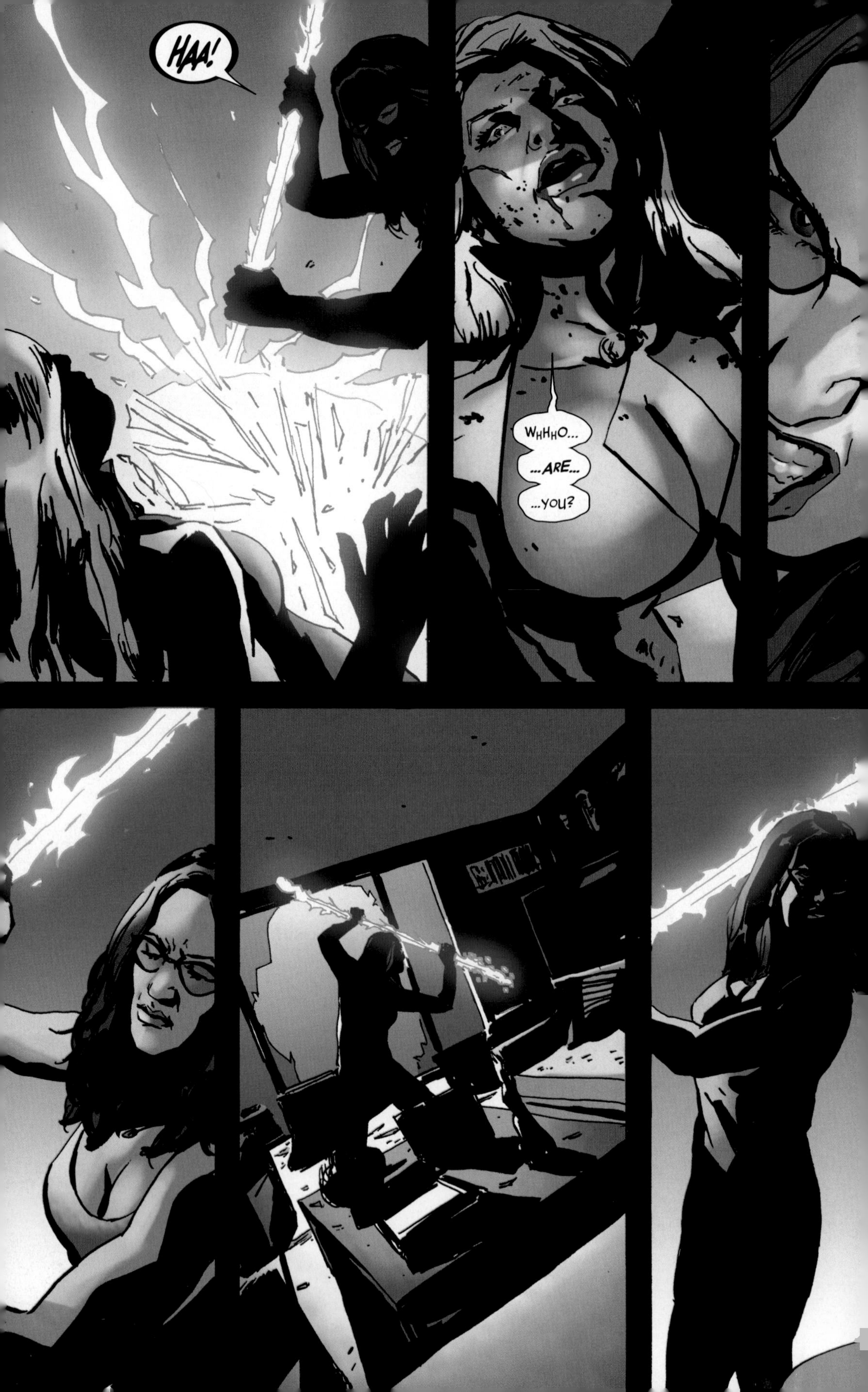
HAA!
WHHHO...
...ARE...
...YOU?

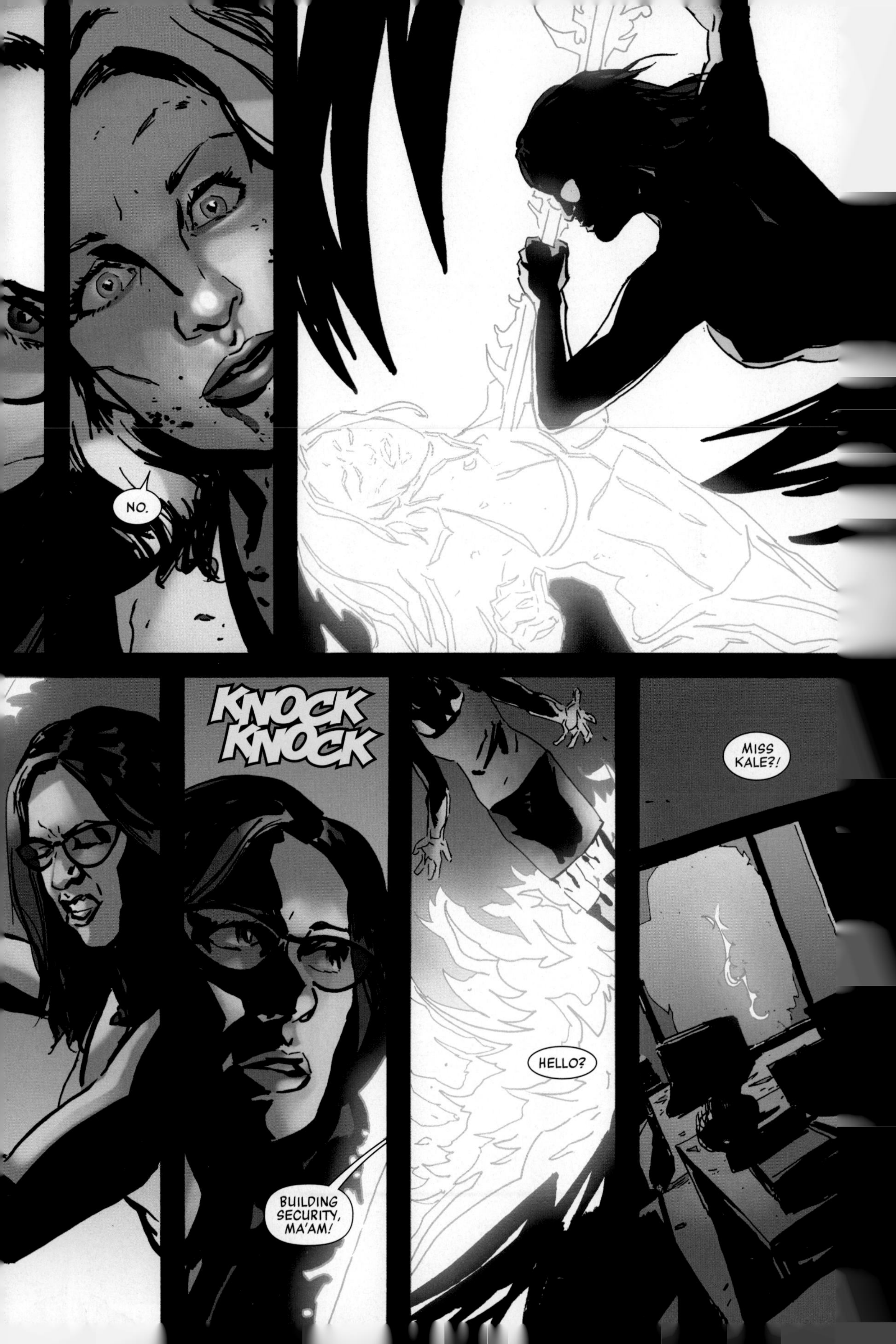
NO.
KNOCK KNOCK
BUILDING SECURITY, MA'AM!
HELLO?
MISS KALE?!

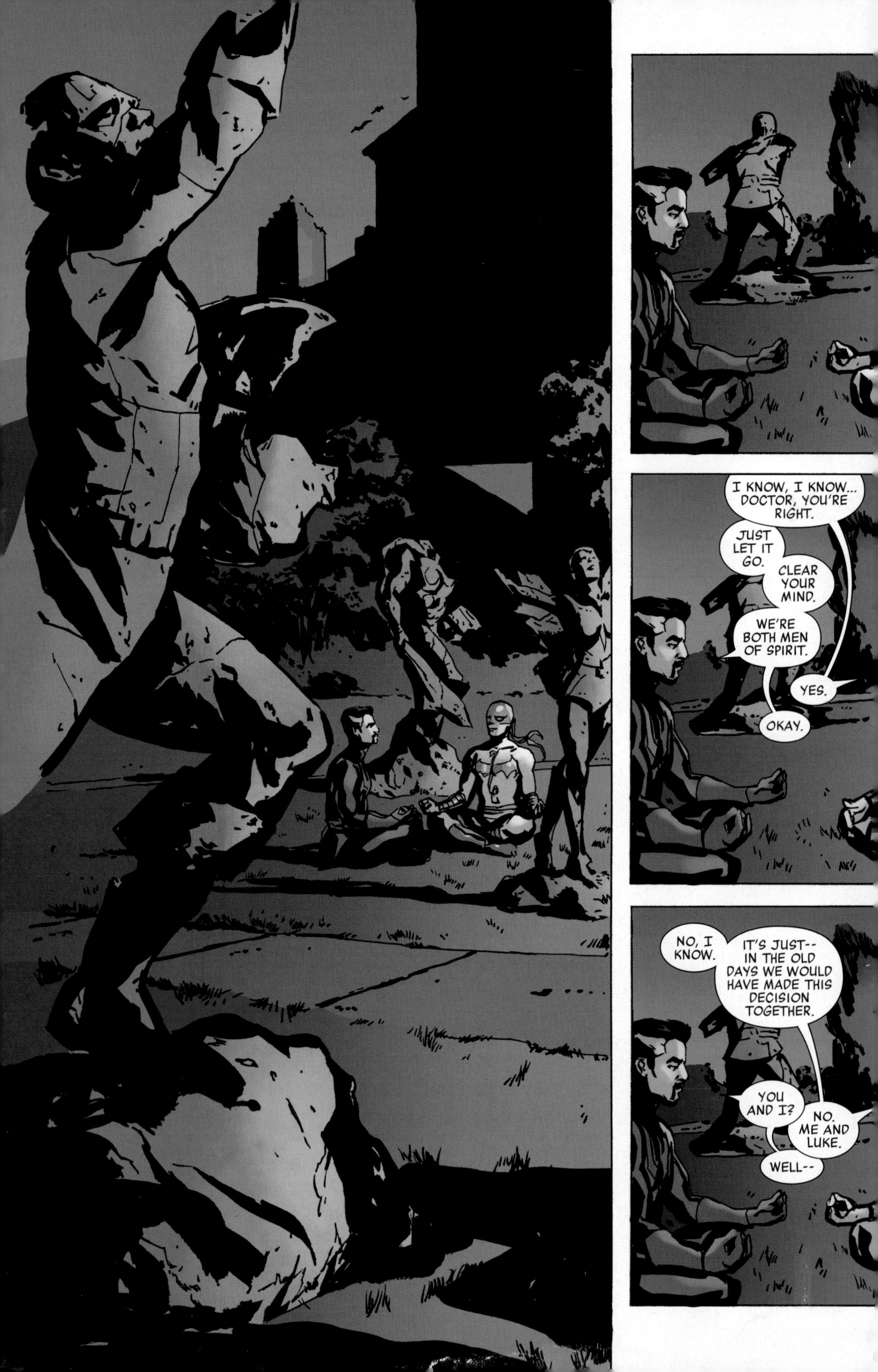
I KNOW, I KNOW... DOCTOR, YOU'RE RIGHT.
JUST LET IT GO.
CLEAR YOUR MIND.
WE'RE BOTH MEN OF SPIRIT.
YES.
OKAY.
NO, I KNOW.
IT'S JUST-- IN THE OLD DAYS WE WOULD HAVE MADE THIS DECISION TOGETHER.
YOU AND I?
NO. ME AND LUKE.
WELL--

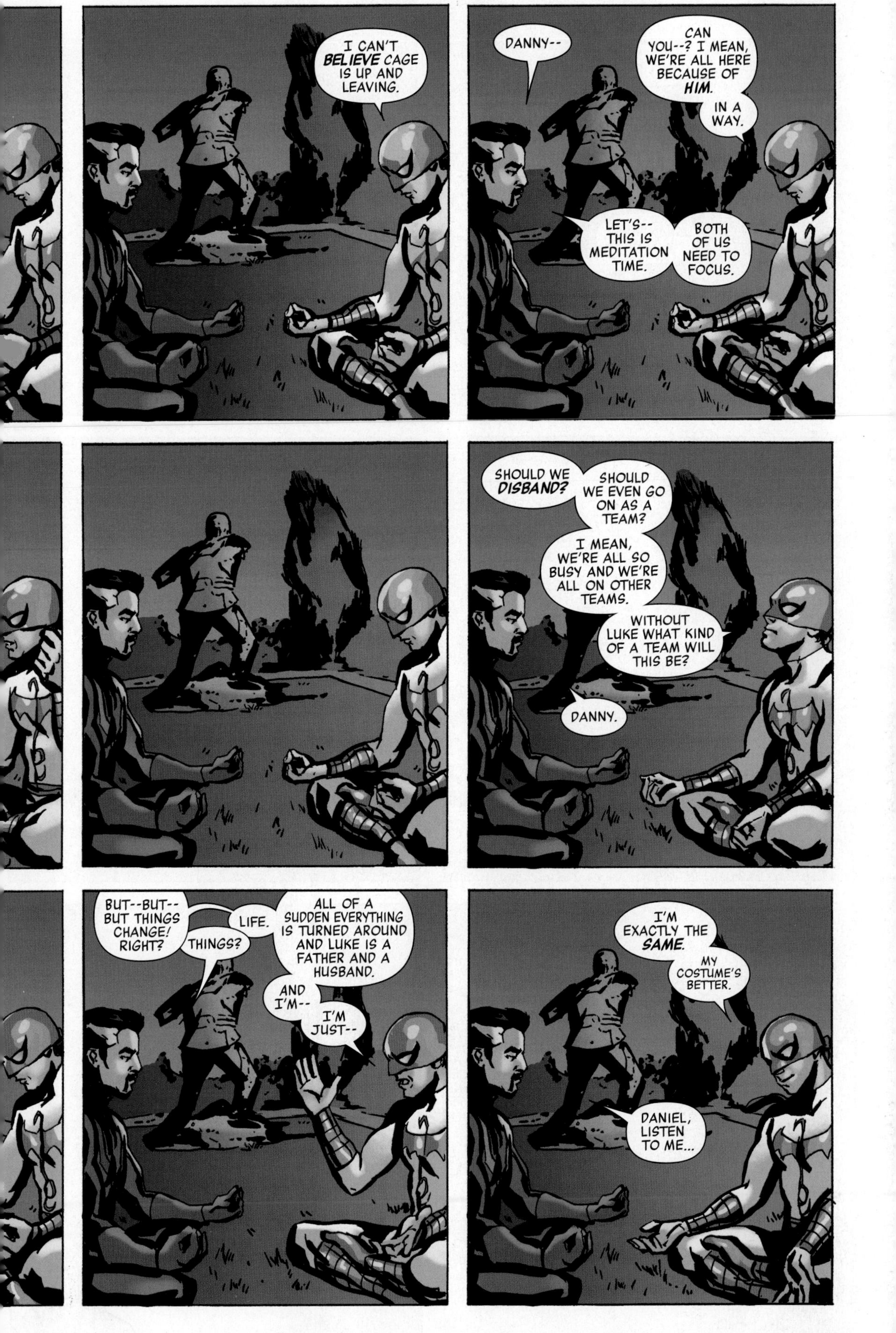
I CAN'T **BELIEVE** CAGE IS UP AND LEAVING.
DANNY--
CAN YOU--? I MEAN, WE'RE ALL HERE BECAUSE OF **HIM**.
IN A WAY.
LET'S-- THIS IS MEDITATION TIME.
BOTH OF US NEED TO FOCUS.
SHOULD WE **DISBAND?**
SHOULD WE EVEN GO ON AS A TEAM?
I MEAN, WE'RE ALL SO BUSY AND WE'RE ALL ON OTHER TEAMS.
WITHOUT LUKE WHAT KIND OF A TEAM WILL THIS BE?
DANNY.
BUT--BUT-- BUT THINGS CHANGE! RIGHT?
THINGS?
LIFE.
ALL OF A SUDDEN EVERYTHING IS TURNED AROUND AND LUKE IS A FATHER AND A HUSBAND.
AND I'M--
I'M JUST--
I'M EXACTLY THE **SAME**.
MY COSTUME'S BETTER.
DANIEL, LISTEN TO ME...

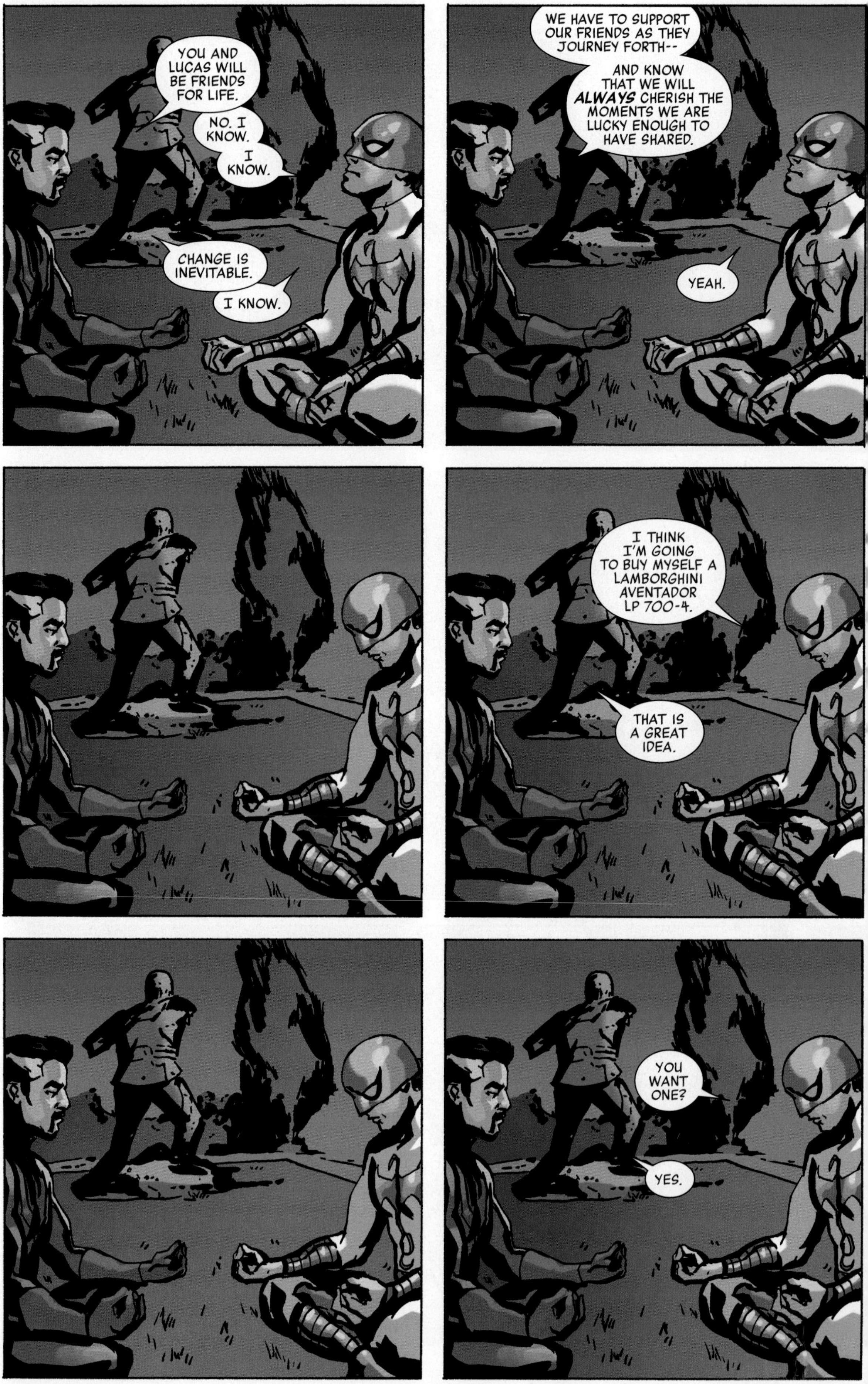
YOU AND LUCAS WILL BE FRIENDS FOR LIFE.
NO. I KNOW.
I KNOW.
CHANGE IS INEVITABLE.
I KNOW.
WE HAVE TO SUPPORT OUR FRIENDS AS THEY JOURNEY FORTH--
AND KNOW THAT WE WILL ALWAYS CHERISH THE MOMENTS WE ARE LUCKY ENOUGH TO HAVE SHARED.
YEAH.
I THINK I'M GOING TO BUY MYSELF A LAMBORGHINI AVENTADOR LP 700-4.
THAT IS A GREAT IDEA.
YOU WANT ONE?
YES.

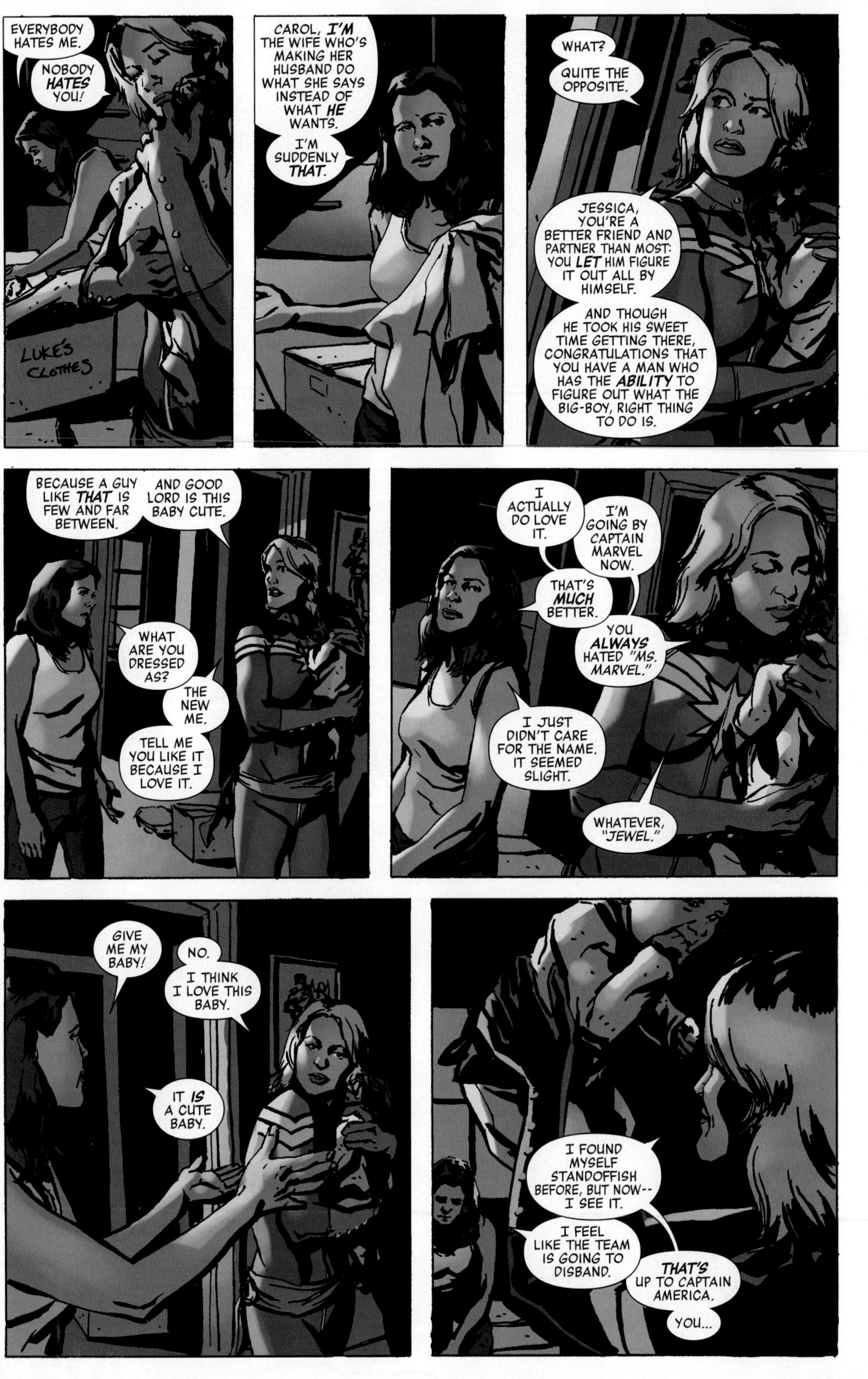
EVERYBODY HATES ME.
NOBODY HATES YOU!
LUKE'S CLOTHES
CAROL, I'M THE WIFE WHO'S MAKING HER HUSBAND DO WHAT SHE SAYS INSTEAD OF WHAT HE WANTS.
I'M SUDDENLY THAT.
WHAT?
QUITE THE OPPOSITE.
JESSICA, YOU'RE A BETTER FRIEND AND PARTNER THAN MOST: YOU LET HIM FIGURE IT OUT ALL BY HIMSELF.
AND THOUGH HE TOOK HIS SWEET TIME GETTING THERE, CONGRATULATIONS THAT YOU HAVE A MAN WHO HAS THE ABILITY TO FIGURE OUT WHAT THE BIG-BOY, RIGHT THING TO DO IS.
BECAUSE A GUY LIKE THAT IS FEW AND FAR BETWEEN.
AND GOOD LORD IS THIS BABY CUTE.
WHAT ARE YOU DRESSED AS?
THE NEW ME.
TELL ME YOU LIKE IT BECAUSE I LOVE IT.
I ACTUALLY DO LOVE IT.
I'M GOING BY CAPTAIN MARVEL NOW.
THAT'S MUCH BETTER.
YOU ALWAYS HATED "MS. MARVEL."
I JUST DIDN'T CARE FOR THE NAME. IT SEEMED SLIGHT.
WHATEVER, "JEWEL."
GIVE ME MY BABY!
NO.
I THINK I LOVE THIS BABY.
IT IS A CUTE BABY.
I FOUND MYSELF STANDOFFISH BEFORE, BUT NOW-- I SEE IT.
I FEEL LIKE THE TEAM IS GOING TO DISBAND.
THAT'S UP TO CAPTAIN AMERICA.
YOU...

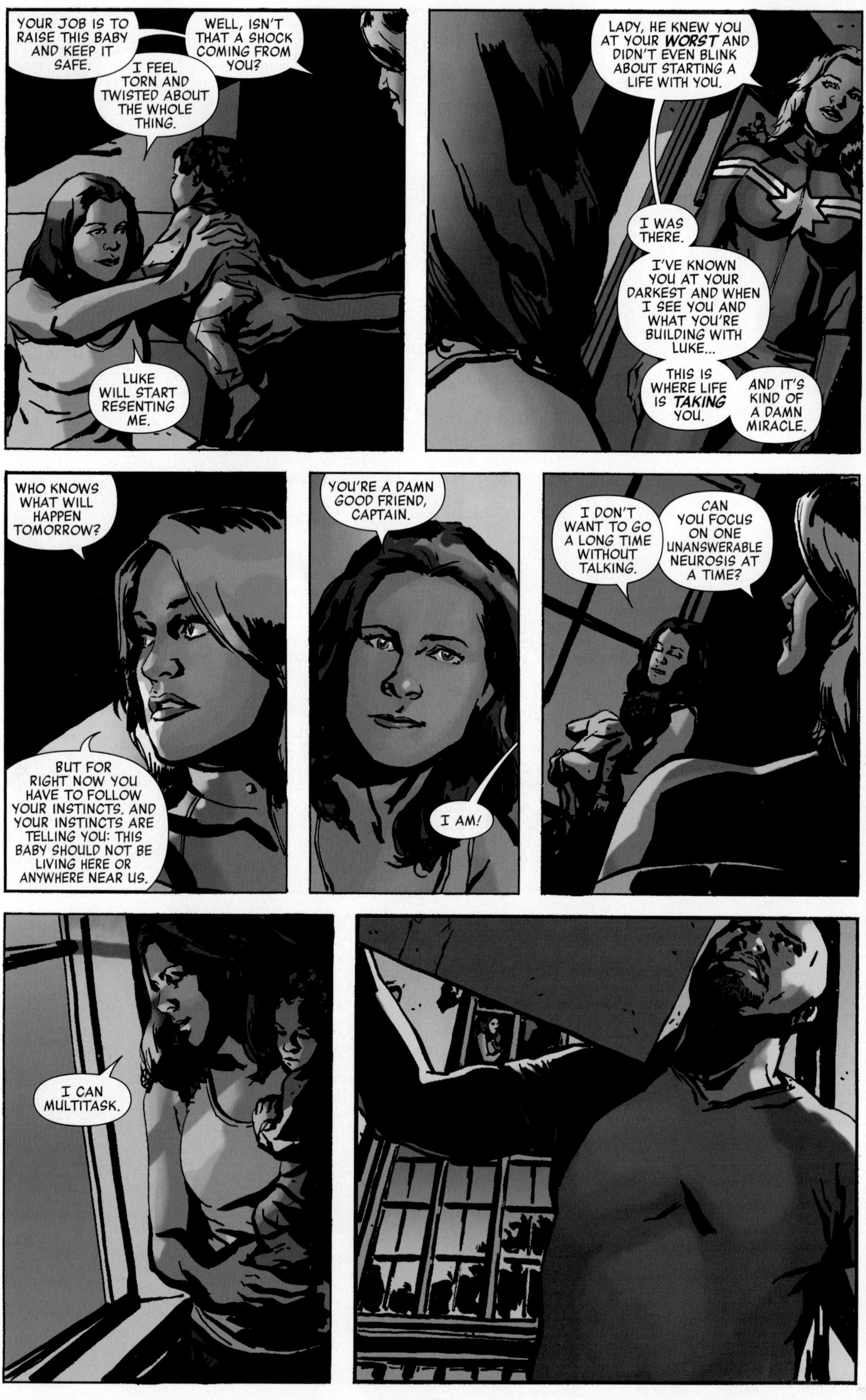
YOUR JOB IS TO RAISE THIS BABY AND KEEP IT SAFE.
WELL, ISN'T THAT A SHOCK COMING FROM YOU?
I FEEL TORN AND TWISTED ABOUT THE WHOLE THING.
LUKE WILL START RESENTING ME.
LADY, HE KNEW YOU AT YOUR *WORST* AND DIDN'T EVEN BLINK ABOUT STARTING A LIFE WITH YOU.
I WAS THERE.
I'VE KNOWN YOU AT YOUR DARKEST AND WHEN I SEE YOU AND WHAT YOU'RE BUILDING WITH LUKE...
THIS IS WHERE LIFE IS *TAKING* YOU.
AND IT'S KIND OF A DAMN MIRACLE.
WHO KNOWS WHAT WILL HAPPEN TOMORROW?
BUT FOR RIGHT NOW YOU HAVE TO FOLLOW YOUR INSTINCTS. AND YOUR INSTINCTS ARE TELLING YOU: THIS BABY SHOULD NOT BE LIVING HERE OR ANYWHERE NEAR US.
YOU'RE A DAMN GOOD FRIEND, CAPTAIN.
I AM!
I DON'T WANT TO GO A LONG TIME WITHOUT TALKING.
CAN YOU FOCUS ON ONE UNANSWERABLE NEUROSIS AT A TIME?
I CAN MULTITASK.

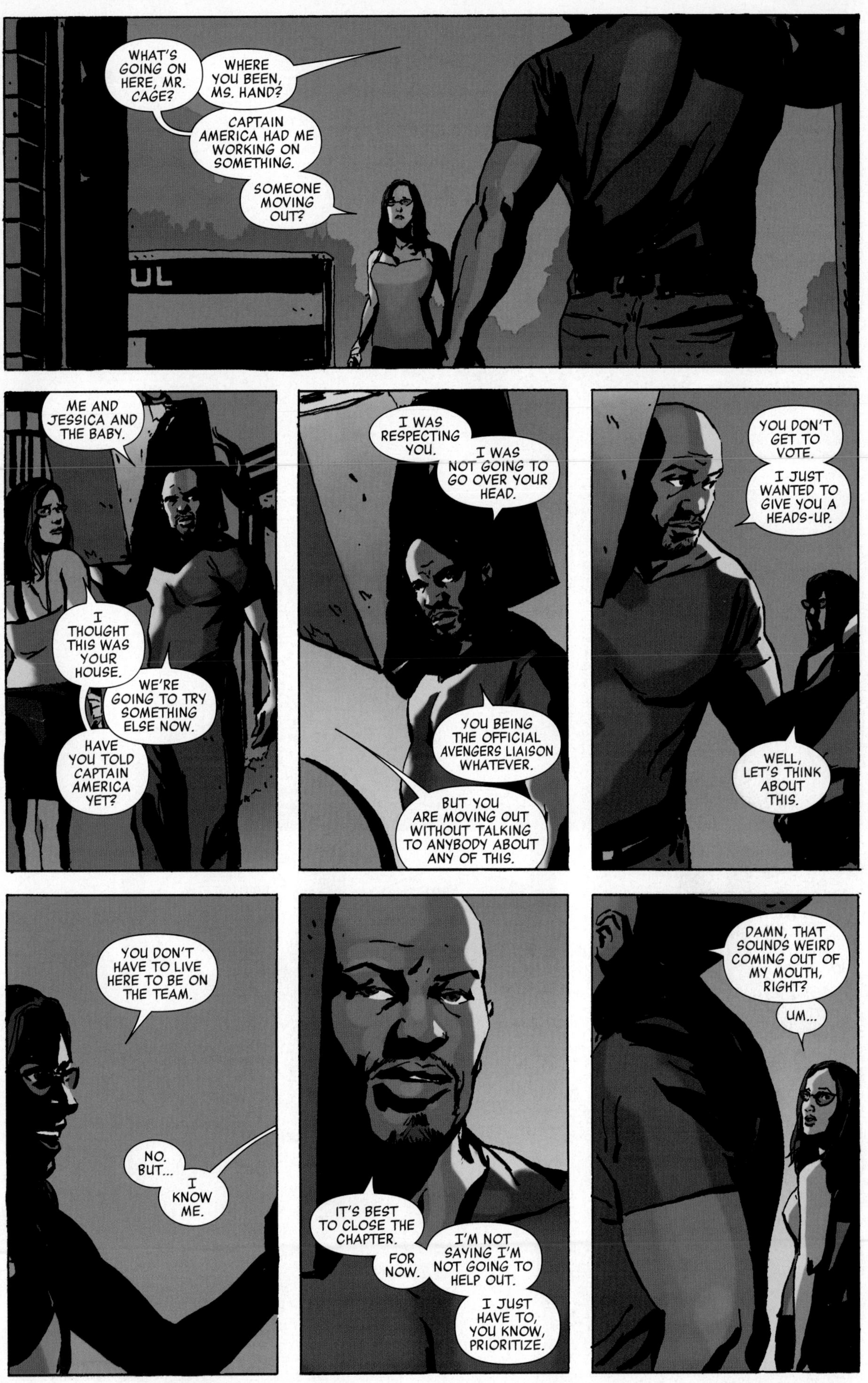
WHAT'S GOING ON HERE, MR. CAGE?
WHERE YOU BEEN, MS. HAND?
CAPTAIN AMERICA HAD ME WORKING ON SOMETHING.
SOMEONE MOVING OUT?
UL
ME AND JESSICA AND THE BABY.
I THOUGHT THIS WAS YOUR HOUSE.
WE'RE GOING TO TRY SOMETHING ELSE NOW.
HAVE YOU TOLD CAPTAIN AMERICA YET?
I WAS RESPECTING YOU.
I WAS NOT GOING TO GO OVER YOUR HEAD.
YOU BEING THE OFFICIAL AVENGERS LIAISON WHATEVER.
BUT YOU ARE MOVING OUT WITHOUT TALKING TO ANYBODY ABOUT ANY OF THIS.
YOU DON'T GET TO VOTE.
I JUST WANTED TO GIVE YOU A HEADS-UP.
WELL, LET'S THINK ABOUT THIS.
YOU DON'T HAVE TO LIVE HERE TO BE ON THE TEAM.
NO. BUT...
I KNOW ME.
IT'S BEST TO CLOSE THE CHAPTER.
FOR NOW.
I'M NOT SAYING I'M NOT GOING TO HELP OUT.
I JUST HAVE TO, YOU KNOW, PRIORITIZE.
DAMN, THAT SOUNDS WEIRD COMING OUT OF MY MOUTH, RIGHT?
UM...

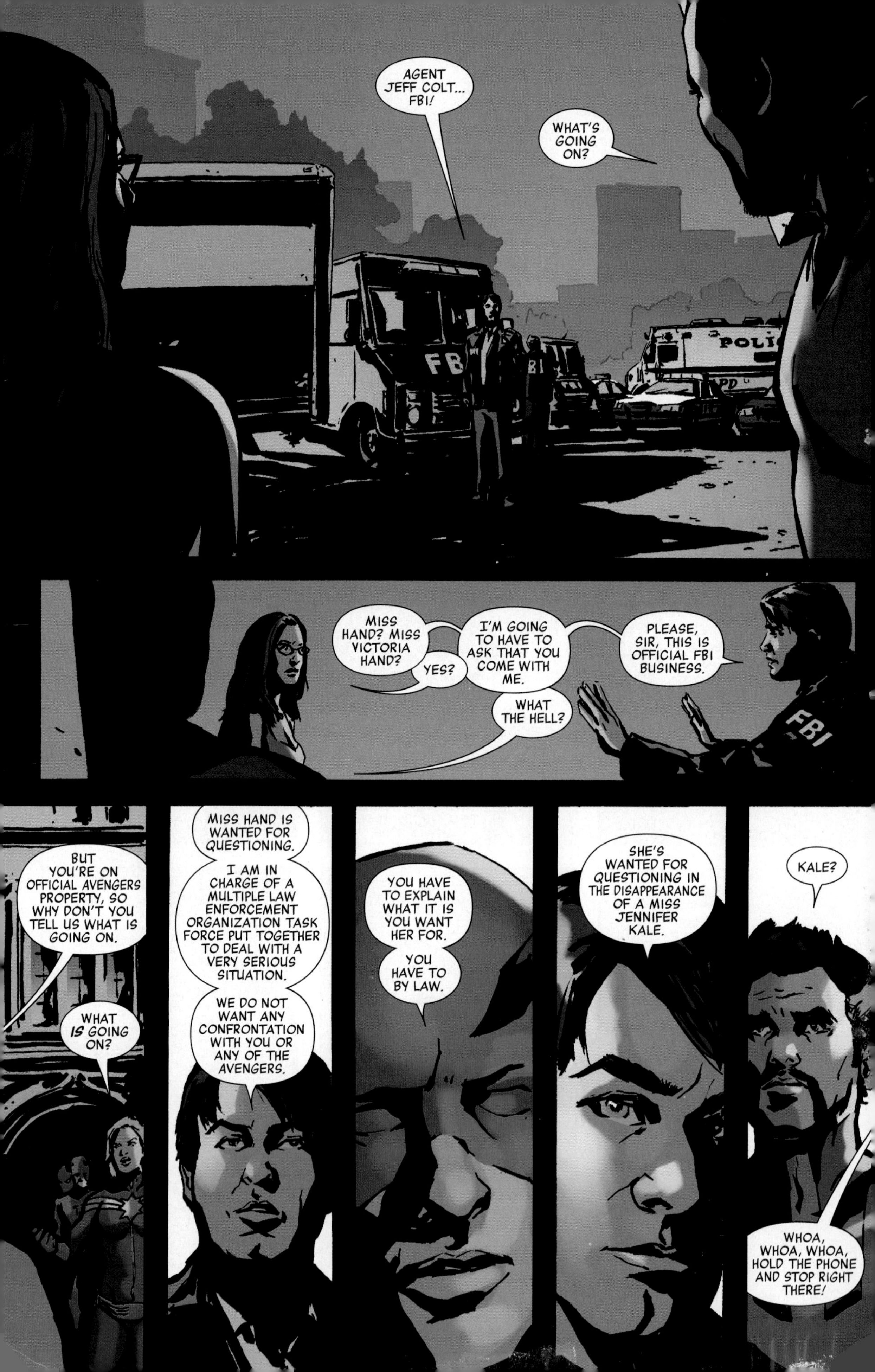
AGENT JEFF COLT... FBI!
WHAT'S GOING ON?
MISS HAND? MISS VICTORIA HAND?
YES?
I'M GOING TO HAVE TO ASK THAT YOU COME WITH ME.
PLEASE, SIR, THIS IS OFFICIAL FBI BUSINESS.
WHAT THE HELL?
FBI
POLI
BUT YOU'RE ON OFFICIAL AVENGERS PROPERTY, SO WHY DON'T YOU TELL US WHAT IS GOING ON.
WHAT *IS* GOING ON?
MISS HAND IS WANTED FOR QUESTIONING.
I AM IN CHARGE OF A MULTIPLE LAW ENFORCEMENT ORGANIZATION TASK FORCE PUT TOGETHER TO DEAL WITH A VERY SERIOUS SITUATION.
WE DO NOT WANT ANY CONFRONTATION WITH YOU OR ANY OF THE AVENGERS.
YOU HAVE TO EXPLAIN WHAT IT IS YOU WANT HER FOR.
YOU HAVE TO BY LAW.
SHE'S WANTED FOR QUESTIONING IN THE DISAPPEARANCE OF A MISS JENNIFER KALE.
KALE?
WHOA, WHOA, WHOA, HOLD THE PHONE AND STOP RIGHT THERE!

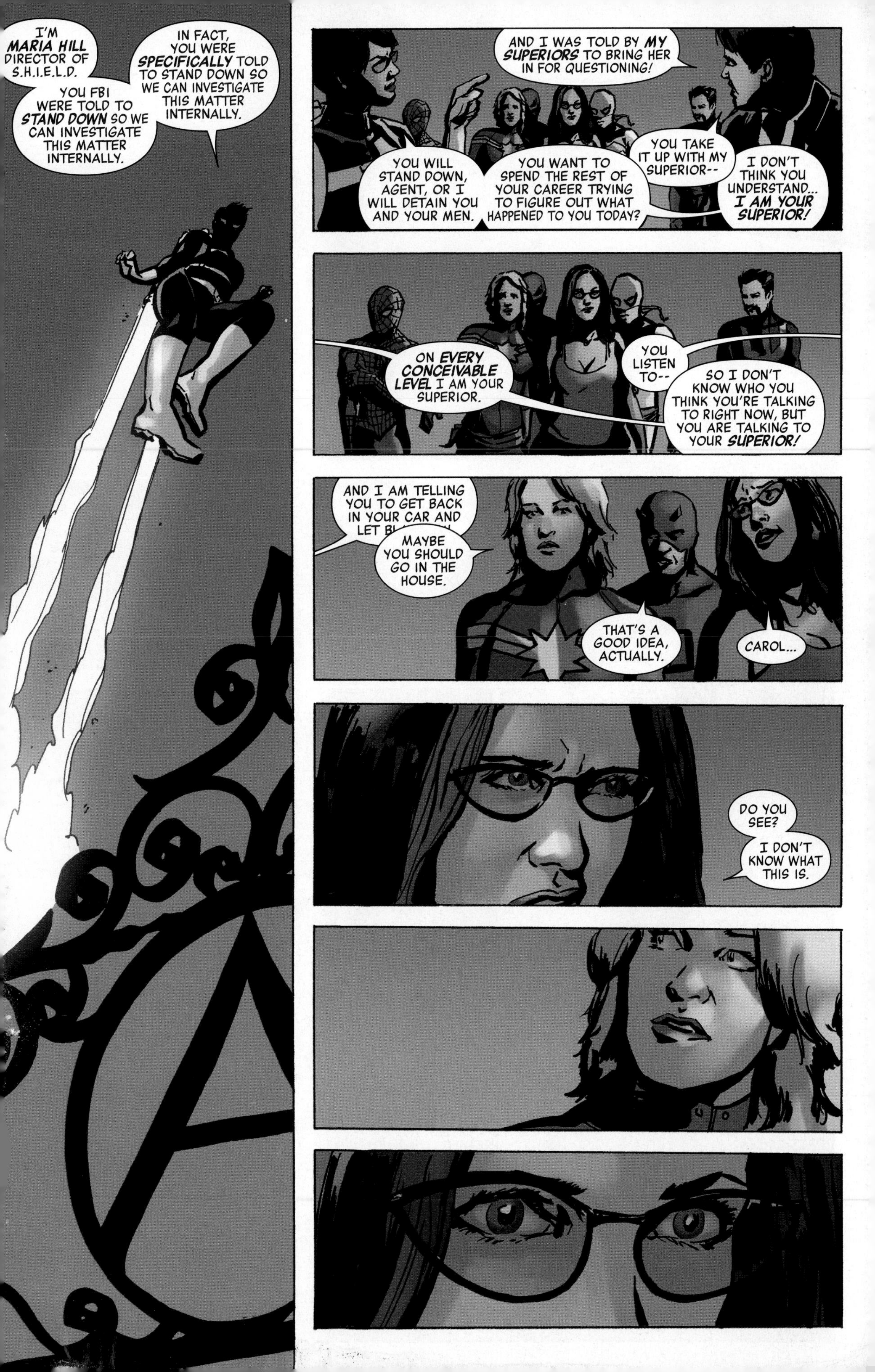

I'M MARIA HILL DIRECTOR OF S.H.I.E.L.D.
YOU FBI WERE TOLD TO STAND DOWN SO WE CAN INVESTIGATE THIS MATTER INTERNALLY.
IN FACT, YOU WERE SPECIFICALLY TOLD TO STAND DOWN SO WE CAN INVESTIGATE THIS MATTER INTERNALLY.
AND I WAS TOLD BY MY SUPERIORS TO BRING HER IN FOR QUESTIONING!
YOU WILL STAND DOWN, AGENT, OR I WILL DETAIN YOU AND YOUR MEN.
YOU WANT TO SPEND THE REST OF YOUR CAREER TRYING TO FIGURE OUT WHAT HAPPENED TO YOU TODAY?
YOU TAKE IT UP WITH MY SUPERIOR--
I DON'T THINK YOU UNDERSTAND... I AM YOUR SUPERIOR!
ON EVERY CONCEIVABLE LEVEL I AM YOUR SUPERIOR.
YOU LISTEN TO--
SO I DON'T KNOW WHO YOU THINK YOU'RE TALKING TO RIGHT NOW, BUT YOU ARE TALKING TO YOUR SUPERIOR!
AND I AM TELLING YOU TO GET BACK IN YOUR CAR AND LET
MAYBE YOU SHOULD GO IN THE HOUSE.
THAT'S A GOOD IDEA, ACTUALLY.
CAROL...
DO YOU SEE?
I DON'T KNOW WHAT THIS IS.

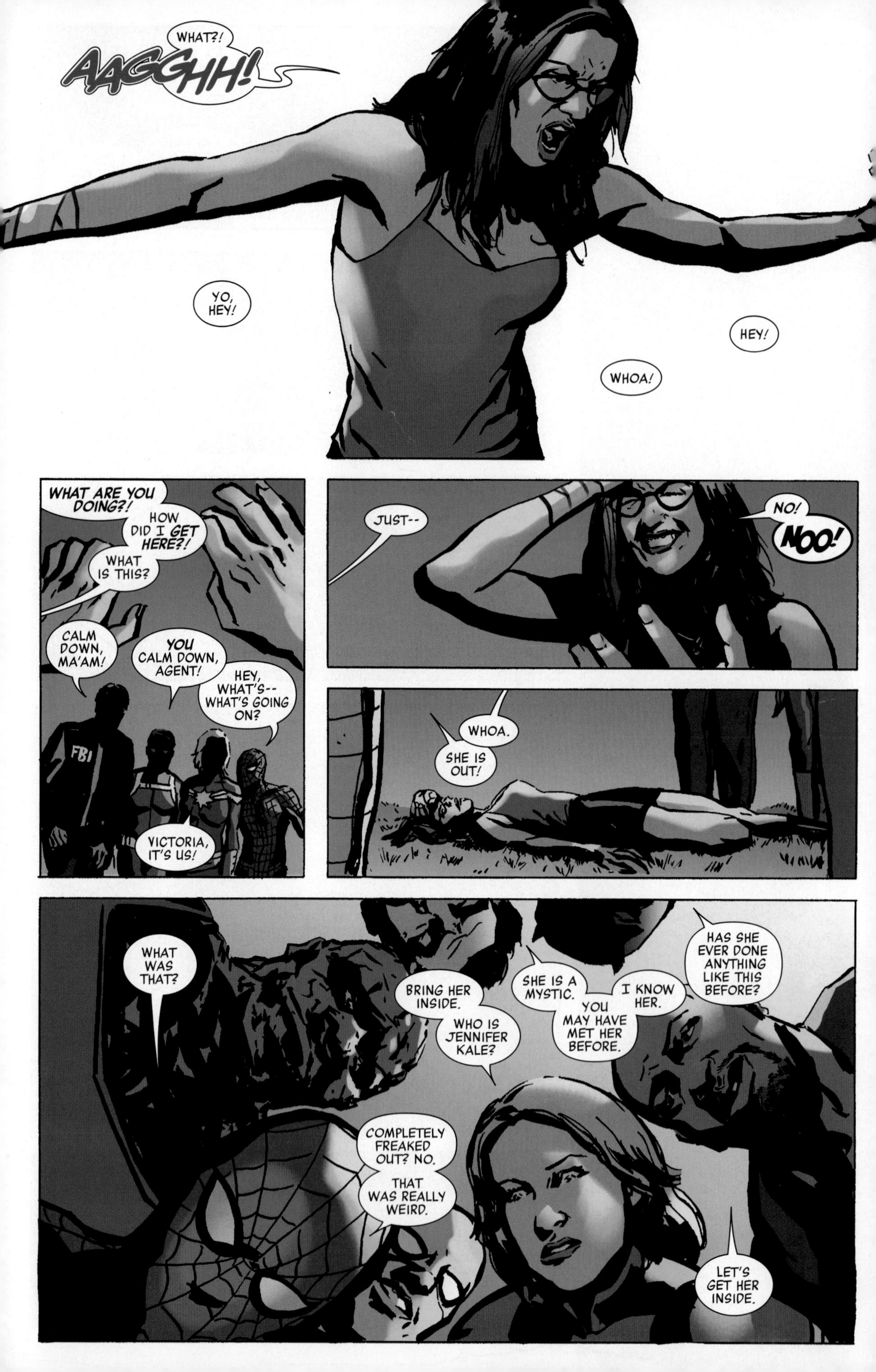

WHAT?!
AAGGHH!
YO, HEY!
WHOA!
HEY!
WHAT ARE YOU DOING?!
HOW DID I GET HERE?!
WHAT IS THIS?
CALM DOWN, MA'AM!
YOU CALM DOWN, AGENT!
HEY, WHAT'S-- WHAT'S GOING ON?
VICTORIA, IT'S US!
FBI
JUST--
NO!
NOO!
WHOA.
SHE IS OUT!
WHAT WAS THAT?
BRING HER INSIDE.
WHO IS JENNIFER KALE?
SHE IS A MYSTIC.
YOU MAY HAVE MET HER BEFORE.
I KNOW HER.
HAS SHE EVER DONE ANYTHING LIKE THIS BEFORE?
COMPLETELY FREAKED OUT? NO.
THAT WAS REALLY WEIRD.
LET'S GET HER INSIDE.

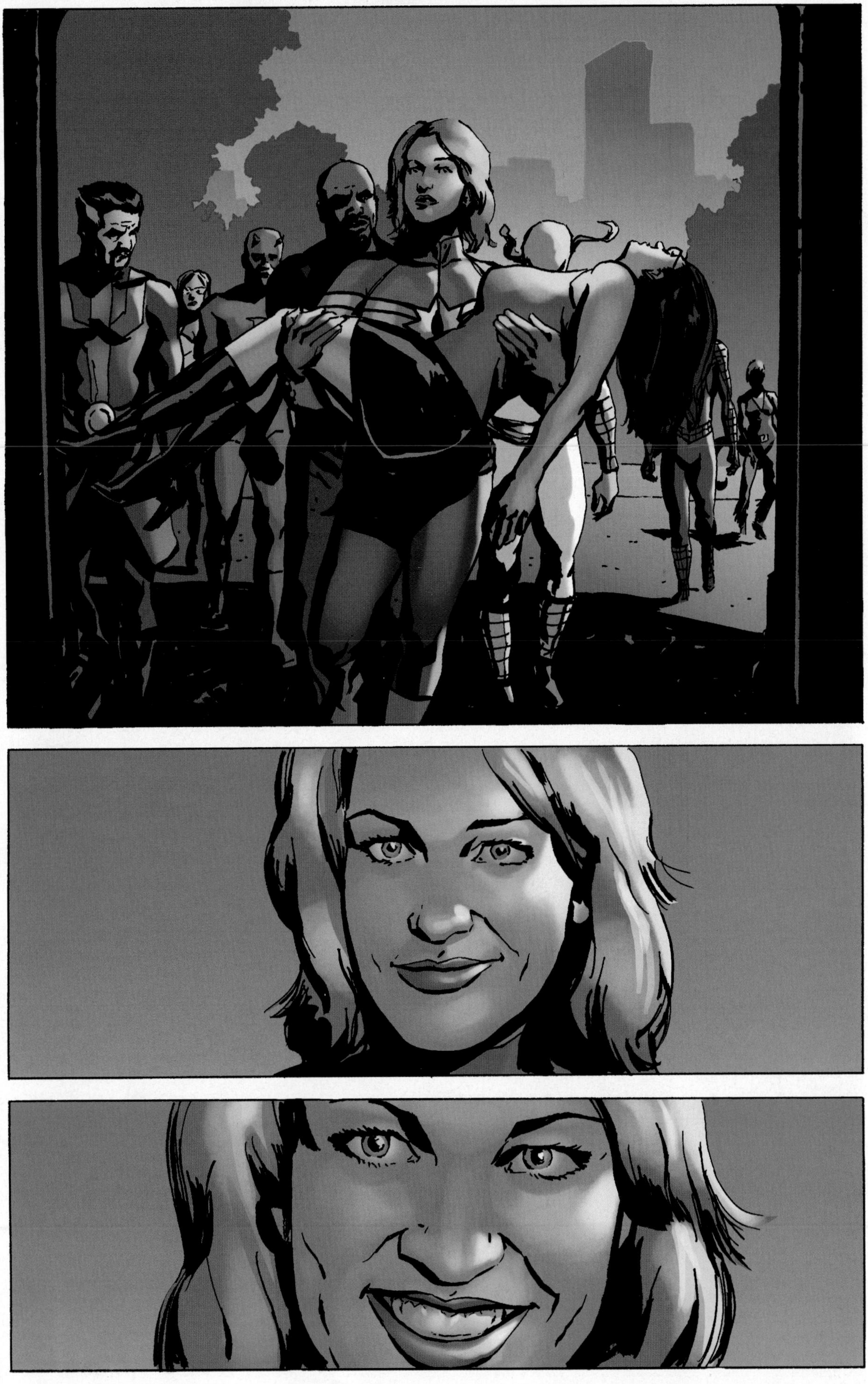

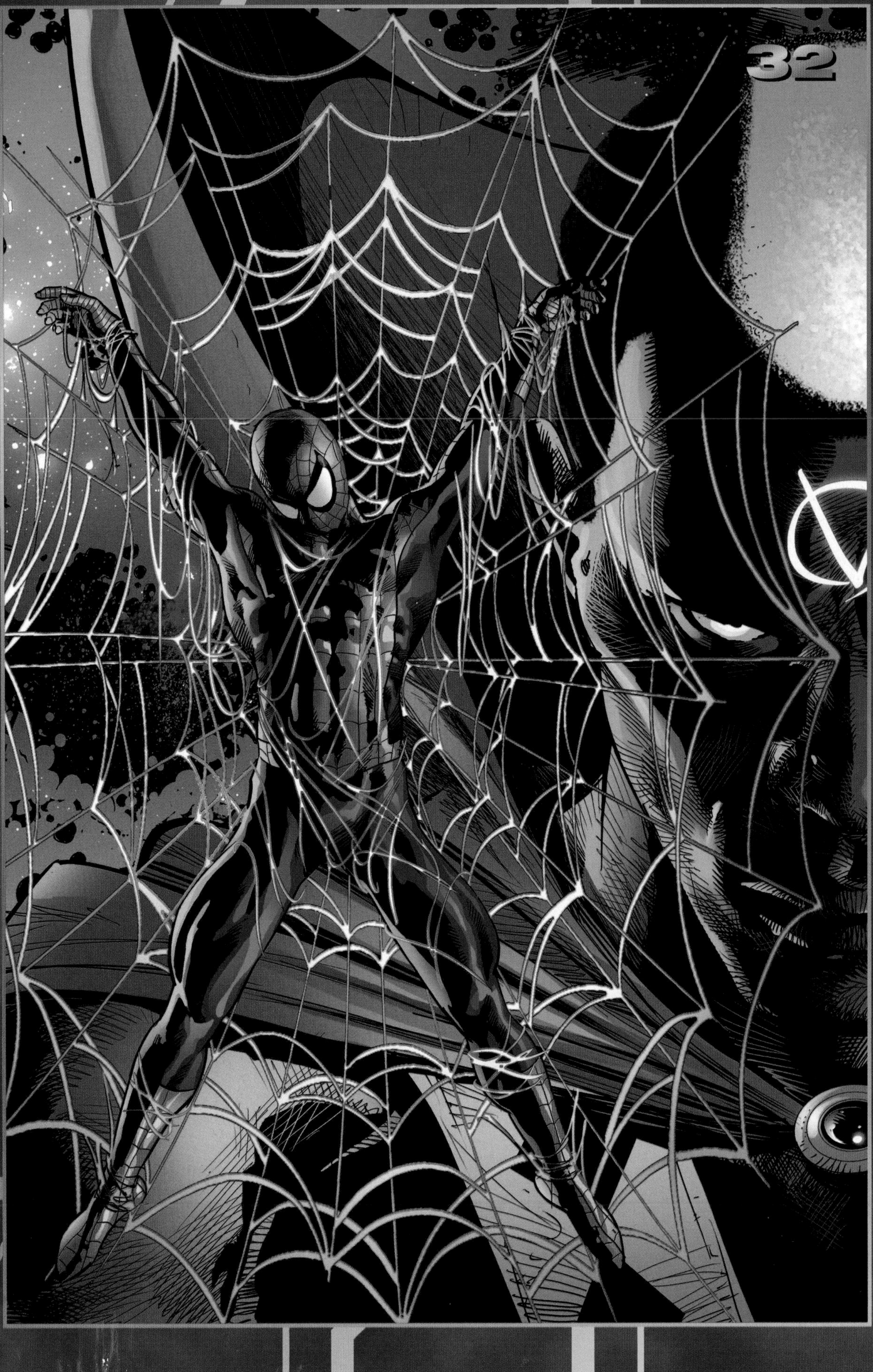
32

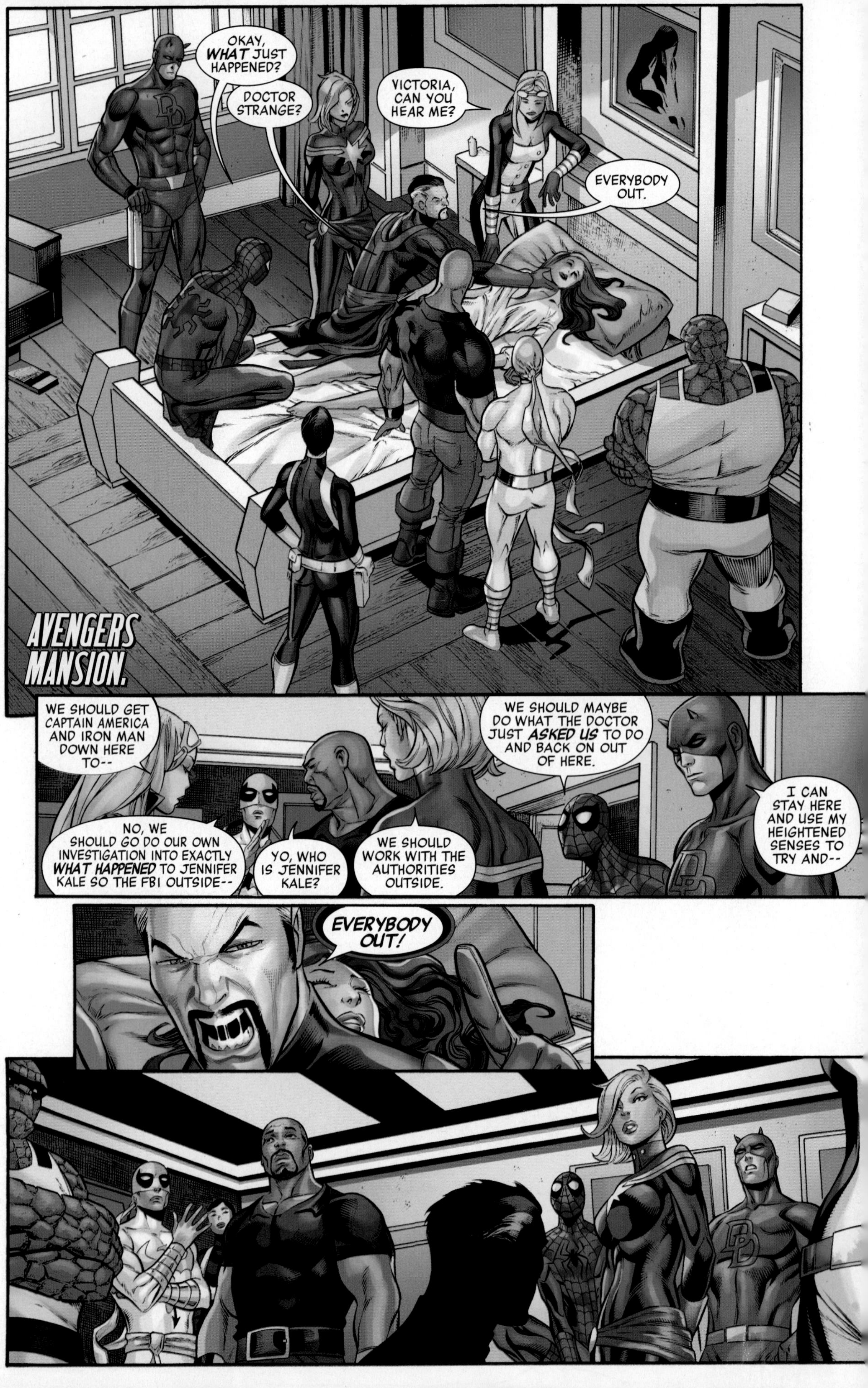
OKAY, WHAT JUST HAPPENED?
DOCTOR STRANGE?
VICTORIA, CAN YOU HEAR ME?
EVERYBODY OUT.
AVENGERS MANSION.
WE SHOULD GET CAPTAIN AMERICA AND IRON MAN DOWN HERE TO--
WE SHOULD MAYBE DO WHAT THE DOCTOR JUST ASKED US TO DO AND BACK ON OUT OF HERE.
NO, WE SHOULD GO DO OUR OWN INVESTIGATION INTO EXACTLY WHAT HAPPENED TO JENNIFER KALE SO THE FBI OUTSIDE--
YO, WHO IS JENNIFER KALE?
WE SHOULD WORK WITH THE AUTHORITIES OUTSIDE.
I CAN STAY HERE AND USE MY HEIGHTENED SENSES TO TRY AND--
EVERYBODY OUT!

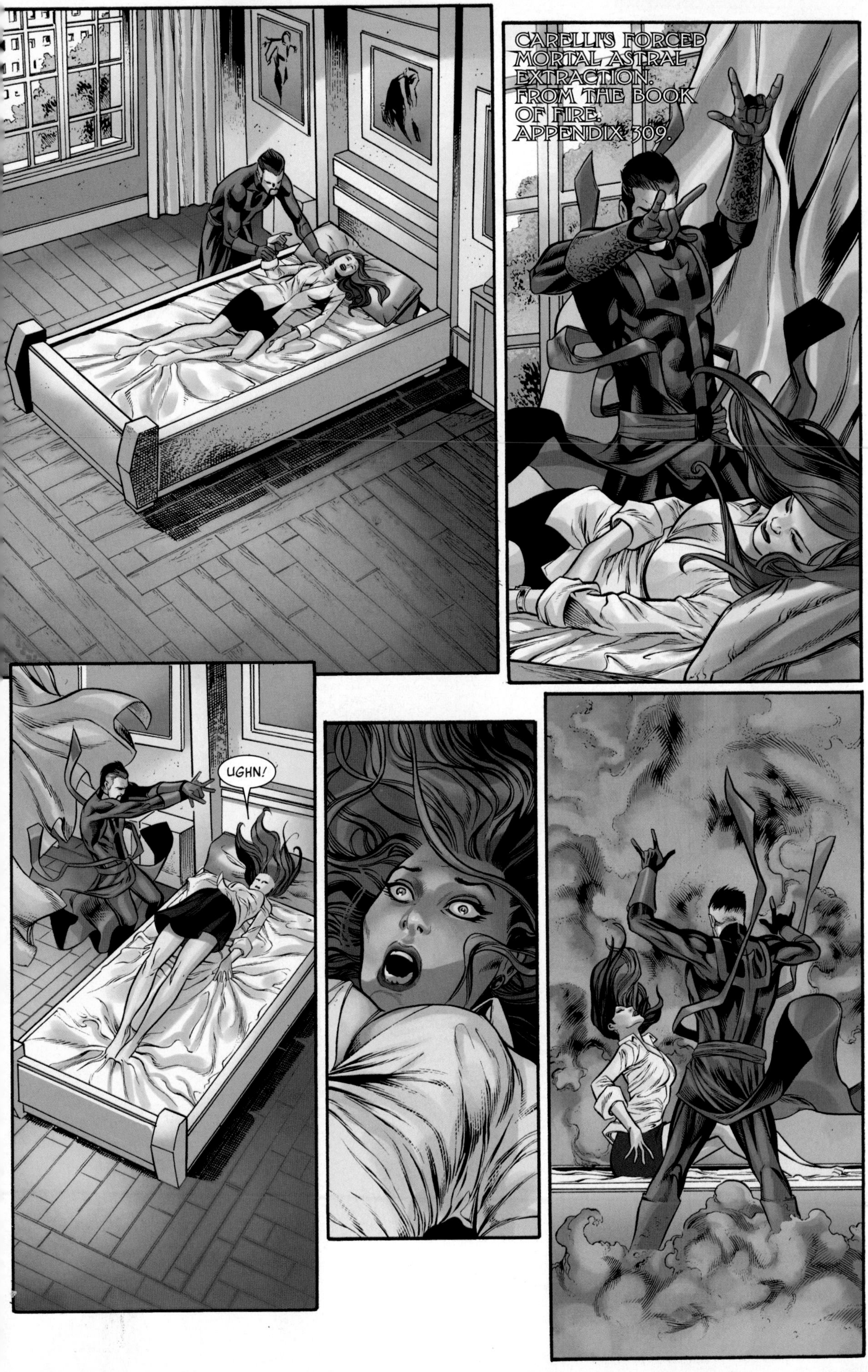
CARELLI'S FORCED MORTAL ASTRAL EXTRACTION. FROM THE BOOK OF FIRE. APPENDIX 309.
UGHN!

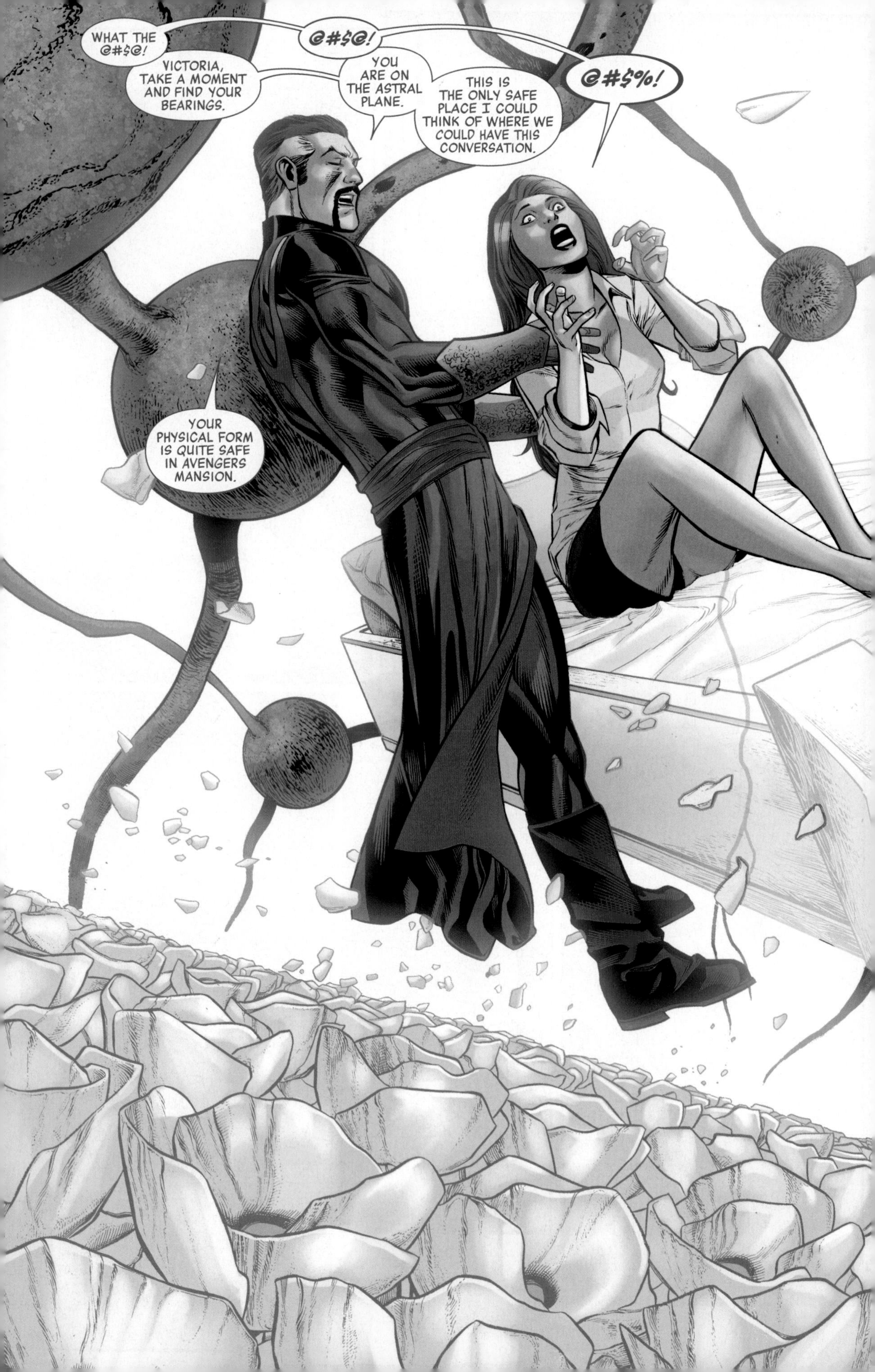
WHAT THE @#$@!
@#$@!
@#$%!
VICTORIA, TAKE A MOMENT AND FIND YOUR BEARINGS.
YOU ARE ON THE ASTRAL PLANE.
THIS IS THE ONLY SAFE PLACE I COULD THINK OF WHERE WE COULD HAVE THIS CONVERSATION.
YOUR PHYSICAL FORM IS QUITE SAFE IN AVENGERS MANSION.

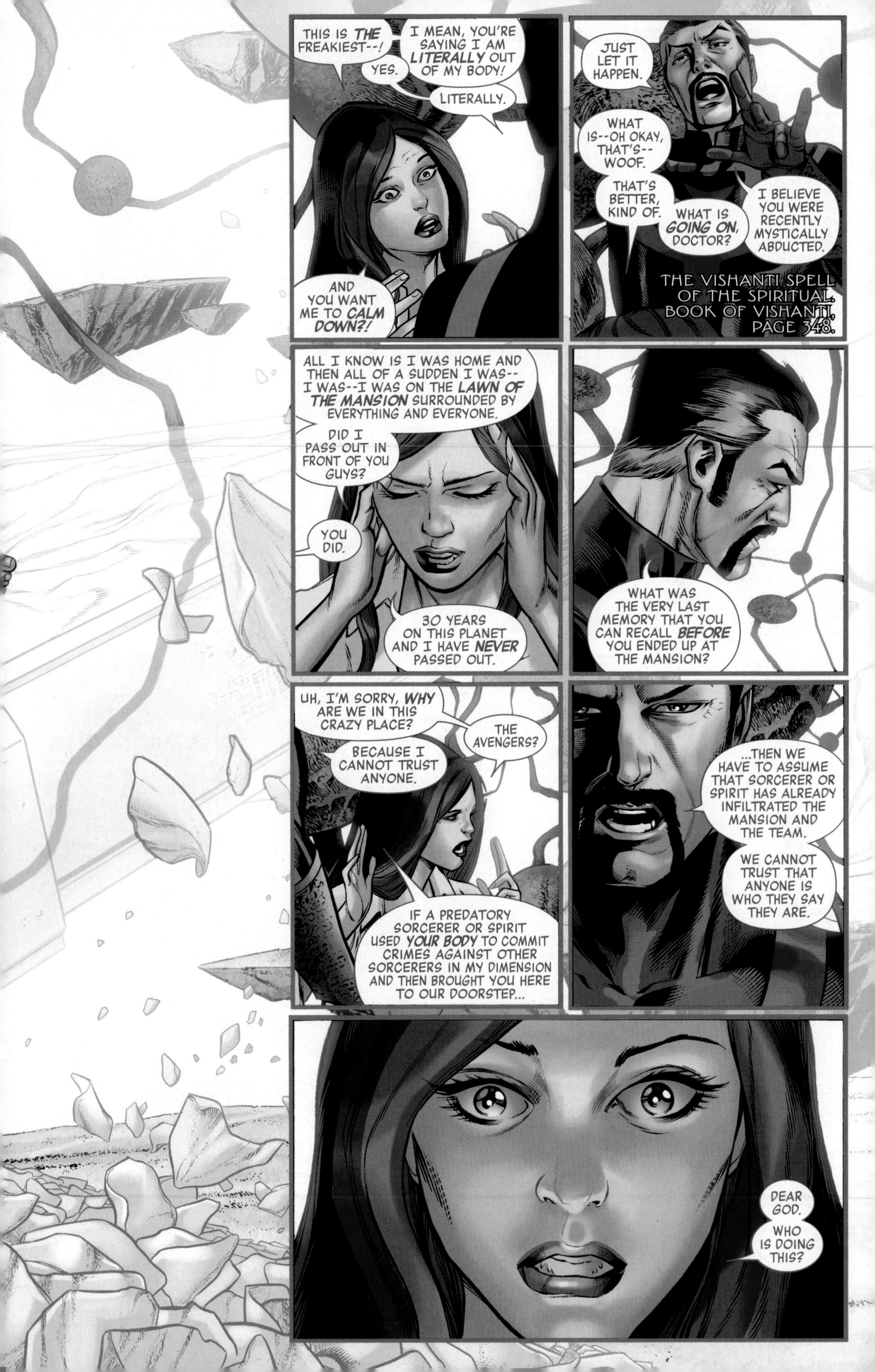

THIS IS THE FREAKIEST--!
I MEAN, YOU'RE SAYING I AM LITERALLY OUT OF MY BODY!
YES.
LITERALLY.
AND YOU WANT ME TO CALM DOWN?!
JUST LET IT HAPPEN.
WHAT IS--OH OKAY, THAT'S-- WOOF.
THAT'S BETTER, KIND OF.
WHAT IS GOING ON, DOCTOR?
I BELIEVE YOU WERE RECENTLY MYSTICALLY ABDUCTED.
THE VISHANTI SPELL OF THE SPIRITUAL, BOOK OF VISHANTI, PAGE 348.
ALL I KNOW IS I WAS HOME AND THEN ALL OF A SUDDEN I WAS-- I WAS--I WAS ON THE LAWN OF THE MANSION SURROUNDED BY EVERYTHING AND EVERYONE.
DID I PASS OUT IN FRONT OF YOU GUYS?
YOU DID.
30 YEARS ON THIS PLANET AND I HAVE NEVER PASSED OUT.
WHAT WAS THE VERY LAST MEMORY THAT YOU CAN RECALL BEFORE YOU ENDED UP AT THE MANSION?
UH, I'M SORRY, WHY ARE WE IN THIS CRAZY PLACE?
THE AVENGERS?
BECAUSE I CANNOT TRUST ANYONE.
IF A PREDATORY SORCERER OR SPIRIT USED YOUR BODY TO COMMIT CRIMES AGAINST OTHER SORCERERS IN MY DIMENSION AND THEN BROUGHT YOU HERE TO OUR DOORSTEP...
...THEN WE HAVE TO ASSUME THAT SORCERER OR SPIRIT HAS ALREADY INFILTRATED THE MANSION AND THE TEAM.
WE CANNOT TRUST THAT ANYONE IS WHO THEY SAY THEY ARE.
DEAR GOD.
WHO IS DOING THIS?

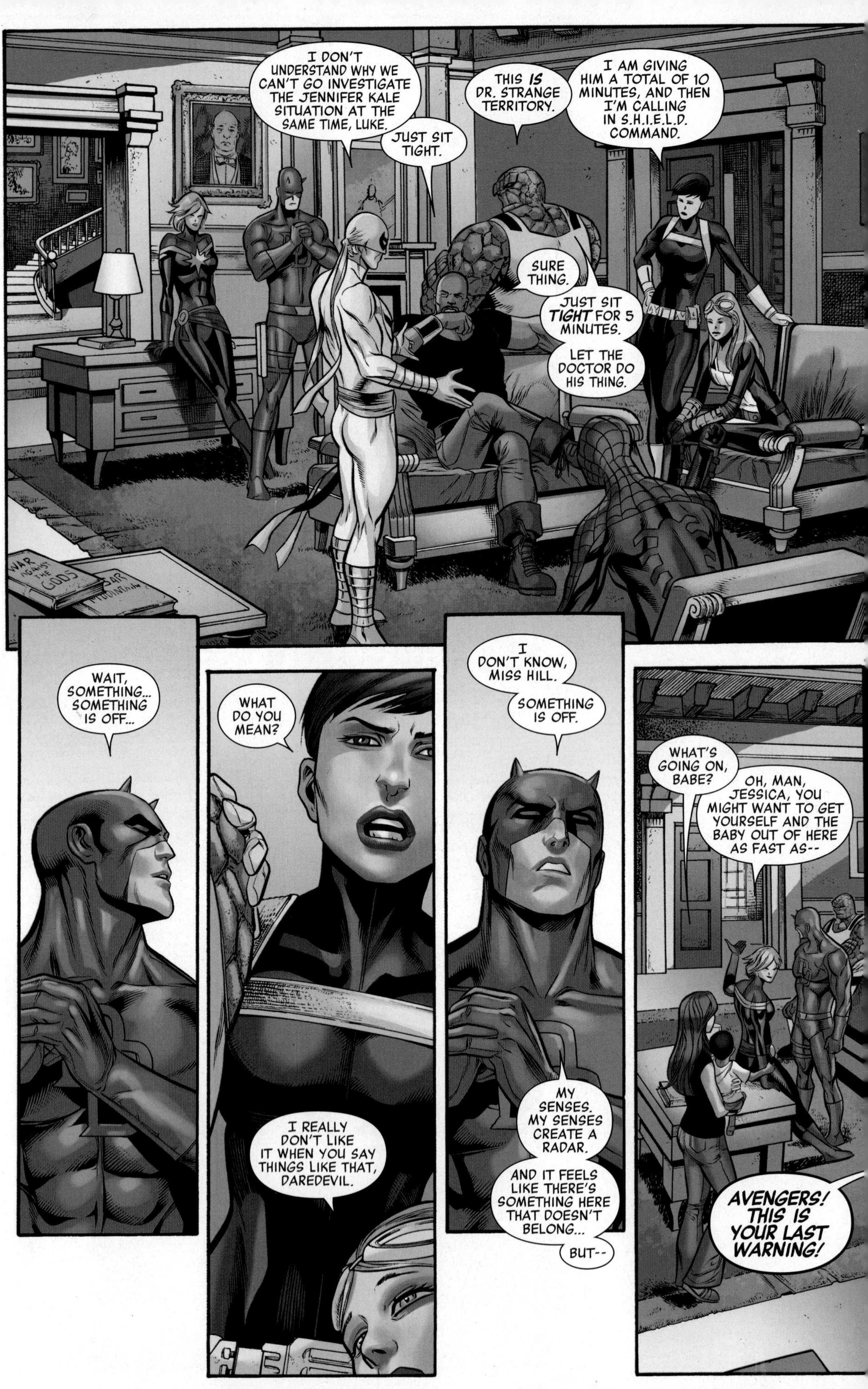
I DON'T UNDERSTAND WHY WE CAN'T GO INVESTIGATE THE JENNIFER KALE SITUATION AT THE SAME TIME, LUKE.
JUST SIT TIGHT.
THIS IS DR. STRANGE TERRITORY.
I AM GIVING HIM A TOTAL OF 10 MINUTES, AND THEN I'M CALLING IN S.H.I.E.L.D. COMMAND.
SURE THING.
JUST SIT TIGHT FOR 5 MINUTES.
LET THE DOCTOR DO HIS THING.
WAR AGAINST THE GODS
WAIT, SOMETHING... SOMETHING IS OFF...
WHAT DO YOU MEAN?
I REALLY DON'T LIKE IT WHEN YOU SAY THINGS LIKE THAT, DAREDEVIL.
I DON'T KNOW, MISS HILL.
SOMETHING IS OFF.
MY SENSES. MY SENSES CREATE A RADAR.
AND IT FEELS LIKE THERE'S SOMETHING HERE THAT DOESN'T BELONG...
BUT--
WHAT'S GOING ON, BABE?
OH, MAN, JESSICA, YOU MIGHT WANT TO GET YOURSELF AND THE BABY OUT OF HERE AS FAST AS--
AVENGERS! THIS IS YOUR LAST WARNING!

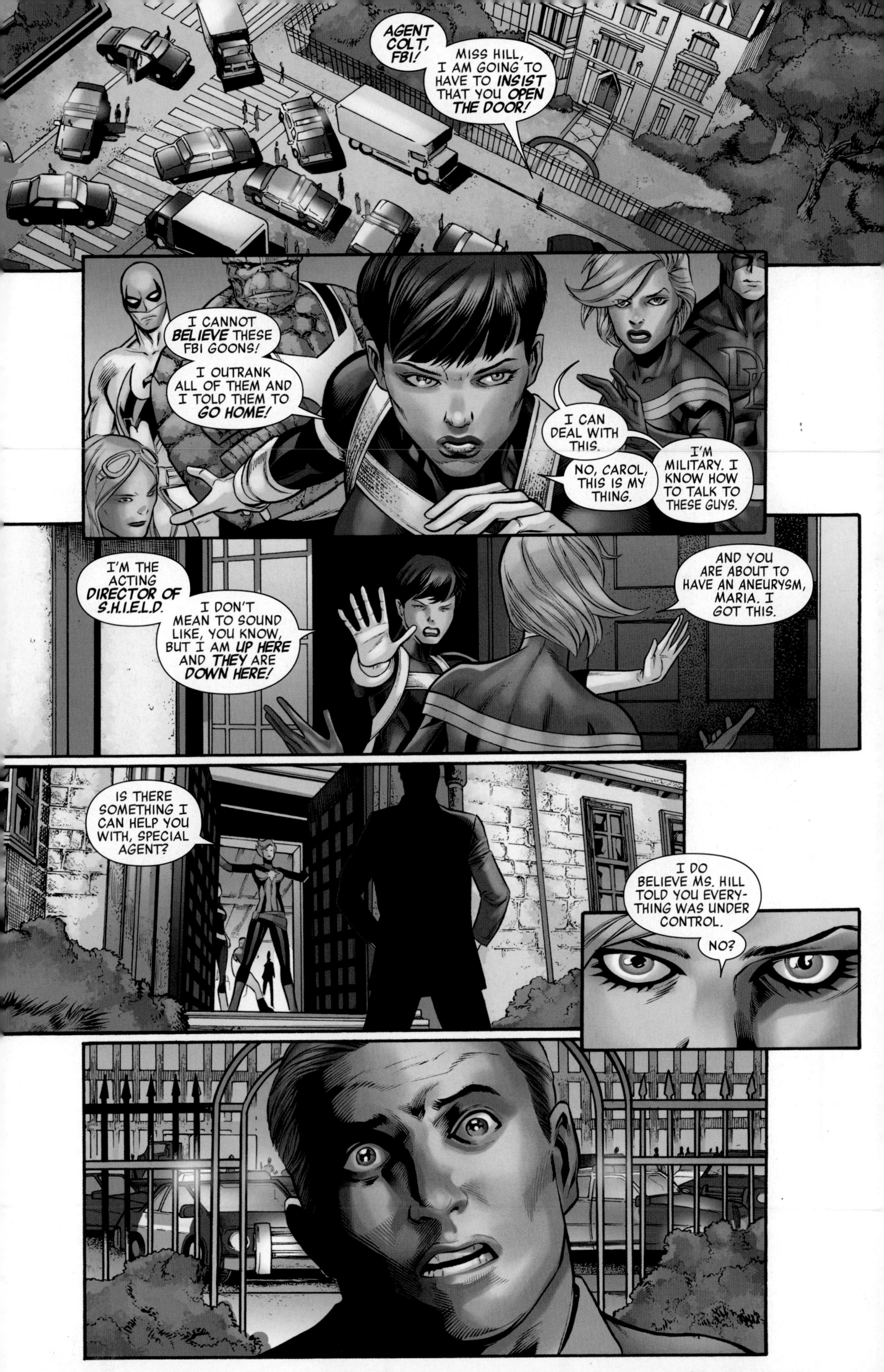
AGENT COLT, FBI!
MISS HILL, I AM GOING TO HAVE TO INSIST THAT YOU OPEN THE DOOR!
I CANNOT BELIEVE THESE FBI GOONS!
I OUTRANK ALL OF THEM AND I TOLD THEM TO GO HOME!
I CAN DEAL WITH THIS.
NO, CAROL, THIS IS MY THING.
I'M MILITARY. I KNOW HOW TO TALK TO THESE GUYS.
I'M THE ACTING DIRECTOR OF S.H.I.E.L.D.
I DON'T MEAN TO SOUND LIKE, YOU KNOW, BUT I AM UP HERE AND THEY ARE DOWN HERE!
AND YOU ARE ABOUT TO HAVE AN ANEURYSM, MARIA. I GOT THIS.
IS THERE SOMETHING I CAN HELP YOU WITH, SPECIAL AGENT?
I DO BELIEVE MS. HILL TOLD YOU EVERY-THING WAS UNDER CONTROL.
NO?

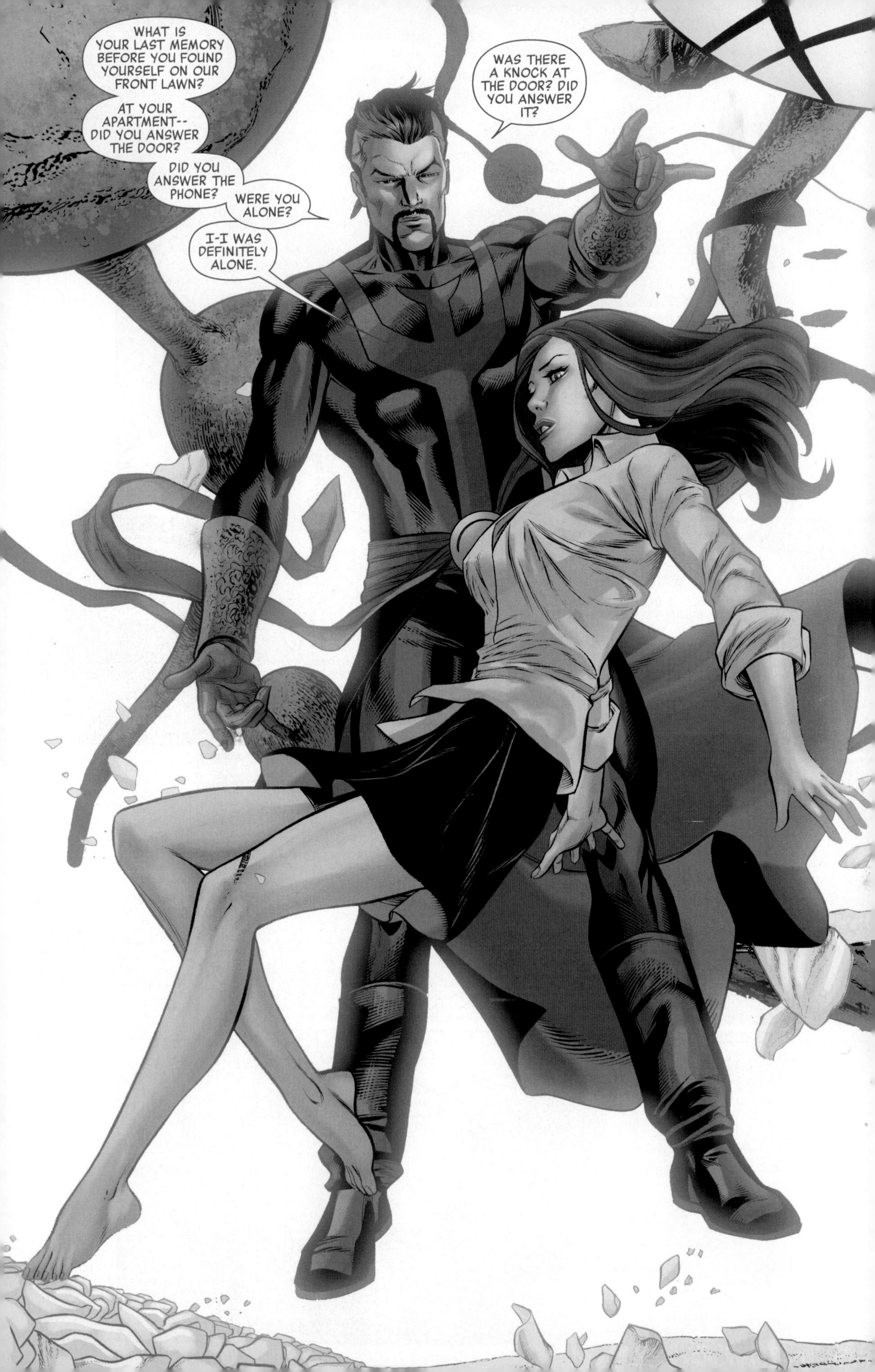
WHAT IS YOUR LAST MEMORY BEFORE YOU FOUND YOURSELF ON OUR FRONT LAWN?
AT YOUR APARTMENT-- DID YOU ANSWER THE DOOR?
DID YOU ANSWER THE PHONE?
WERE YOU ALONE?
I-I WAS DEFINITELY ALONE.
WAS THERE A KNOCK AT THE DOOR? DID YOU ANSWER IT?

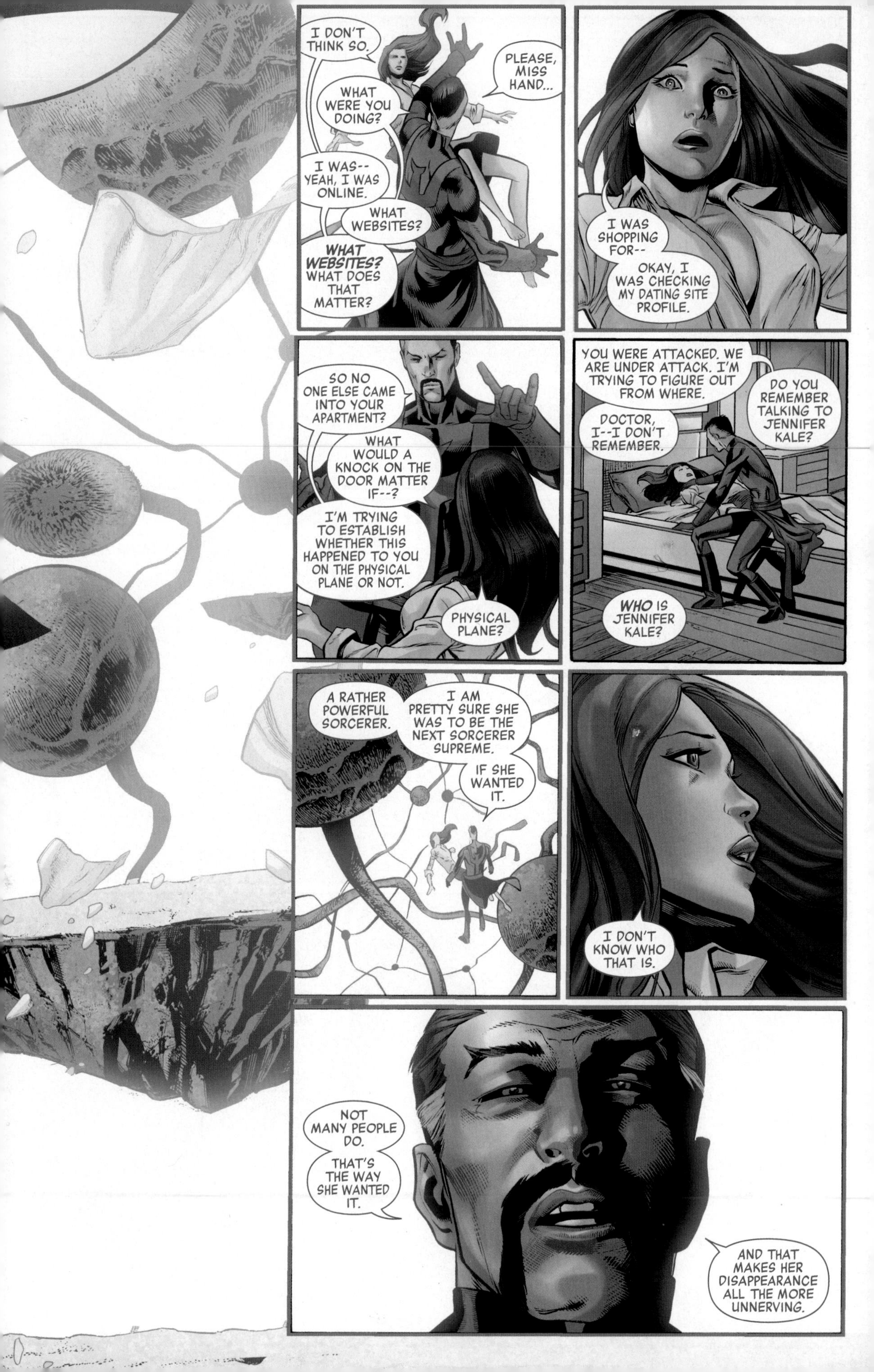
I DON'T THINK SO.
PLEASE, MISS HAND...
WHAT WERE YOU DOING?
I WAS-- YEAH, I WAS ONLINE.
WHAT WEBSITES?
WHAT WEBSITES? WHAT DOES THAT MATTER?
I WAS SHOPPING FOR--
OKAY, I WAS CHECKING MY DATING SITE PROFILE.
SO NO ONE ELSE CAME INTO YOUR APARTMENT?
WHAT WOULD A KNOCK ON THE DOOR MATTER IF--?
I'M TRYING TO ESTABLISH WHETHER THIS HAPPENED TO YOU ON THE PHYSICAL PLANE OR NOT.
PHYSICAL PLANE?
YOU WERE ATTACKED. WE ARE UNDER ATTACK. I'M TRYING TO FIGURE OUT FROM WHERE.
DO YOU REMEMBER TALKING TO JENNIFER KALE?
DOCTOR, I--I DON'T REMEMBER.
WHO IS JENNIFER KALE?
A RATHER POWERFUL SORCERER.
I AM PRETTY SURE SHE WAS TO BE THE NEXT SORCERER SUPREME.
IF SHE WANTED IT.
I DON'T KNOW WHO THAT IS.
NOT MANY PEOPLE DO.
THAT'S THE WAY SHE WANTED IT.
AND THAT MAKES HER DISAPPEARANCE ALL THE MORE UNNERVING.

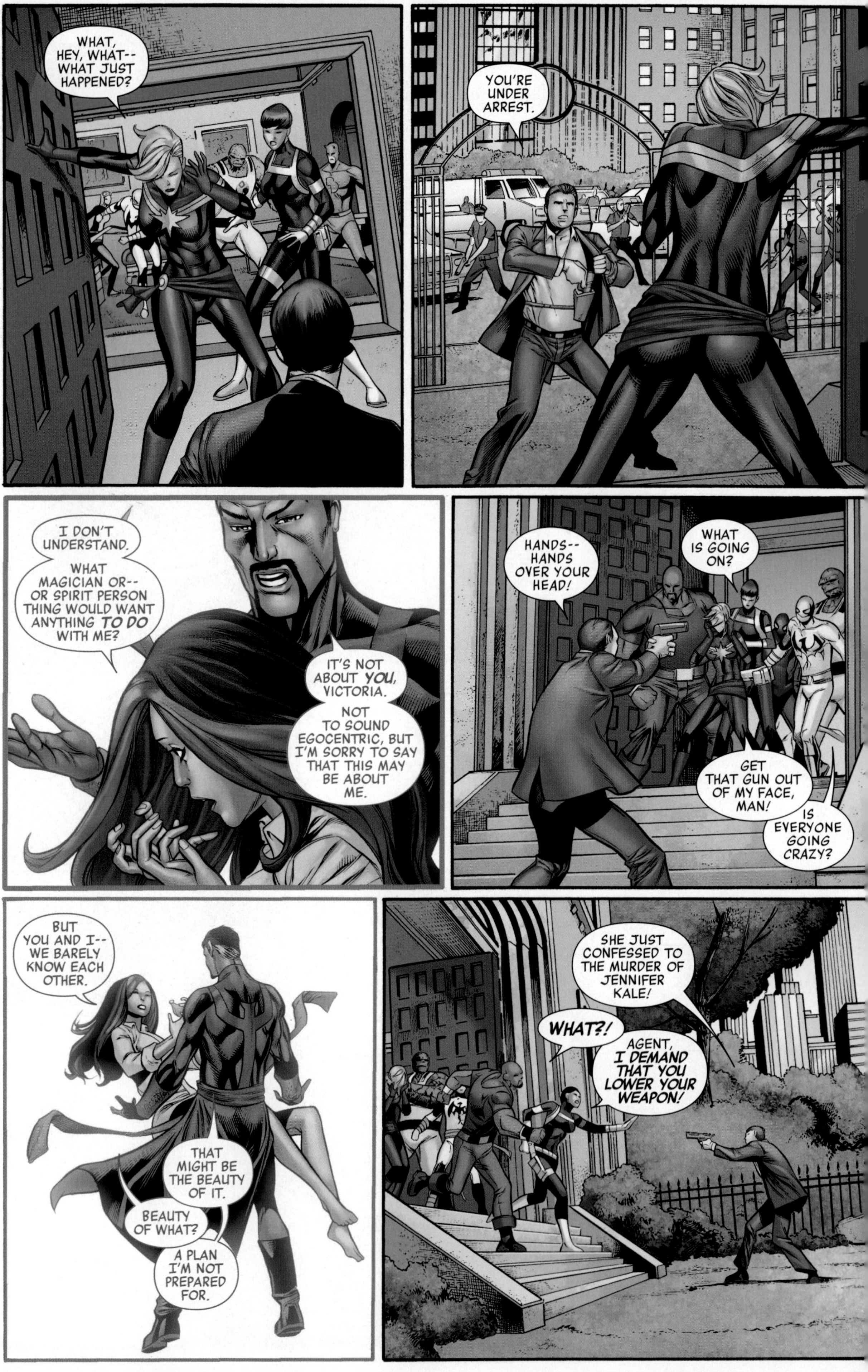
WHAT, HEY, WHAT-- WHAT JUST HAPPENED?
YOU'RE UNDER ARREST.
I DON'T UNDERSTAND.
WHAT MAGICIAN OR-- OR SPIRIT PERSON THING WOULD WANT ANYTHING TO DO WITH ME?
IT'S NOT ABOUT YOU, VICTORIA.
NOT TO SOUND EGOCENTRIC, BUT I'M SORRY TO SAY THAT THIS MAY BE ABOUT ME.
HANDS-- HANDS OVER YOUR HEAD!
WHAT IS GOING ON?
GET THAT GUN OUT OF MY FACE, MAN!
IS EVERYONE GOING CRAZY?
BUT YOU AND I-- WE BARELY KNOW EACH OTHER.
THAT MIGHT BE THE BEAUTY OF IT.
BEAUTY OF WHAT?
A PLAN I'M NOT PREPARED FOR.
SHE JUST CONFESSED TO THE MURDER OF JENNIFER KALE!
WHAT?!
AGENT, I DEMAND THAT YOU LOWER YOUR WEAPON!

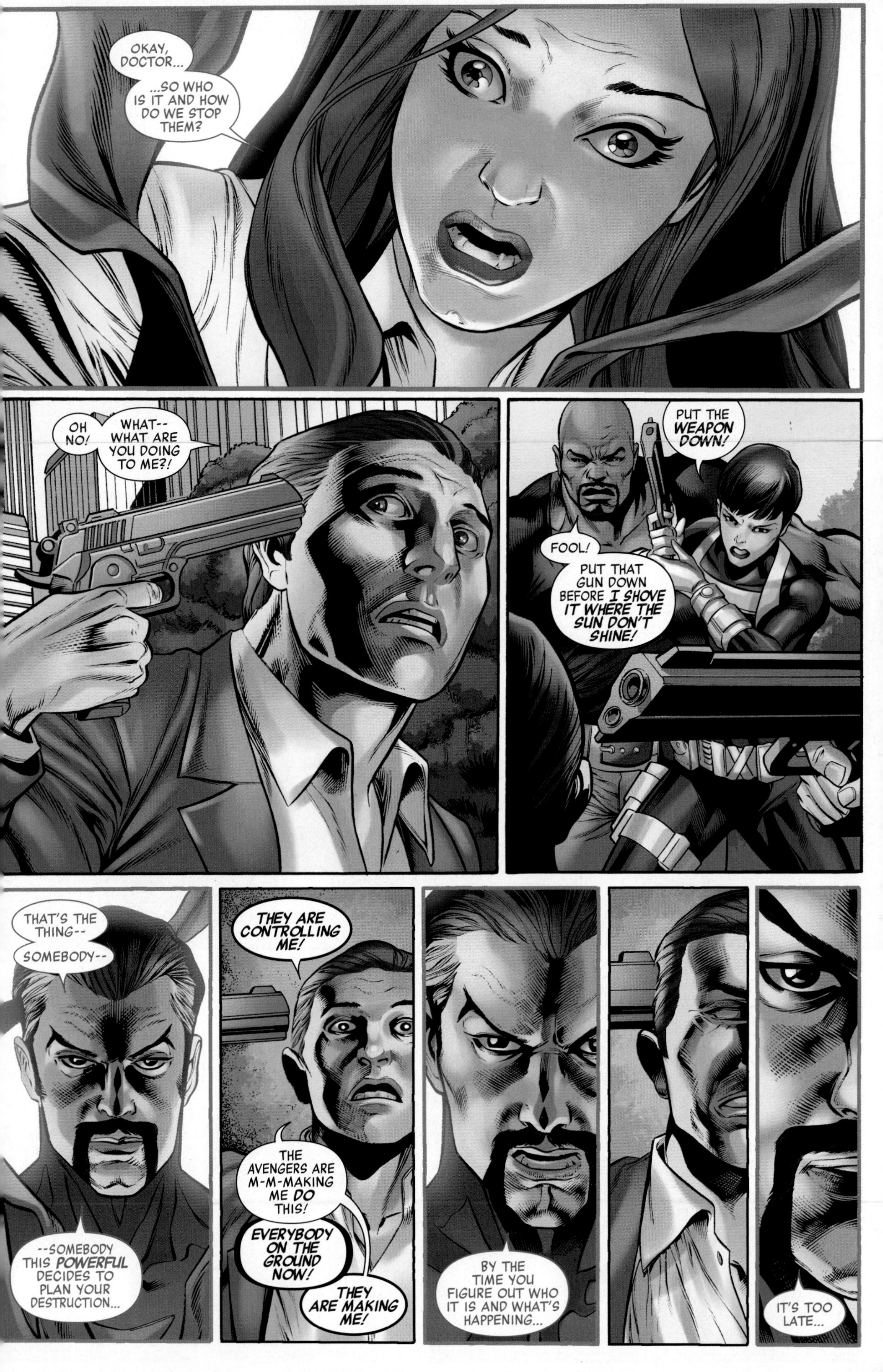

OKAY, DOCTOR...
...SO WHO IS IT AND HOW DO WE STOP THEM?
OH NO!
WHAT-- WHAT ARE YOU DOING TO ME?!
PUT THE WEAPON DOWN!
FOOL!
PUT THAT GUN DOWN BEFORE I SHOVE IT WHERE THE SUN DON'T SHINE!
THAT'S THE THING--
SOMEBODY--
--SOMEBODY THIS POWERFUL DECIDES TO PLAN YOUR DESTRUCTION...
THEY ARE CONTROLLING ME!
THE AVENGERS ARE M-M-MAKING ME DO THIS!
EVERYBODY ON THE GROUND NOW!
THEY ARE MAKING ME!
BY THE TIME YOU FIGURE OUT WHO IT IS AND WHAT'S HAPPENING...
IT'S TOO LATE...

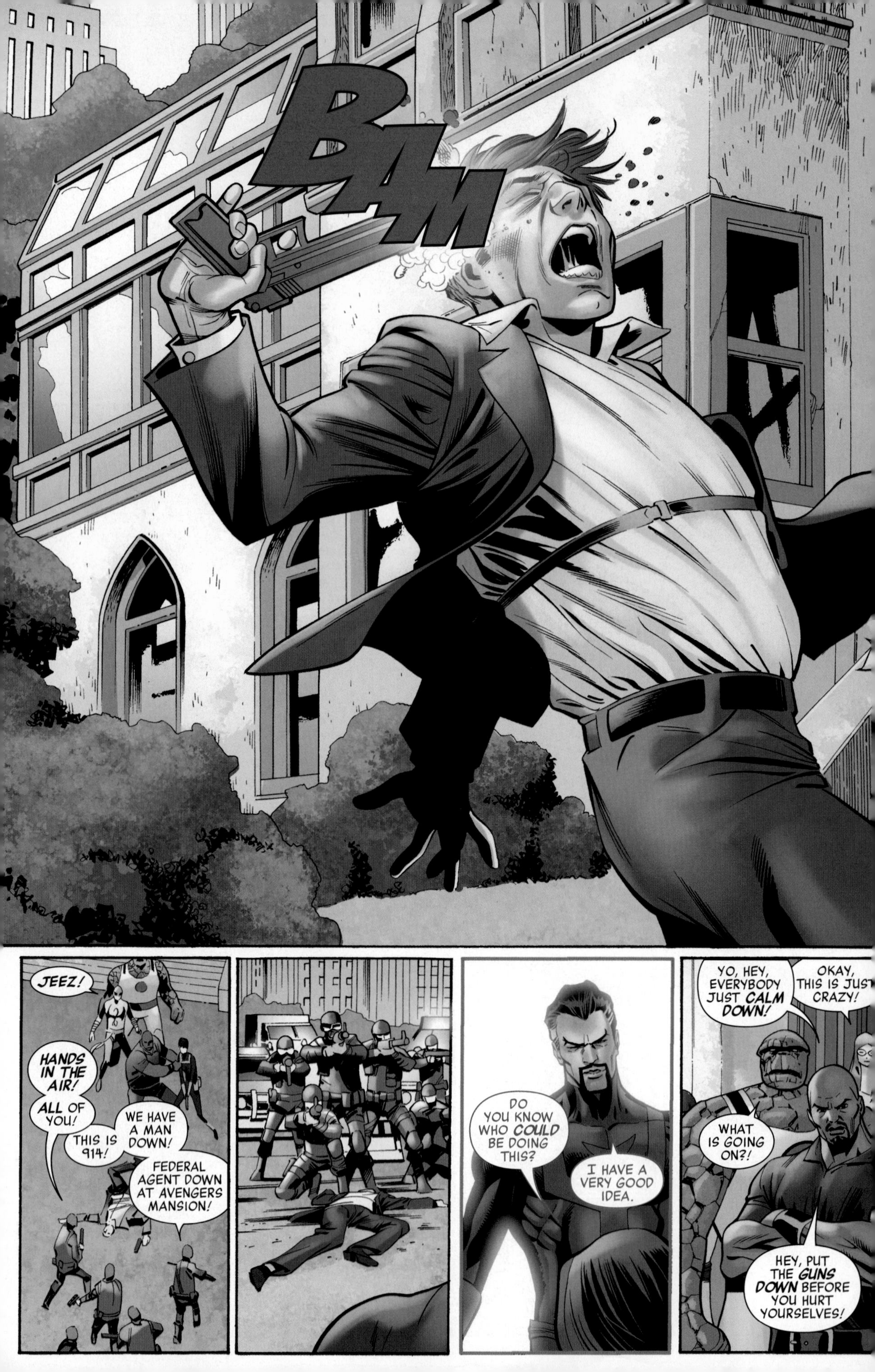
BAM
JEEZ!
HANDS IN THE AIR!
ALL OF YOU!
THIS IS 914!
WE HAVE A MAN DOWN!
FEDERAL AGENT DOWN AT AVENGERS MANSION!
DO YOU KNOW WHO COULD BE DOING THIS?
I HAVE A VERY GOOD IDEA.
YO, HEY, EVERYBODY JUST CALM DOWN!
OKAY, THIS IS JUST CRAZY!
WHAT IS GOING ON?!
HEY, PUT THE GUNS DOWN BEFORE YOU HURT YOURSELVES!

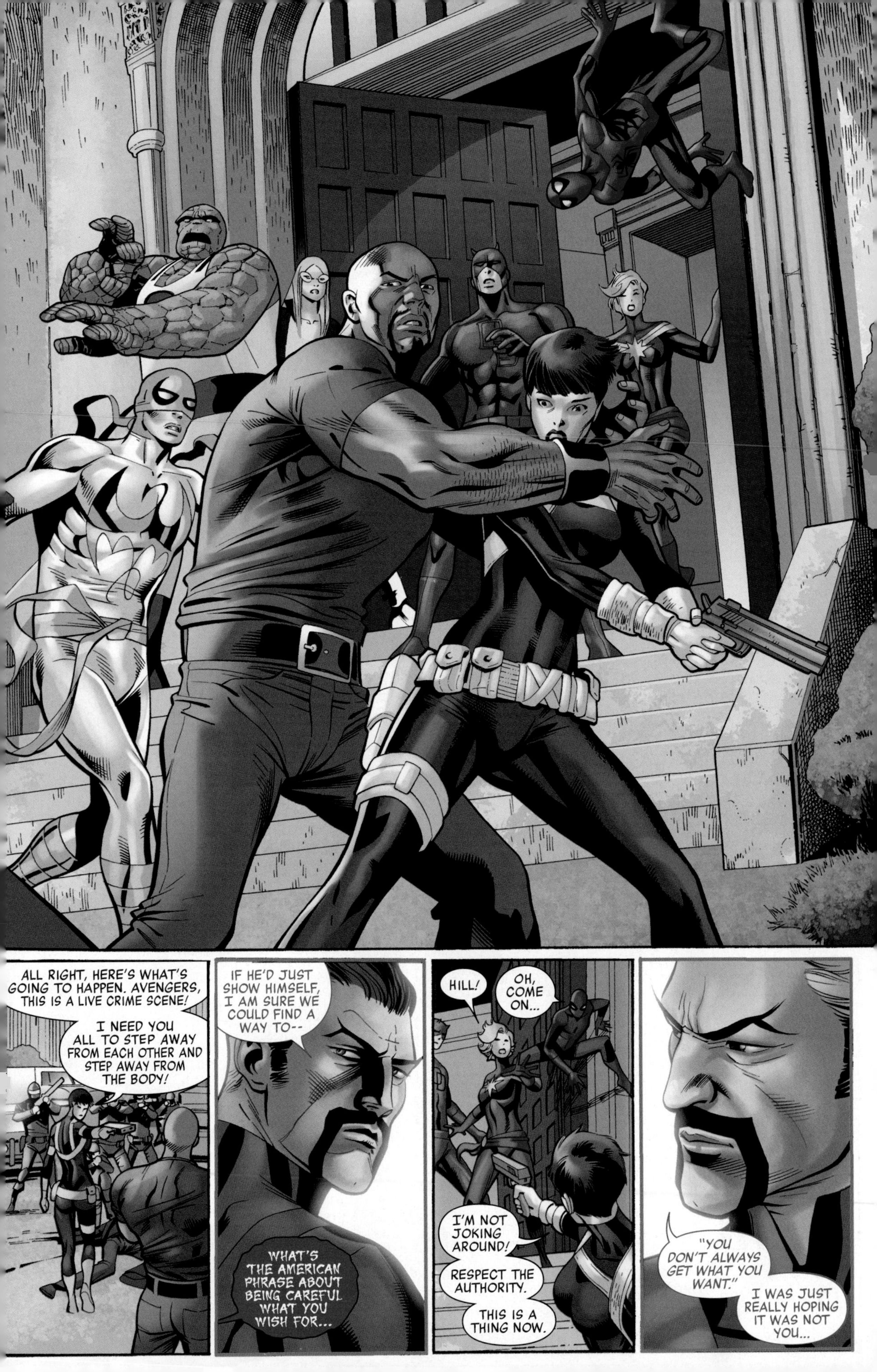
ALL RIGHT, HERE'S WHAT'S GOING TO HAPPEN. AVENGERS, THIS IS A LIVE CRIME SCENE!
I NEED YOU ALL TO STEP AWAY FROM EACH OTHER AND STEP AWAY FROM THE BODY!
IF HE'D JUST SHOW HIMSELF, I AM SURE WE COULD FIND A WAY TO--
WHAT'S THE AMERICAN PHRASE ABOUT BEING CAREFUL WHAT YOU WISH FOR...
HILL!
OH, COME ON...
I'M NOT JOKING AROUND!
RESPECT THE AUTHORITY.
THIS IS A THING NOW.
"YOU DON'T ALWAYS GET WHAT YOU WANT."
I WAS JUST REALLY HOPING IT WAS NOT YOU...

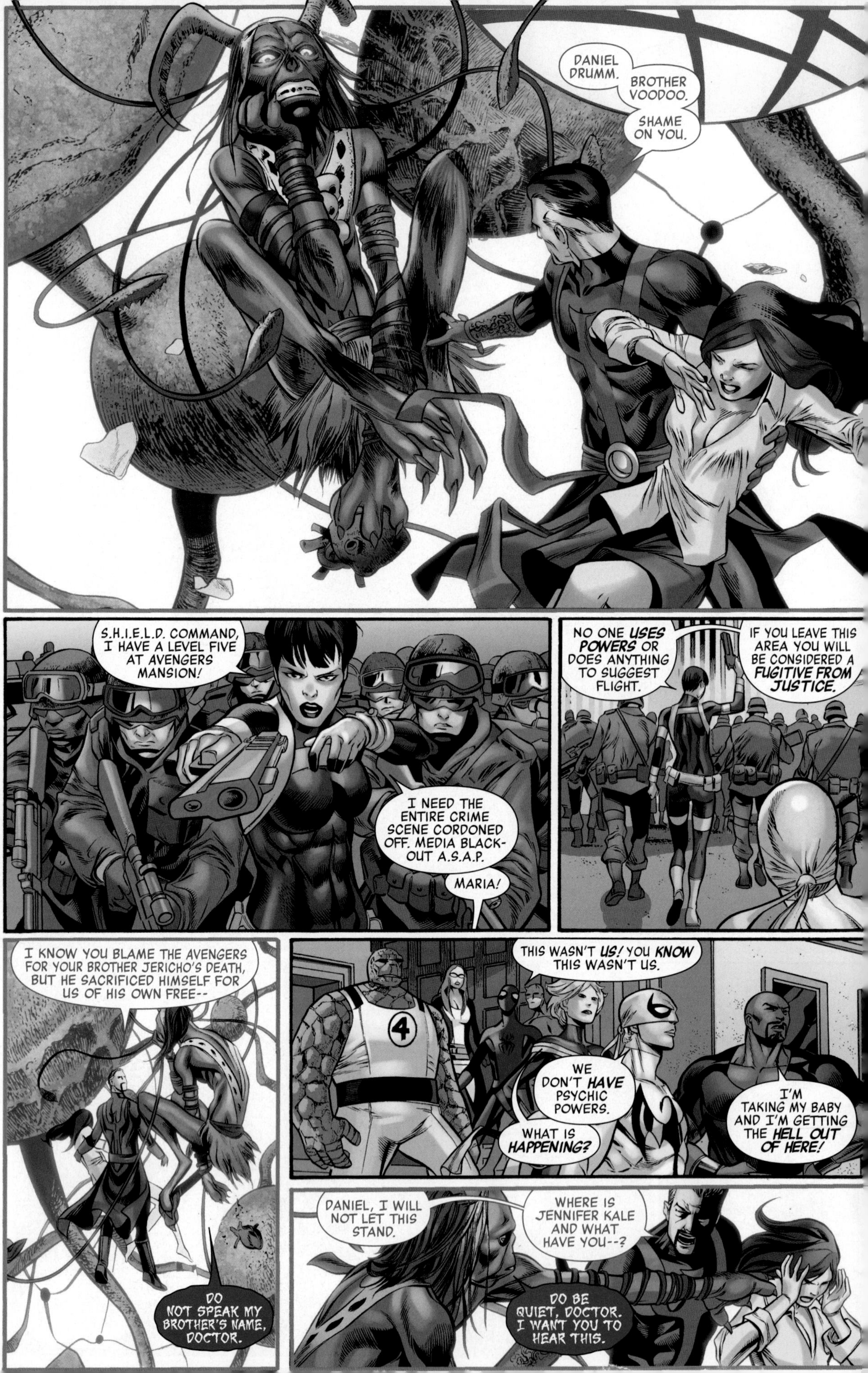

DANIEL DRUMM.
BROTHER VOODOO.
SHAME ON YOU.
S.H.I.E.L.D. COMMAND, I HAVE A LEVEL FIVE AT AVENGERS MANSION!
I NEED THE ENTIRE CRIME SCENE CORDONED OFF. MEDIA BLACK-OUT A.S.A.P.
MARIA!
NO ONE USES POWERS OR DOES ANYTHING TO SUGGEST FLIGHT.
IF YOU LEAVE THIS AREA YOU WILL BE CONSIDERED A FUGITIVE FROM JUSTICE.
I KNOW YOU BLAME THE AVENGERS FOR YOUR BROTHER JERICHO'S DEATH, BUT HE SACRIFICED HIMSELF FOR US OF HIS OWN FREE--
DO NOT SPEAK MY BROTHER'S NAME, DOCTOR.
THIS WASN'T US! YOU KNOW THIS WASN'T US.
WE DON'T HAVE PSYCHIC POWERS.
WHAT IS HAPPENING?
I'M TAKING MY BABY AND I'M GETTING THE HELL OUT OF HERE!
DANIEL, I WILL NOT LET THIS STAND.
WHERE IS JENNIFER KALE AND WHAT HAVE YOU--?
DO BE QUIET, DOCTOR. I WANT YOU TO HEAR THIS.

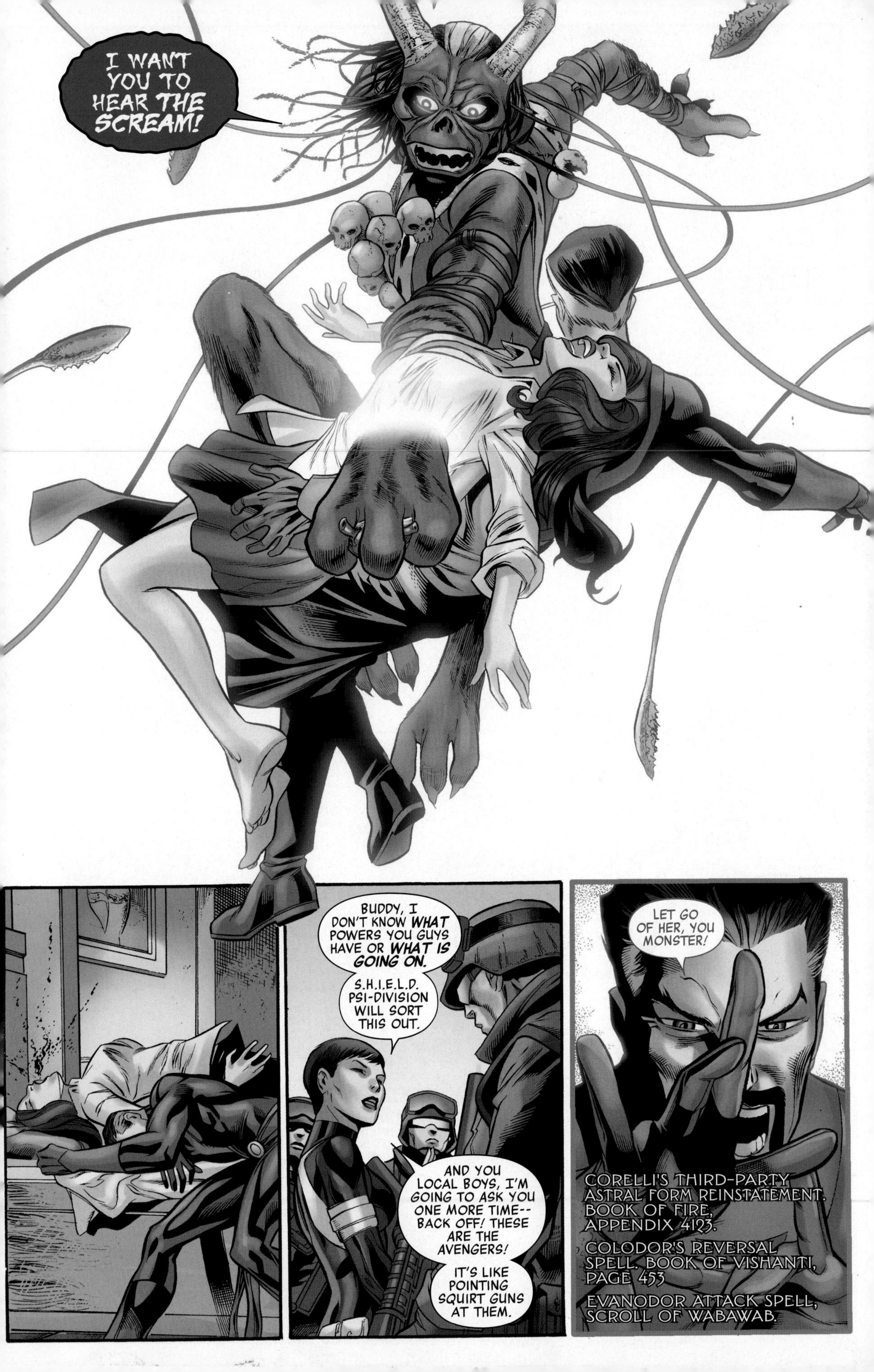
I WANT YOU TO HEAR THE SCREAM!
BUDDY, I DON'T KNOW WHAT POWERS YOU GUYS HAVE OR WHAT IS GOING ON.
S.H.I.E.L.D. PSI-DIVISION WILL SORT THIS OUT.
AND YOU LOCAL BOYS, I'M GOING TO ASK YOU ONE MORE TIME-- BACK OFF! THESE ARE THE AVENGERS!
IT'S LIKE POINTING SQUIRT GUNS AT THEM.
LET GO OF HER, YOU MONSTER!
CORELLI'S THIRD-PARTY ASTRAL FORM REINSTATEMENT. BOOK OF FIRE, APPENDIX 4123.
COLODOR'S REVERSAL SPELL. BOOK OF VISHANTI, PAGE 453
EVANODOR ATTACK SPELL, SCROLL OF WABAWAB.

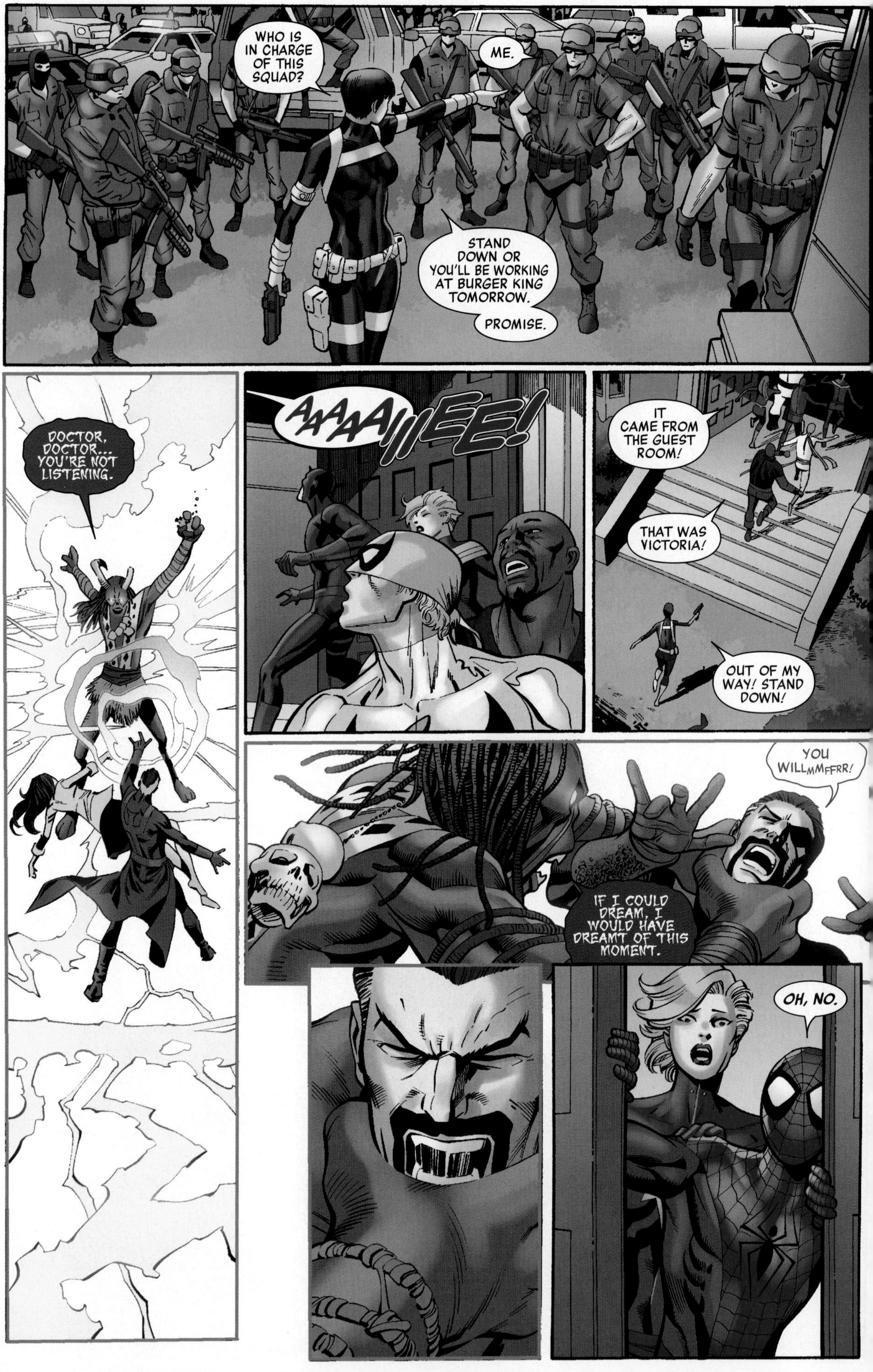

WHO IS IN CHARGE OF THIS SQUAD?
ME.
STAND DOWN OR YOU'LL BE WORKING AT BURGER KING TOMORROW.
PROMISE.
DOCTOR, DOCTOR... YOU'RE NOT LISTENING.
AAAAAIIIIEEE!
IT CAME FROM THE GUEST ROOM!
THAT WAS VICTORIA!
OUT OF MY WAY! STAND DOWN!
YOU WILLMMFFRR!
IF I COULD DREAM, I WOULD HAVE DREAMT OF THIS MOMENT.
OH, NO.

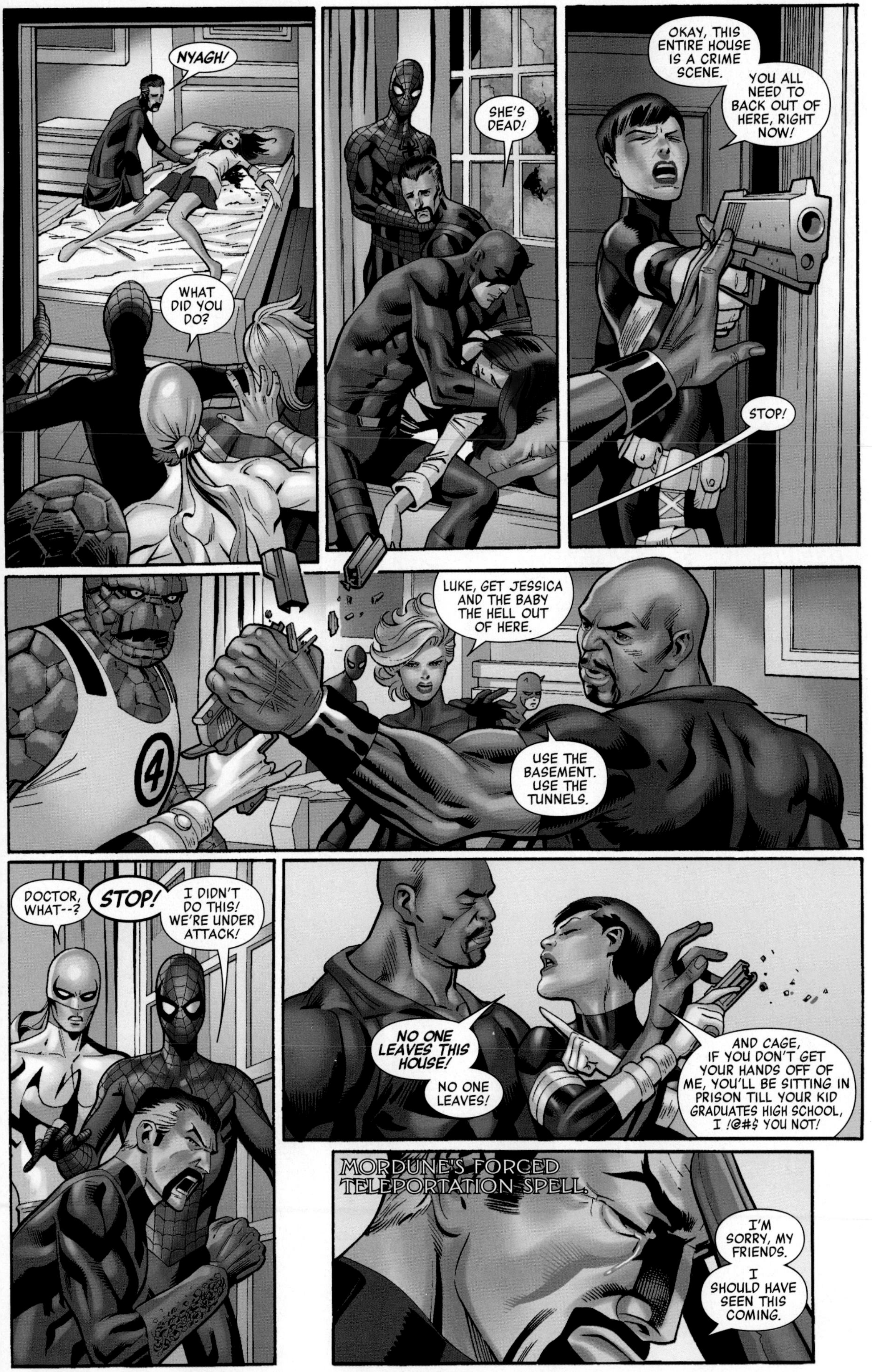
NYAGH!
WHAT DID YOU DO?
SHE'S DEAD!
OKAY, THIS ENTIRE HOUSE IS A CRIME SCENE.
YOU ALL NEED TO BACK OUT OF HERE, RIGHT NOW!
STOP!
LUKE, GET JESSICA AND THE BABY THE HELL OUT OF HERE.
USE THE BASEMENT. USE THE TUNNELS.
DOCTOR, WHAT--?
STOP!
I DIDN'T DO THIS! WE'RE UNDER ATTACK!
NO ONE LEAVES THIS HOUSE!
NO ONE LEAVES!
AND CAGE, IF YOU DON'T GET YOUR HANDS OFF OF ME, YOU'LL BE SITTING IN PRISON TILL YOUR KID GRADUATES HIGH SCHOOL, I !@#$ YOU NOT!
MORDUNE'S FORCED TELEPORTATION SPELL.
I'M SORRY, MY FRIENDS.
I SHOULD HAVE SEEN THIS COMING.

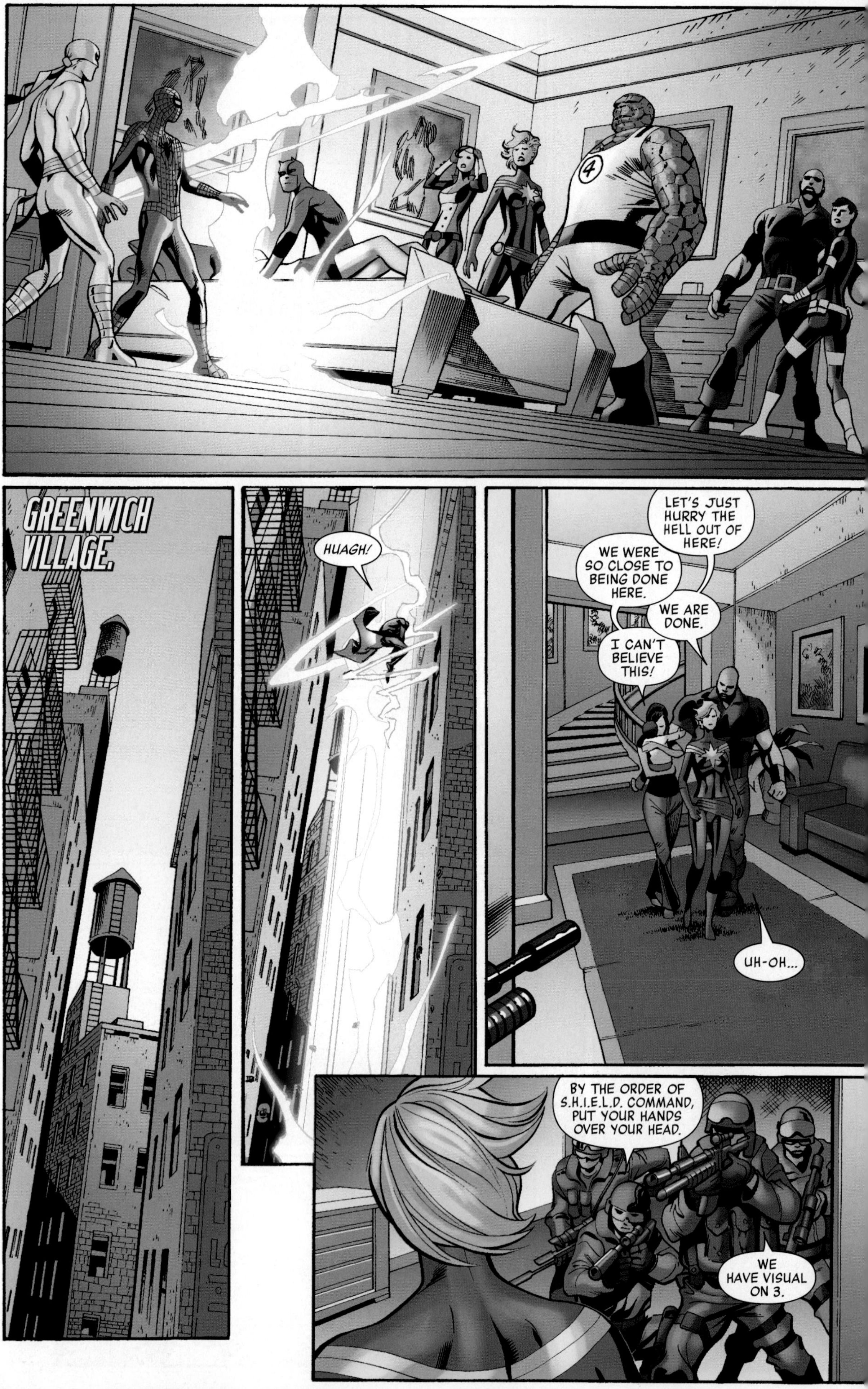
GREENWICH VILLAGE.
HUAGH!
LET'S JUST HURRY THE HELL OUT OF HERE!
WE WERE SO CLOSE TO BEING DONE HERE.
WE ARE DONE.
I CAN'T BELIEVE THIS!
UH-OH...
BY THE ORDER OF S.H.I.E.L.D. COMMAND, PUT YOUR HANDS OVER YOUR HEAD.
WE HAVE VISUAL ON 3.

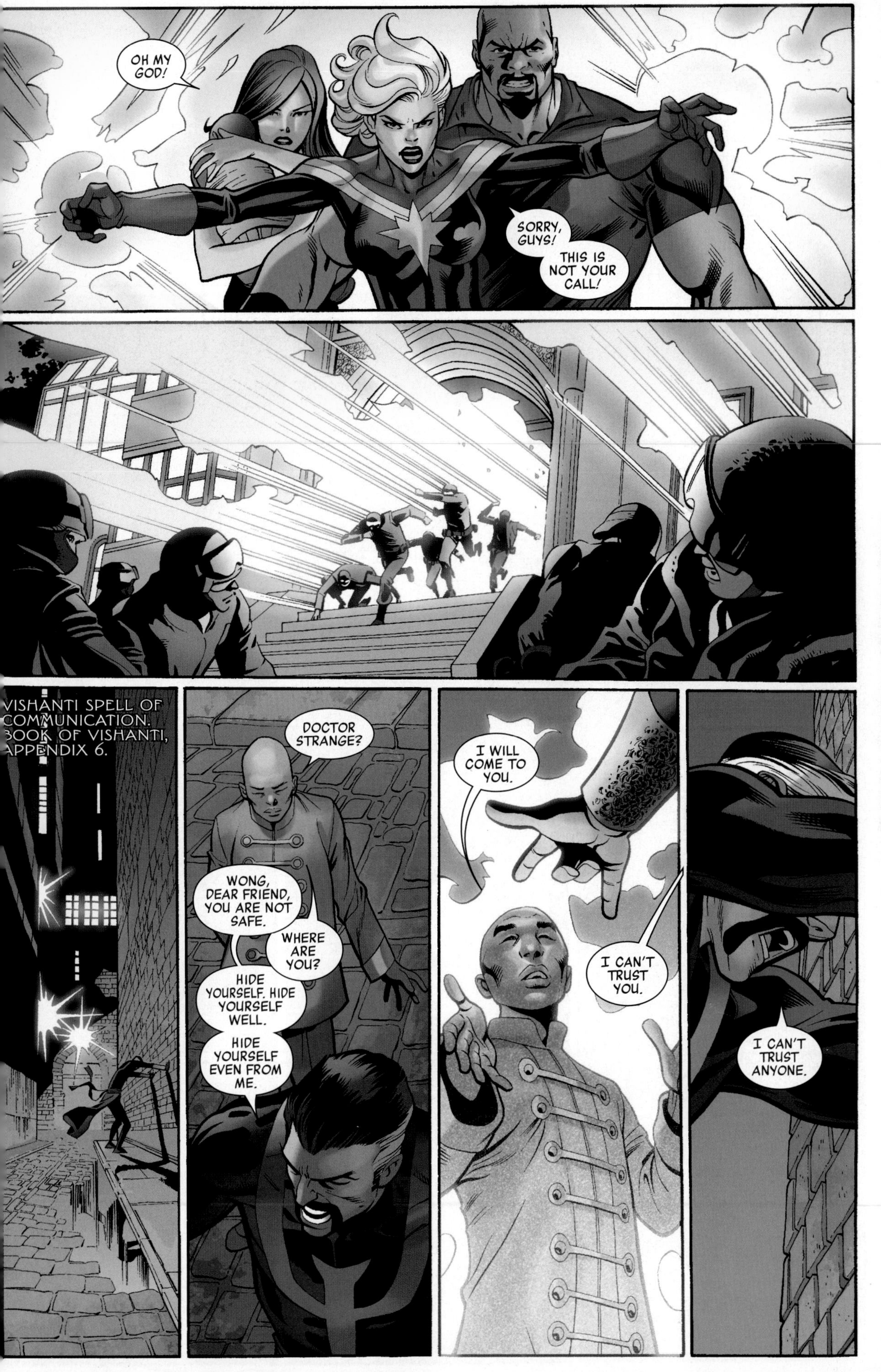
OH MY GOD!
SORRY, GUYS!
THIS IS NOT YOUR CALL!
VISHANTI SPELL OF COMMUNICATION. BOOK OF VISHANTI, APPENDIX 6.
DOCTOR STRANGE?
WONG, DEAR FRIEND, YOU ARE NOT SAFE.
WHERE ARE YOU?
HIDE YOURSELF. HIDE YOURSELF WELL.
HIDE YOURSELF EVEN FROM ME.
I WILL COME TO YOU.
I CAN'T TRUST YOU.
I CAN'T TRUST ANYONE.

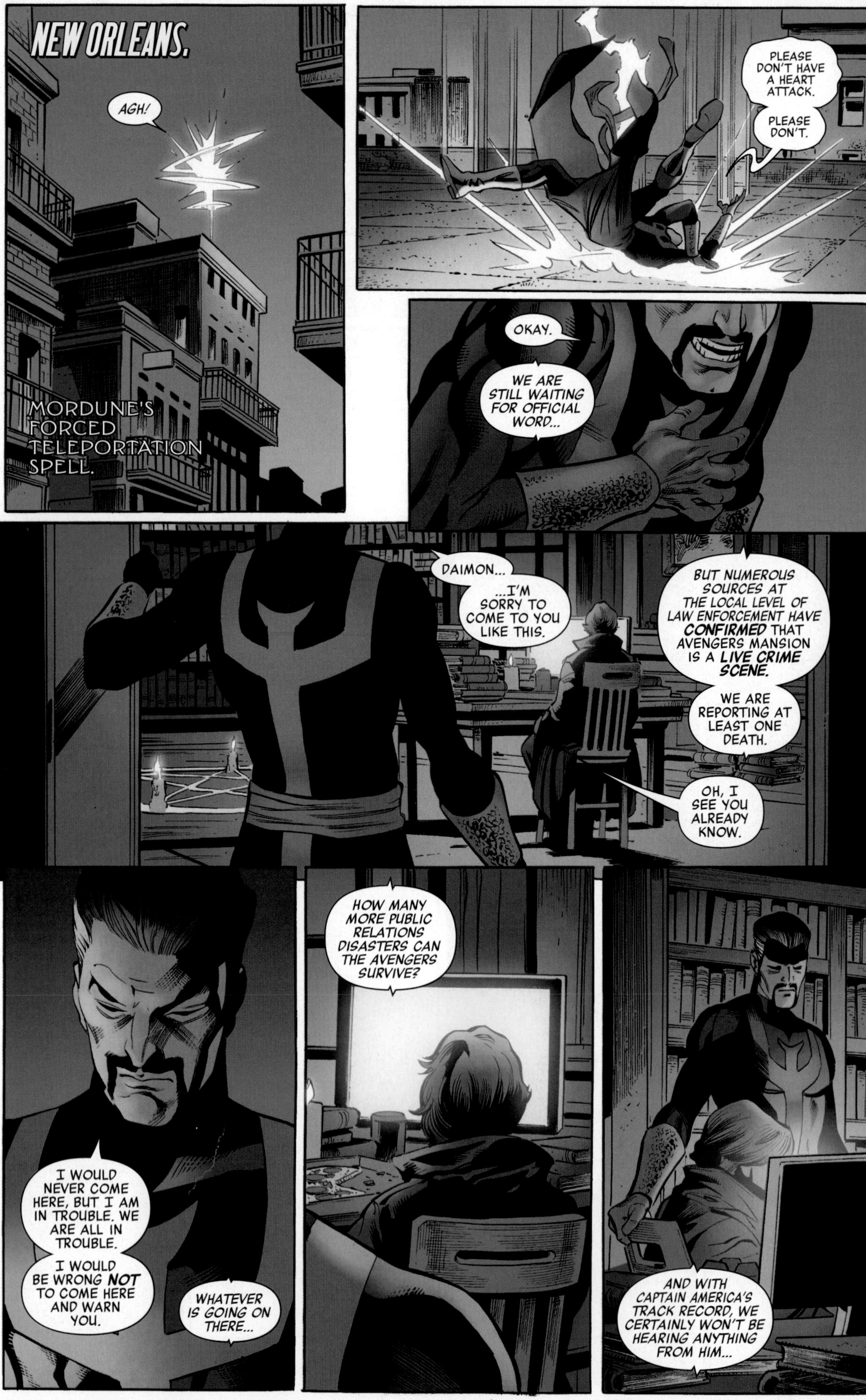
NEW ORLEANS.
AGH!
MORDUNE'S FORCED TELEPORTATION SPELL.
PLEASE DON'T HAVE A HEART ATTACK.
PLEASE DON'T.
OKAY.
WE ARE STILL WAITING FOR OFFICIAL WORD...
DAIMON...
...I'M SORRY TO COME TO YOU LIKE THIS.
BUT NUMEROUS SOURCES AT THE LOCAL LEVEL OF LAW ENFORCEMENT HAVE CONFIRMED THAT AVENGERS MANSION IS A LIVE CRIME SCENE.
WE ARE REPORTING AT LEAST ONE DEATH.
OH, I SEE YOU ALREADY KNOW.
I WOULD NEVER COME HERE, BUT I AM IN TROUBLE. WE ARE ALL IN TROUBLE.
I WOULD BE WRONG NOT TO COME HERE AND WARN YOU.
WHATEVER IS GOING ON THERE...
HOW MANY MORE PUBLIC RELATIONS DISASTERS CAN THE AVENGERS SURVIVE?
AND WITH CAPTAIN AMERICA'S TRACK RECORD, WE CERTAINLY WON'T BE HEARING ANYTHING FROM HIM...

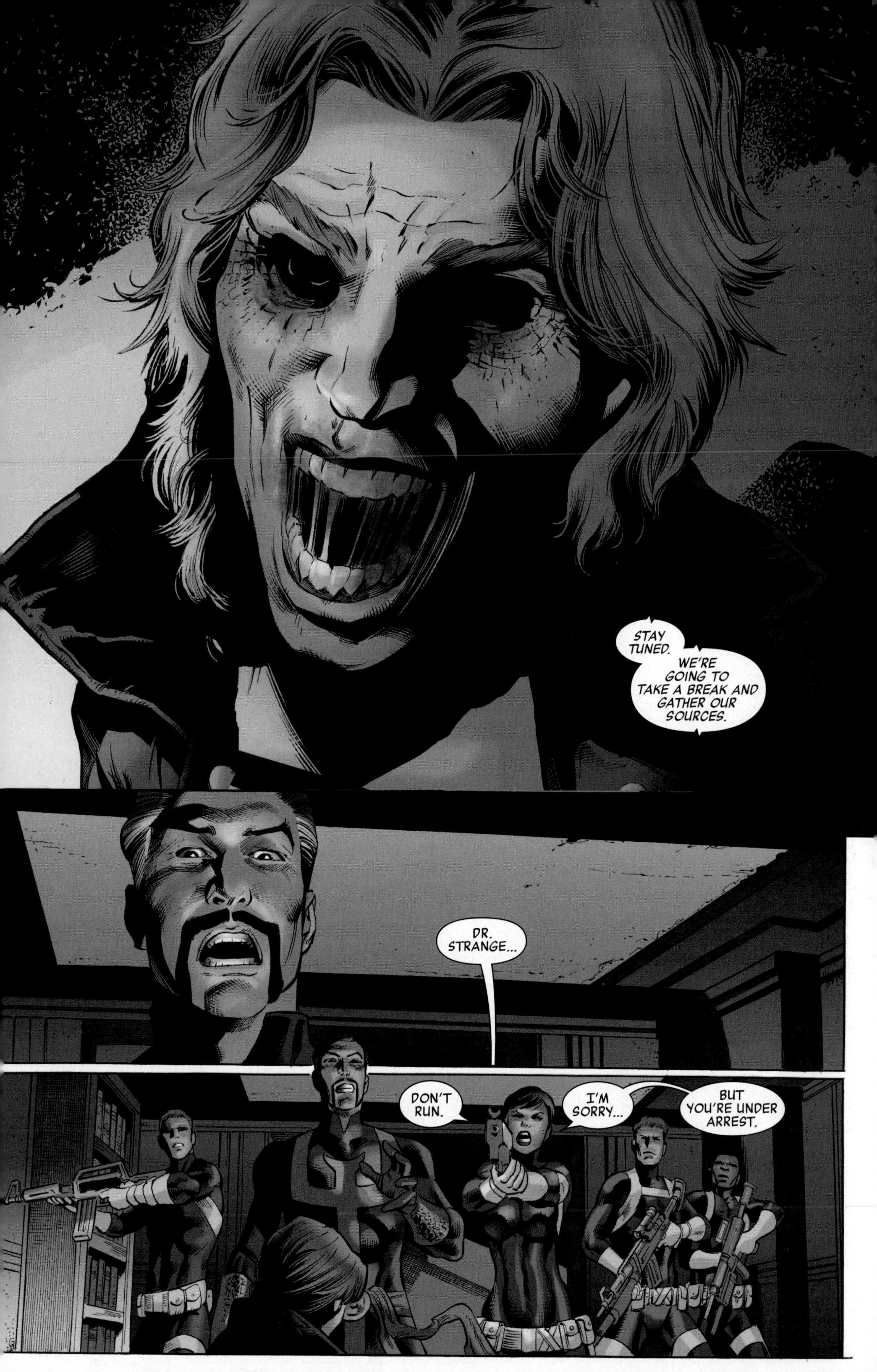
STAY TUNED.
WE'RE GOING TO TAKE A BREAK AND GATHER OUR SOURCES.
DR. STRANGE...
DON'T RUN.
I'M SORRY...
BUT YOU'RE UNDER ARREST.

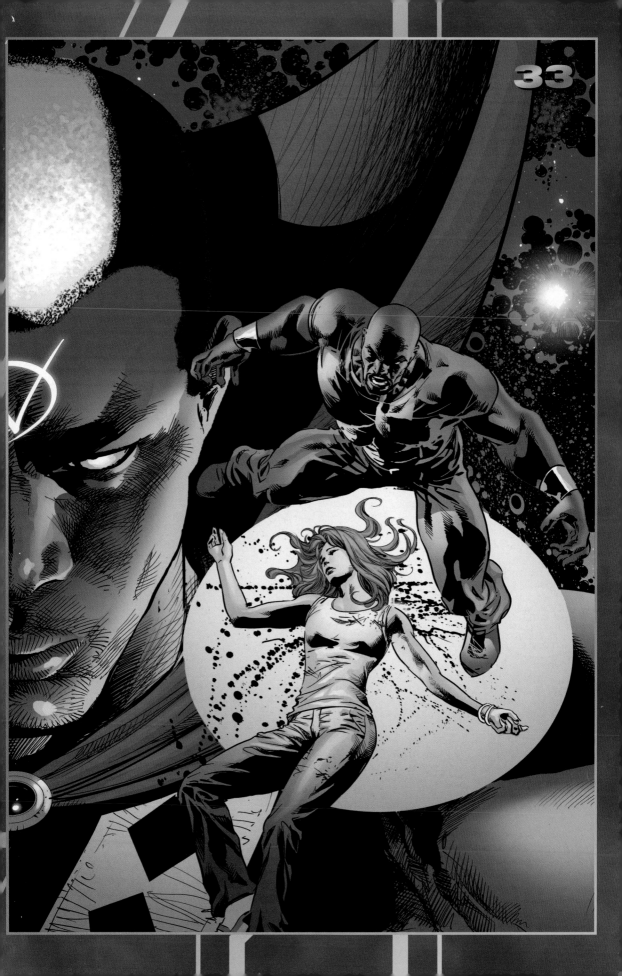

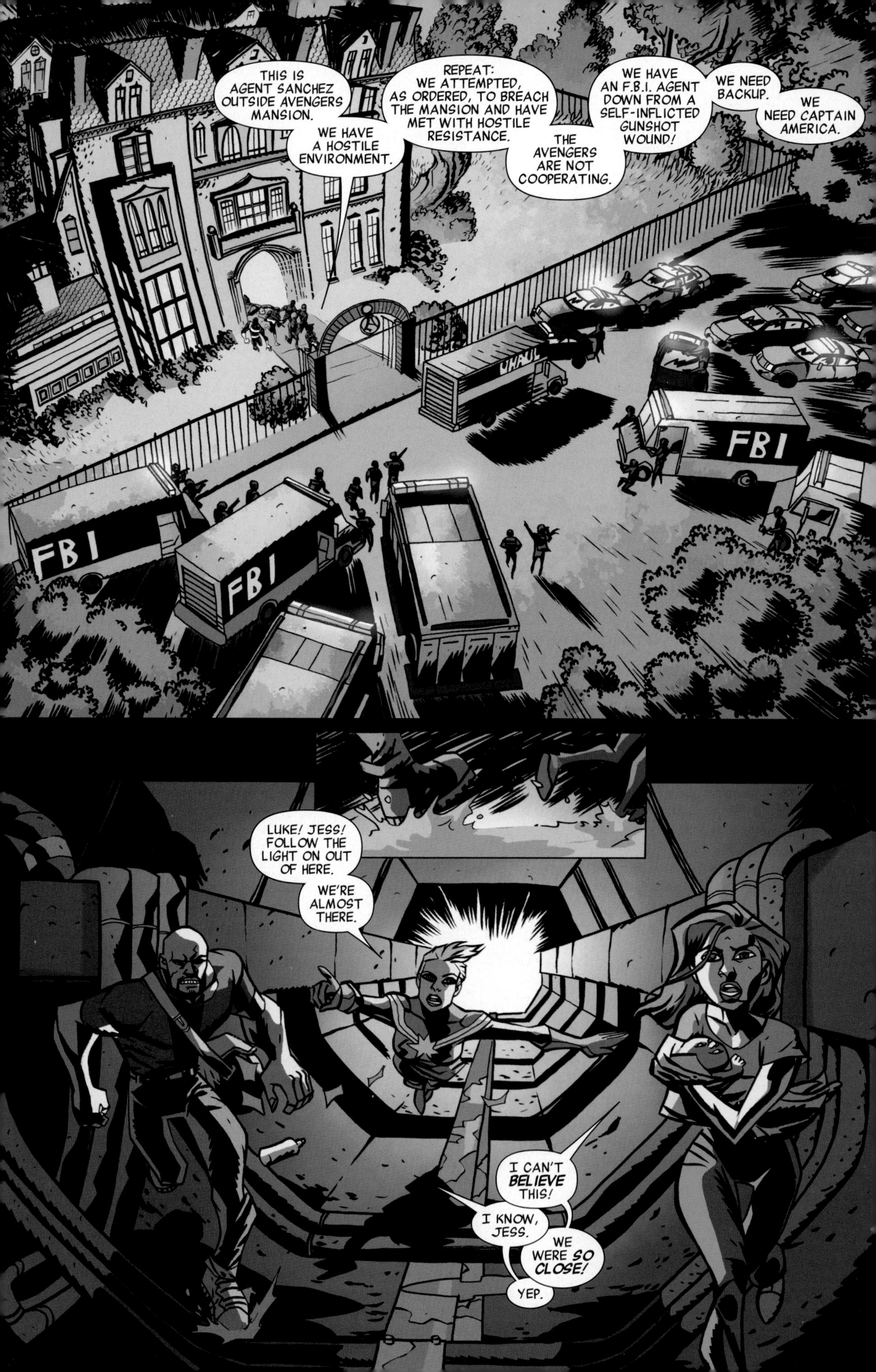
THIS IS AGENT SANCHEZ OUTSIDE AVENGERS MANSION.
WE HAVE A HOSTILE ENVIRONMENT.
REPEAT: WE ATTEMPTED, AS ORDERED, TO BREACH THE MANSION AND HAVE MET WITH HOSTILE RESISTANCE.
THE AVENGERS ARE NOT COOPERATING.
WE HAVE AN F.B.I. AGENT DOWN FROM A SELF-INFLICTED GUNSHOT WOUND!
WE NEED BACKUP.
WE NEED CAPTAIN AMERICA.
U-HAUL
FBI
FBI
FBI
LUKE! JESS! FOLLOW THE LIGHT ON OUT OF HERE.
WE'RE ALMOST THERE.
I CAN'T *BELIEVE* THIS!
I KNOW, JESS.
WE WERE *SO CLOSE!*
YEP.

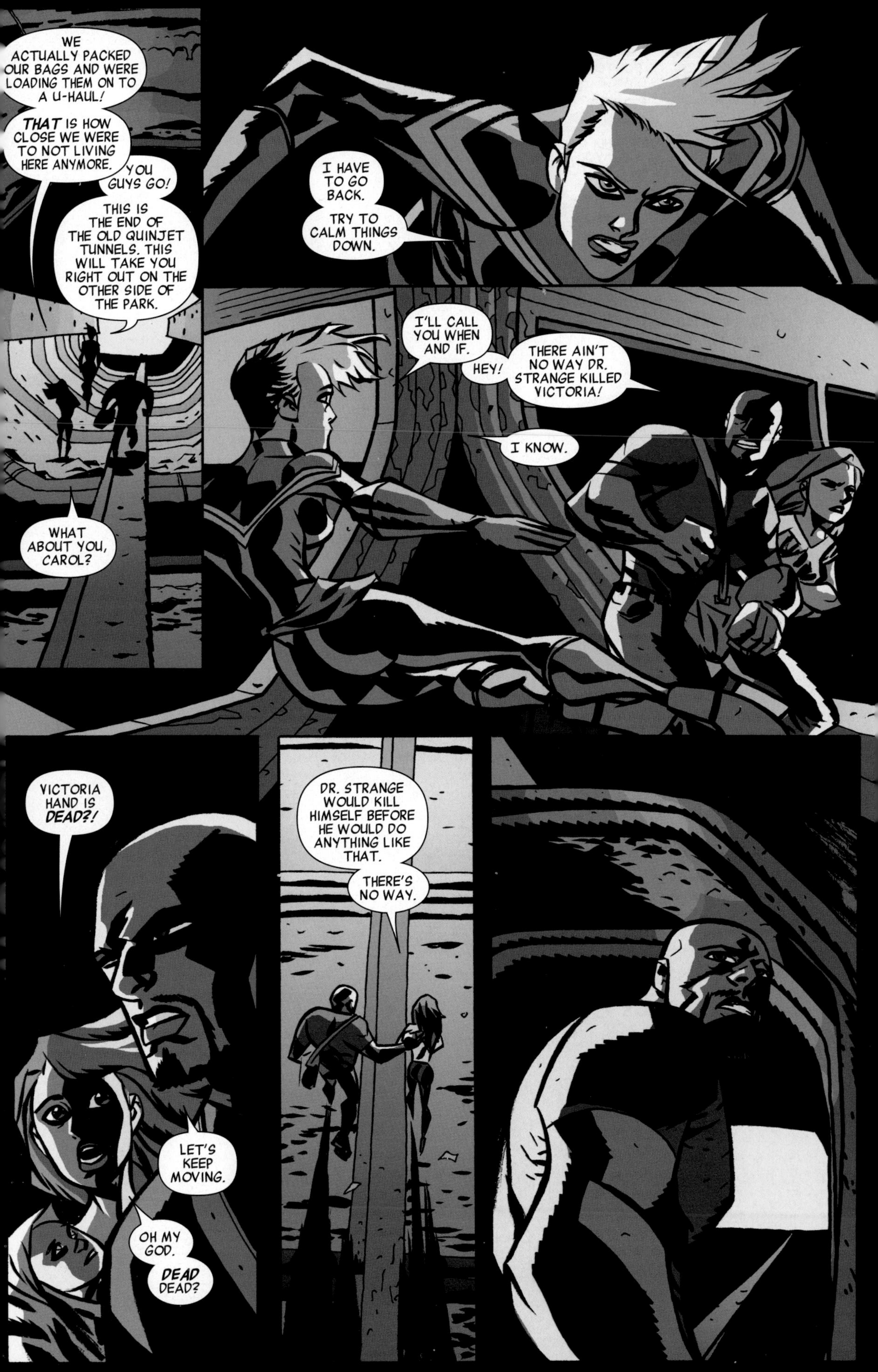

WE ACTUALLY PACKED OUR BAGS AND WERE LOADING THEM ON TO A U-HAUL!
THAT IS HOW CLOSE WE WERE TO NOT LIVING HERE ANYMORE.
YOU GUYS GO!
THIS IS THE END OF THE OLD QUINJET TUNNELS. THIS WILL TAKE YOU RIGHT OUT ON THE OTHER SIDE OF THE PARK.
I HAVE TO GO BACK.
TRY TO CALM THINGS DOWN.
WHAT ABOUT YOU, CAROL?
I'LL CALL YOU WHEN AND IF.
HEY!
THERE AIN'T NO WAY DR. STRANGE KILLED VICTORIA!
I KNOW.
VICTORIA HAND IS DEAD?!
LET'S KEEP MOVING.
OH MY GOD.
DEAD DEAD?
DR. STRANGE WOULD KILL HIMSELF BEFORE HE WOULD DO ANYTHING LIKE THAT.
THERE'S NO WAY.

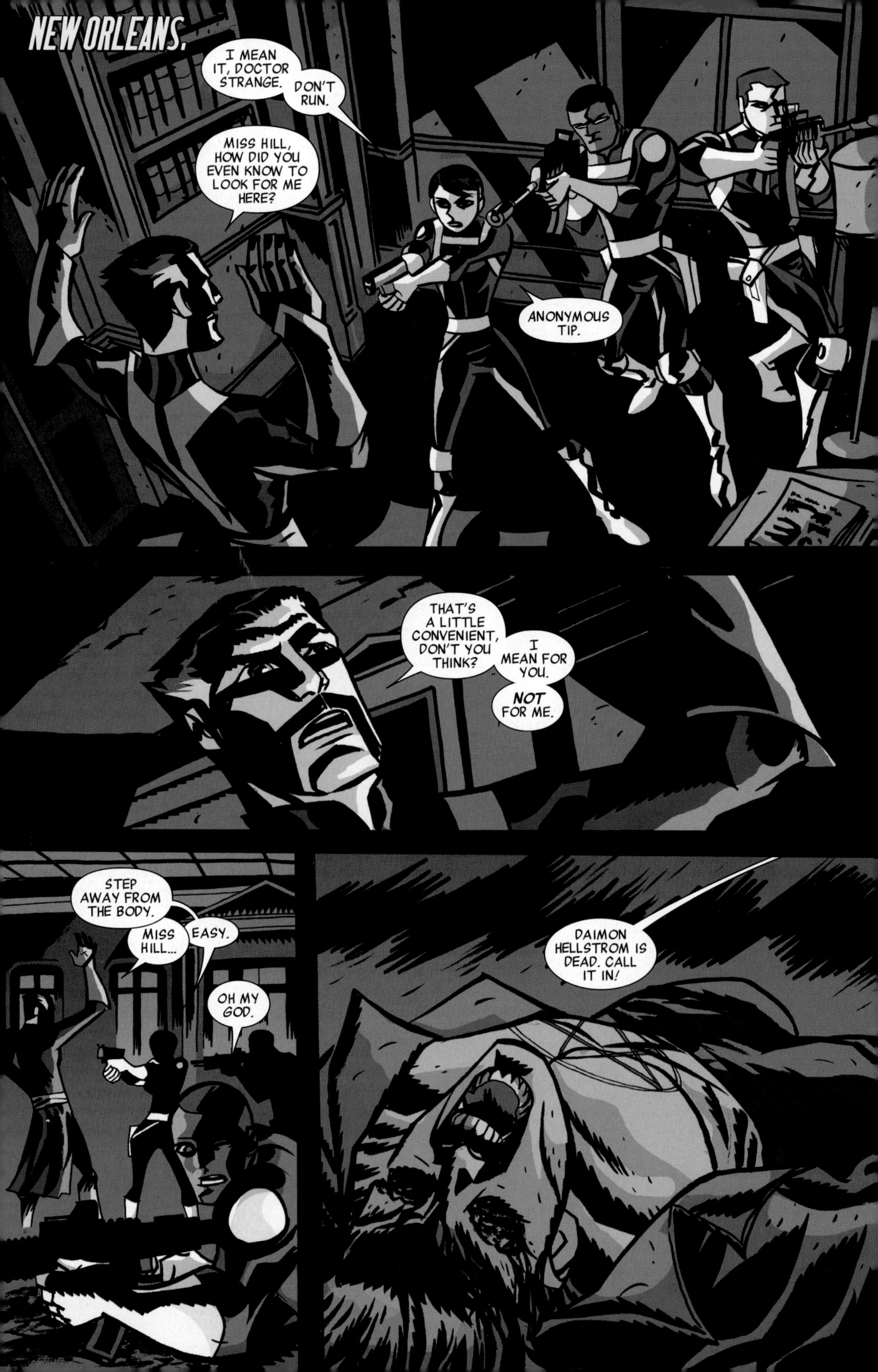
NEW ORLEANS.
I MEAN IT, DOCTOR STRANGE.
DON'T RUN.
MISS HILL, HOW DID YOU EVEN KNOW TO LOOK FOR ME HERE?
ANONYMOUS TIP.
THAT'S A LITTLE CONVENIENT, DON'T YOU THINK?
I MEAN FOR YOU.
NOT FOR ME.
STEP AWAY FROM THE BODY.
MISS HILL...
EASY.
OH MY GOD.
DAIMON HELLSTROM IS DEAD. CALL IT IN!

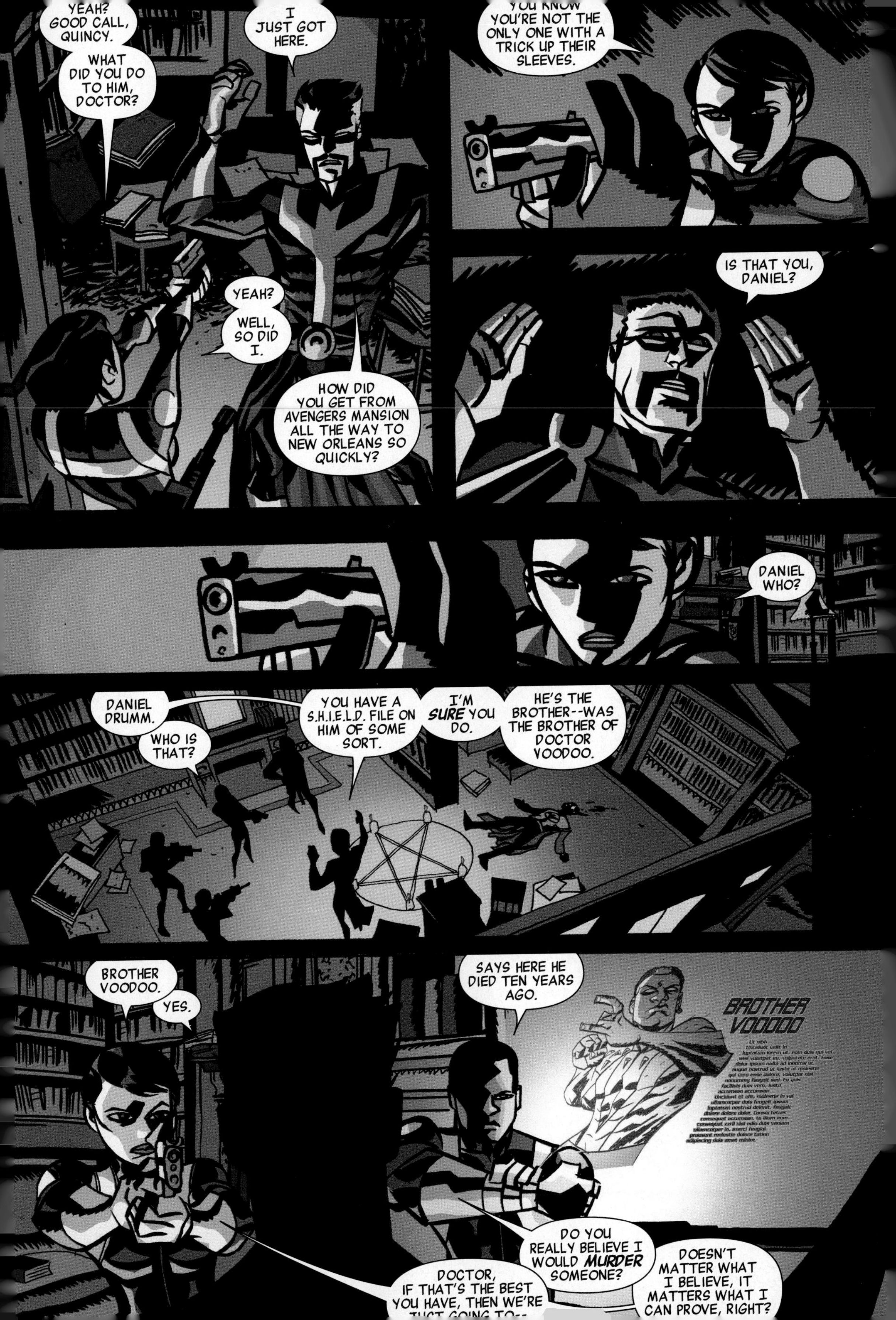

YEAH? GOOD CALL, QUINCY.
WHAT DID YOU DO TO HIM, DOCTOR?
I JUST GOT HERE.
YEAH?
WELL, SO DID I.
HOW DID YOU GET FROM AVENGERS MANSION ALL THE WAY TO NEW ORLEANS SO QUICKLY?
YOU KNOW YOU'RE NOT THE ONLY ONE WITH A TRICK UP THEIR SLEEVES.
IS THAT YOU, DANIEL?
DANIEL WHO?
DANIEL DRUMM.
WHO IS THAT?
YOU HAVE A S.H.I.E.L.D. FILE ON HIM OF SOME SORT.
I'M SURE YOU DO.
HE'S THE BROTHER--WAS THE BROTHER OF DOCTOR VOODOO.
BROTHER VOODOO.
YES.
SAYS HERE HE DIED TEN YEARS AGO.
BROTHER VOODOO
DO YOU REALLY BELIEVE I WOULD MURDER SOMEONE?
DOESN'T MATTER WHAT I BELIEVE, IT MATTERS WHAT I CAN PROVE, RIGHT?
DOCTOR, IF THAT'S THE BEST YOU HAVE, THEN WE'RE

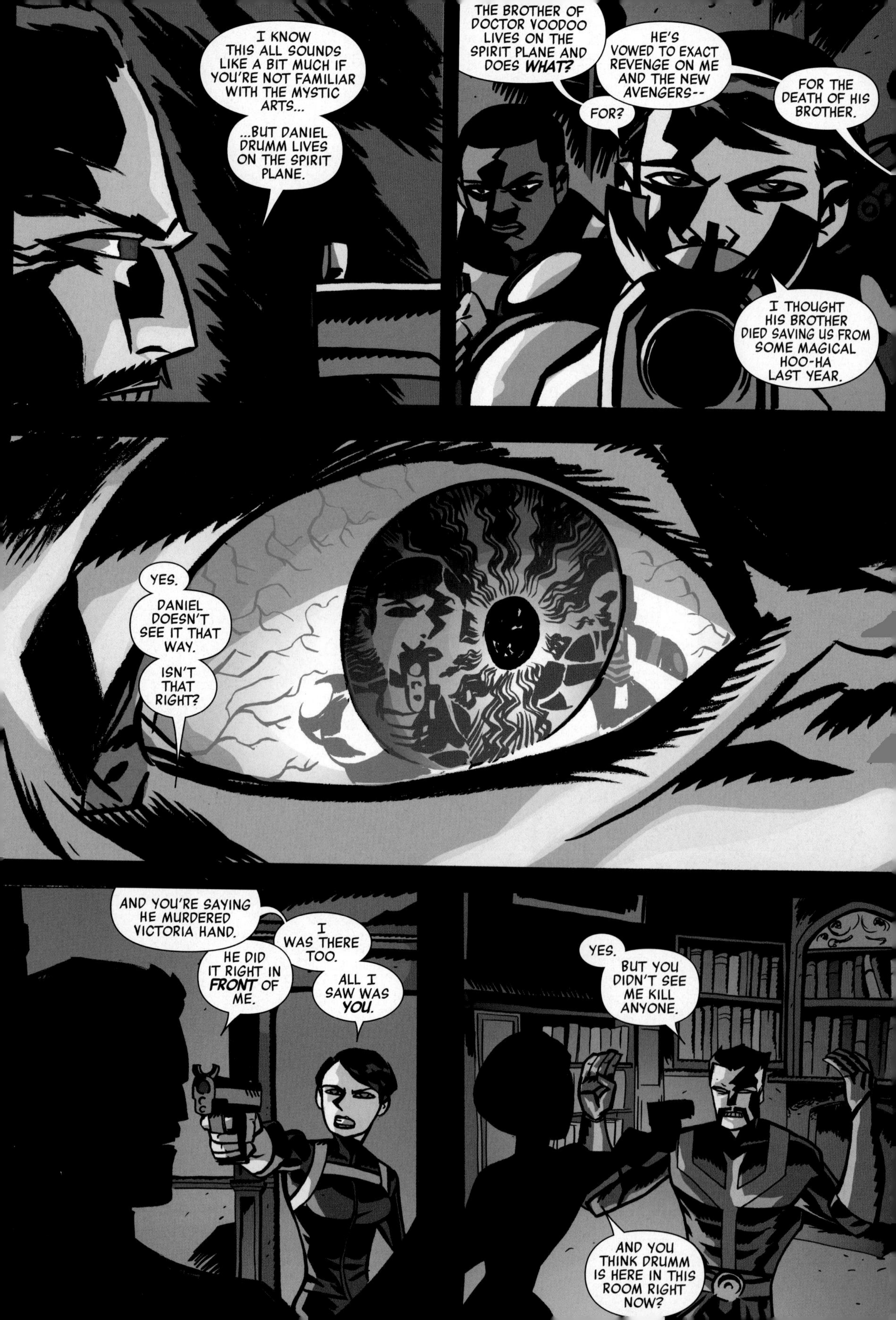
I KNOW THIS ALL SOUNDS LIKE A BIT MUCH IF YOU'RE NOT FAMILIAR WITH THE MYSTIC ARTS...
...BUT DANIEL DRUMM LIVES ON THE SPIRIT PLANE.
THE BROTHER OF DOCTOR VOODOO LIVES ON THE SPIRIT PLANE AND DOES *WHAT?*
HE'S VOWED TO EXACT REVENGE ON ME AND THE NEW AVENGERS--
FOR?
FOR THE DEATH OF HIS BROTHER.
I THOUGHT HIS BROTHER DIED SAVING US FROM SOME MAGICAL HOO-HA LAST YEAR.
YES.
DANIEL DOESN'T SEE IT THAT WAY.
ISN'T THAT RIGHT?
AND YOU'RE SAYING HE MURDERED VICTORIA HAND.
HE DID IT RIGHT IN *FRONT* OF ME.
I WAS THERE TOO.
ALL I SAW WAS *YOU*.
YES.
BUT YOU DIDN'T SEE ME KILL ANYONE.
AND YOU THINK DRUMM IS HERE IN THIS ROOM RIGHT NOW?

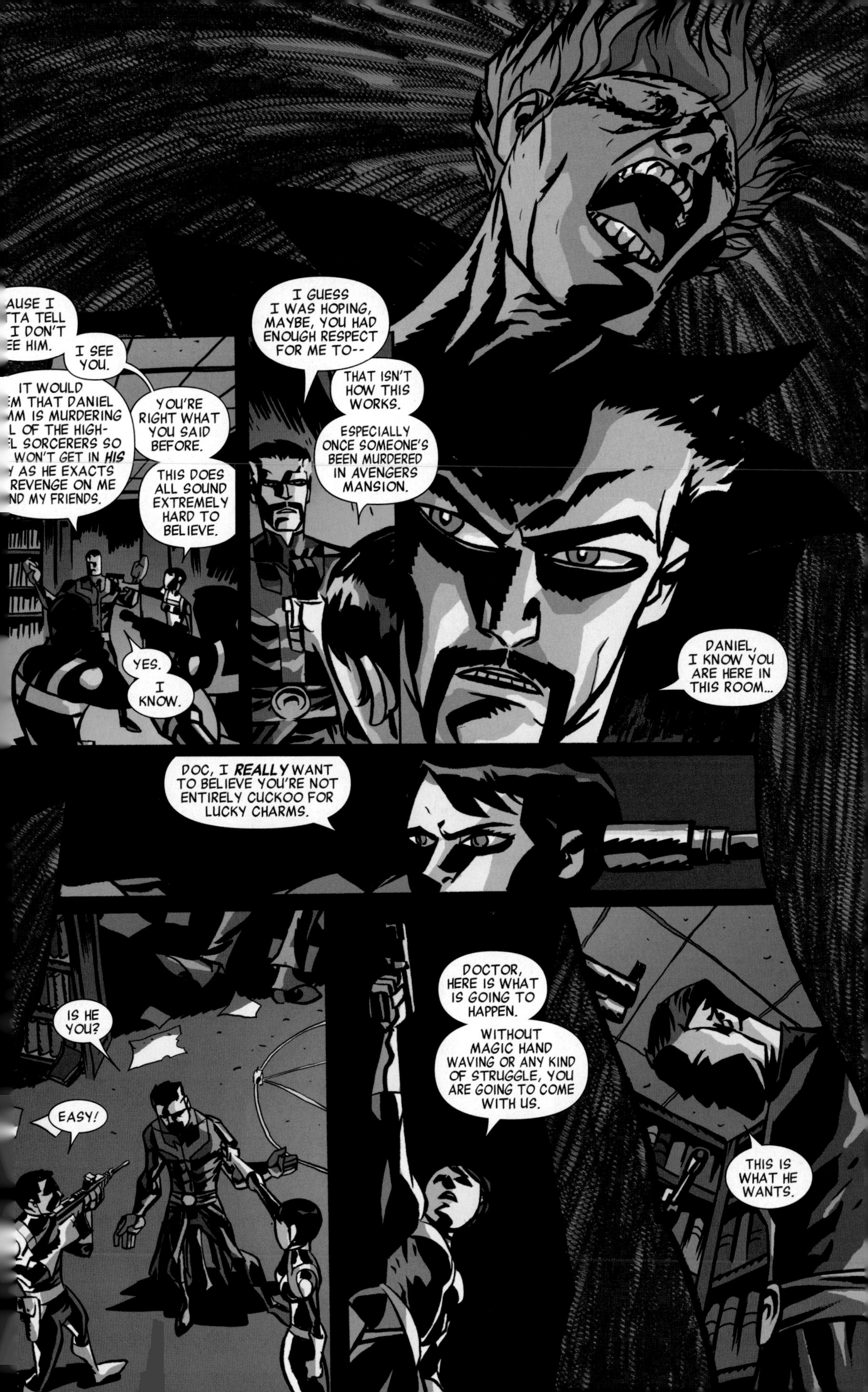

AUSE I TTA TELL I DON'T EE HIM.
I SEE YOU.
IT WOULD EM THAT DANIEL MM IS MURDERING L OF THE HIGH- L SORCERERS SO WON'T GET IN HIS Y AS HE EXACTS REVENGE ON ME ND MY FRIENDS.
YOU'RE RIGHT WHAT YOU SAID BEFORE.
THIS DOES ALL SOUND EXTREMELY HARD TO BELIEVE.
YES.
I KNOW.
I GUESS I WAS HOPING, MAYBE, YOU HAD ENOUGH RESPECT FOR ME TO--
THAT ISN'T HOW THIS WORKS.
ESPECIALLY ONCE SOMEONE'S BEEN MURDERED IN AVENGERS MANSION.
DANIEL, I KNOW YOU ARE HERE IN THIS ROOM...
DOC, I REALLY WANT TO BELIEVE YOU'RE NOT ENTIRELY CUCKOO FOR LUCKY CHARMS.
IS HE YOU?
EASY!
DOCTOR, HERE IS WHAT IS GOING TO HAPPEN.
WITHOUT MAGIC HAND WAVING OR ANY KIND OF STRUGGLE, YOU ARE GOING TO COME WITH US.
THIS IS WHAT HE WANTS.

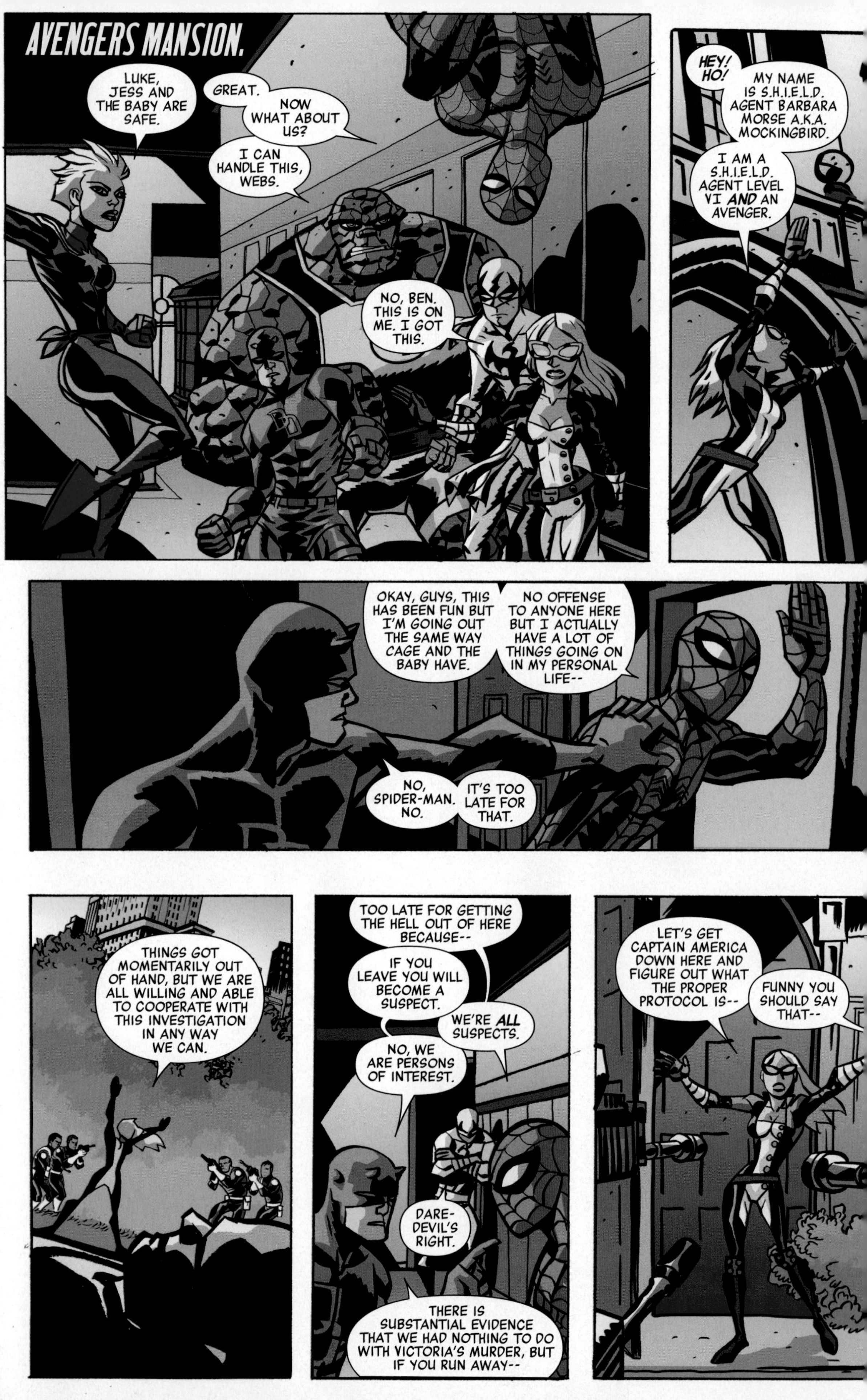
AVENGERS MANSION.
LUKE, JESS AND THE BABY ARE SAFE.
GREAT.
NOW WHAT ABOUT US?
I CAN HANDLE THIS, WEBS.
NO, BEN. THIS IS ON ME. I GOT THIS.
HEY! HO!
MY NAME IS S.H.I.E.L.D. AGENT BARBARA MORSE A.K.A. MOCKINGBIRD.
I AM A S.H.I.E.L.D. AGENT LEVEL VI AND AN AVENGER.
OKAY, GUYS, THIS HAS BEEN FUN BUT I'M GOING OUT THE SAME WAY CAGE AND THE BABY HAVE.
NO OFFENSE TO ANYONE HERE BUT I ACTUALLY HAVE A LOT OF THINGS GOING ON IN MY PERSONAL LIFE--
NO, SPIDER-MAN. NO.
IT'S TOO LATE FOR THAT.
THINGS GOT MOMENTARILY OUT OF HAND, BUT WE ARE ALL WILLING AND ABLE TO COOPERATE WITH THIS INVESTIGATION IN ANY WAY WE CAN.
TOO LATE FOR GETTING THE HELL OUT OF HERE BECAUSE--
IF YOU LEAVE YOU WILL BECOME A SUSPECT.
WE'RE ALL SUSPECTS.
NO, WE ARE PERSONS OF INTEREST.
DARE-DEVIL'S RIGHT.
THERE IS SUBSTANTIAL EVIDENCE THAT WE HAD NOTHING TO DO WITH VICTORIA'S MURDER, BUT IF YOU RUN AWAY--
LET'S GET CAPTAIN AMERICA DOWN HERE AND FIGURE OUT WHAT THE PROPER PROTOCOL IS--
FUNNY YOU SHOULD SAY THAT--

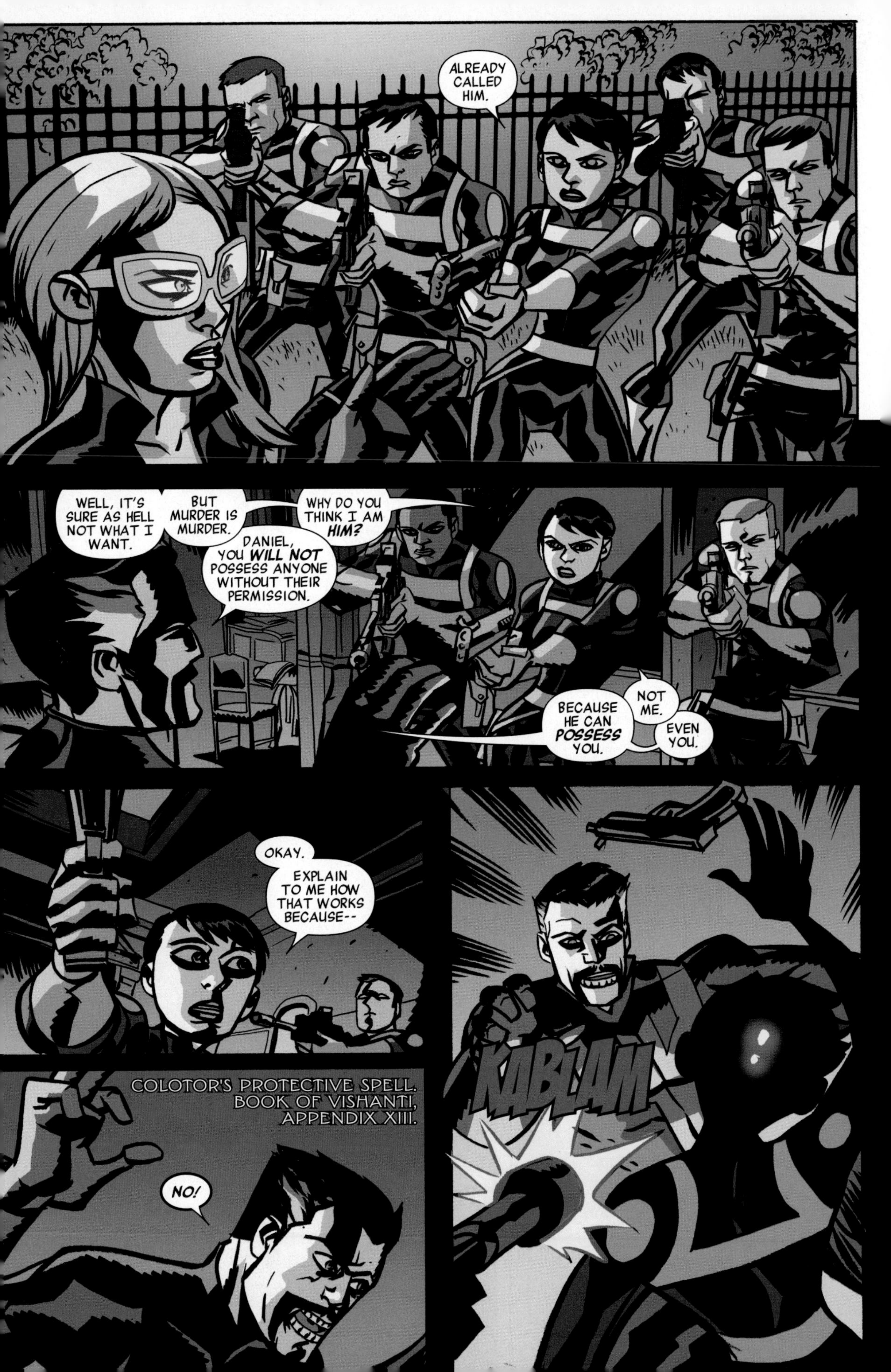
ALREADY CALLED HIM.
WELL, IT'S SURE AS HELL NOT WHAT I WANT.
BUT MURDER IS MURDER.
WHY DO YOU THINK I AM HIM?
DANIEL, YOU WILL NOT POSSESS ANYONE WITHOUT THEIR PERMISSION.
BECAUSE HE CAN POSSESS YOU.
NOT ME.
EVEN YOU.
OKAY.
EXPLAIN TO ME HOW THAT WORKS BECAUSE--
COLOTOR'S PROTECTIVE SPELL. BOOK OF VISHANTI, APPENDIX XIII.
NO!
KABLAM

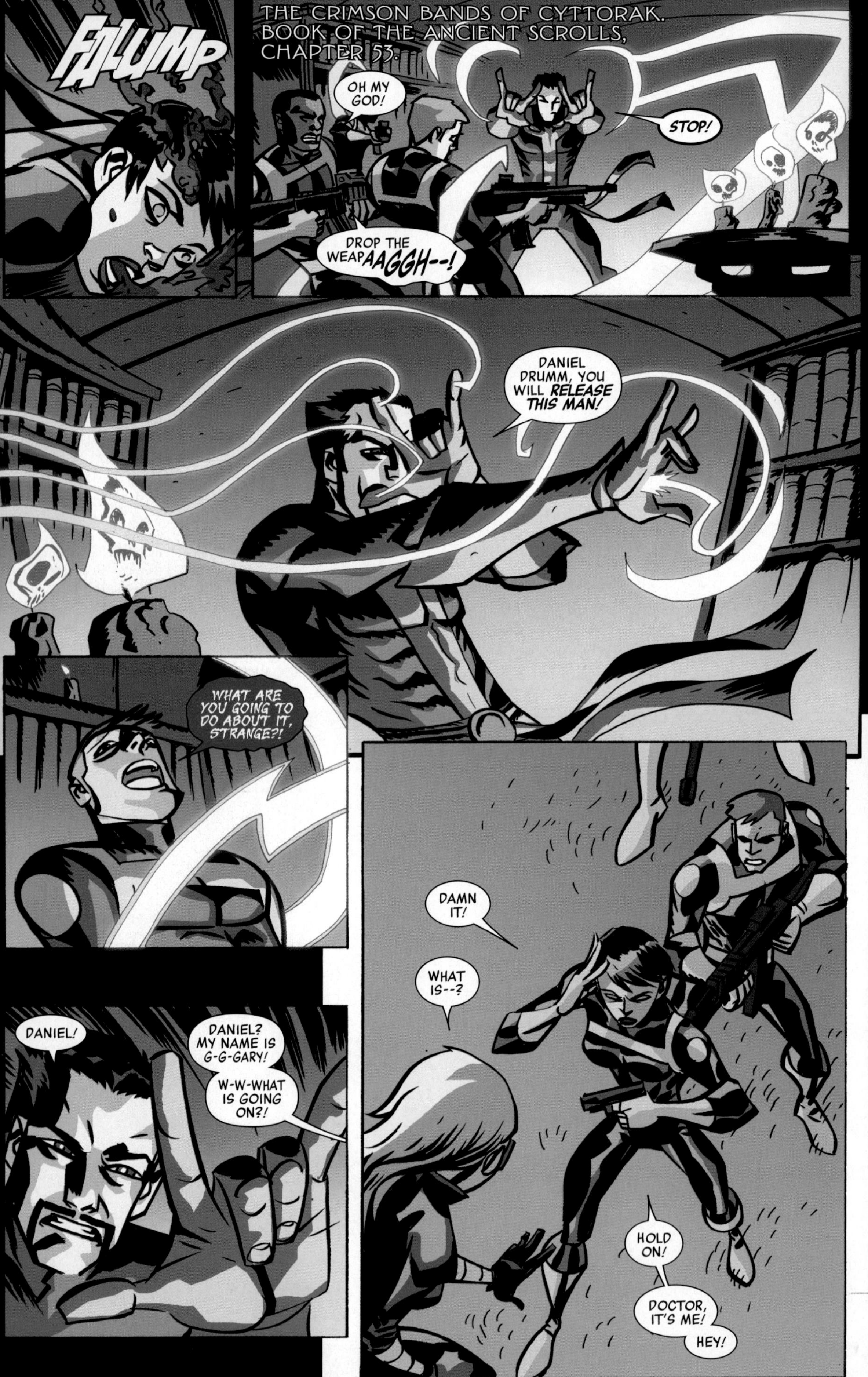
FALUMP
THE CRIMSON BANDS OF CYTTORAK. BOOK OF THE ANCIENT SCROLLS, CHAPTER 53.
OH MY GOD!
STOP!
DROP THE WEAPAAGGH--!
DANIEL DRUMM, YOU WILL RELEASE THIS MAN!
WHAT ARE YOU GOING TO DO ABOUT IT, STRANGE?!
DAMN IT!
WHAT IS--?
DANIEL!
DANIEL? MY NAME IS G-G-GARY!
W-W-WHAT IS GOING ON?!
HOLD ON!
DOCTOR, IT'S ME!
HEY!

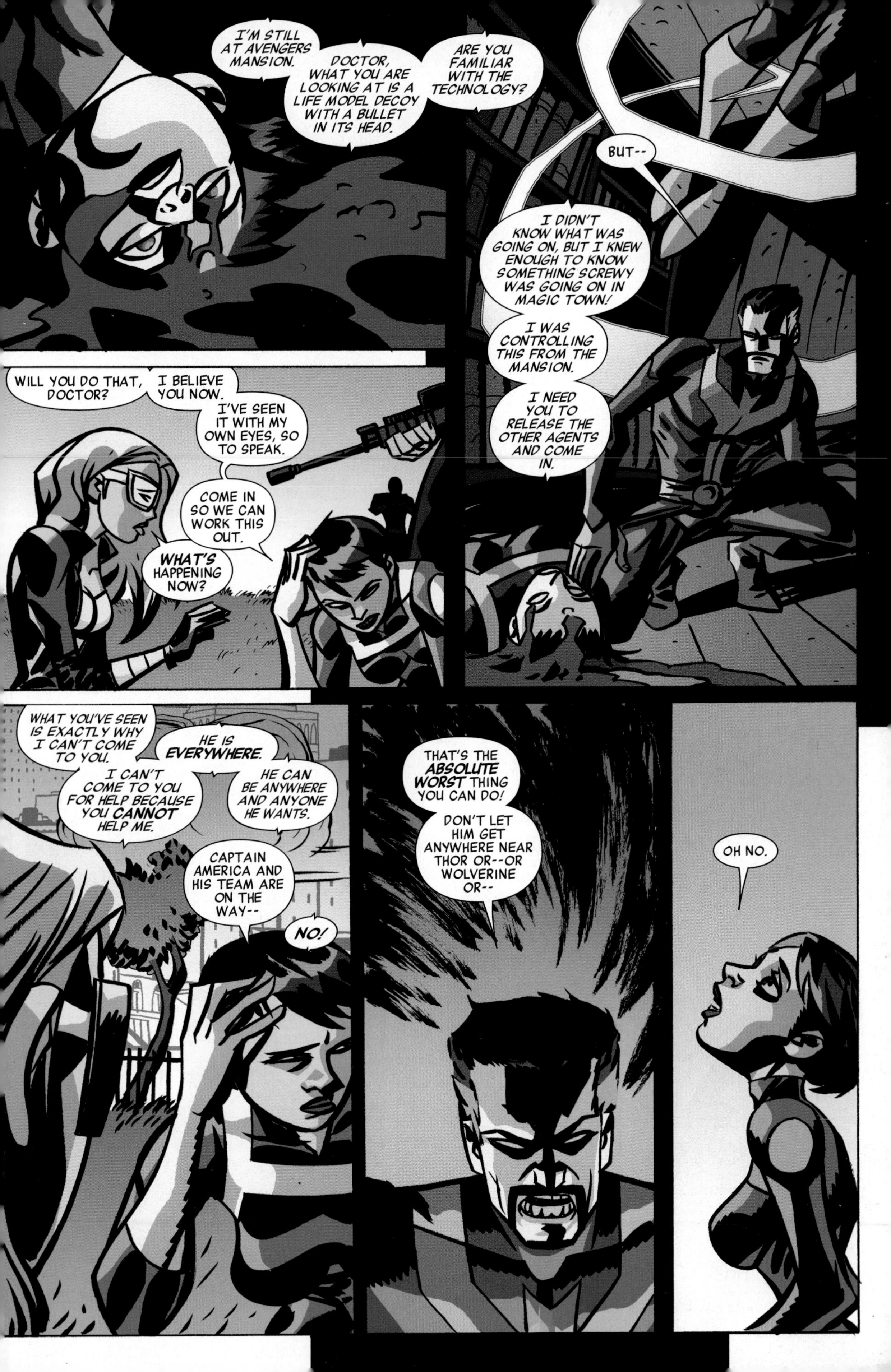
I'M STILL AT AVENGERS MANSION.
DOCTOR, WHAT YOU ARE LOOKING AT IS A LIFE MODEL DECOY WITH A BULLET IN ITS HEAD.
ARE YOU FAMILIAR WITH THE TECHNOLOGY?
BUT--
I DIDN'T KNOW WHAT WAS GOING ON, BUT I KNEW ENOUGH TO KNOW SOMETHING SCREWY WAS GOING ON IN MAGIC TOWN!
I WAS CONTROLLING THIS FROM THE MANSION.
I NEED YOU TO RELEASE THE OTHER AGENTS AND COME IN.
WILL YOU DO THAT, DOCTOR?
I BELIEVE YOU NOW.
I'VE SEEN IT WITH MY OWN EYES, SO TO SPEAK.
COME IN SO WE CAN WORK THIS OUT.
WHAT'S HAPPENING NOW?
WHAT YOU'VE SEEN IS EXACTLY WHY I CAN'T COME TO YOU.
HE IS EVERYWHERE.
I CAN'T COME TO YOU FOR HELP BECAUSE YOU CANNOT HELP ME.
HE CAN BE ANYWHERE AND ANYONE HE WANTS.
CAPTAIN AMERICA AND HIS TEAM ARE ON THE WAY--
NO!
THAT'S THE ABSOLUTE WORST THING YOU CAN DO!
DON'T LET HIM GET ANYWHERE NEAR THOR OR--OR WOLVERINE OR--
OH NO.

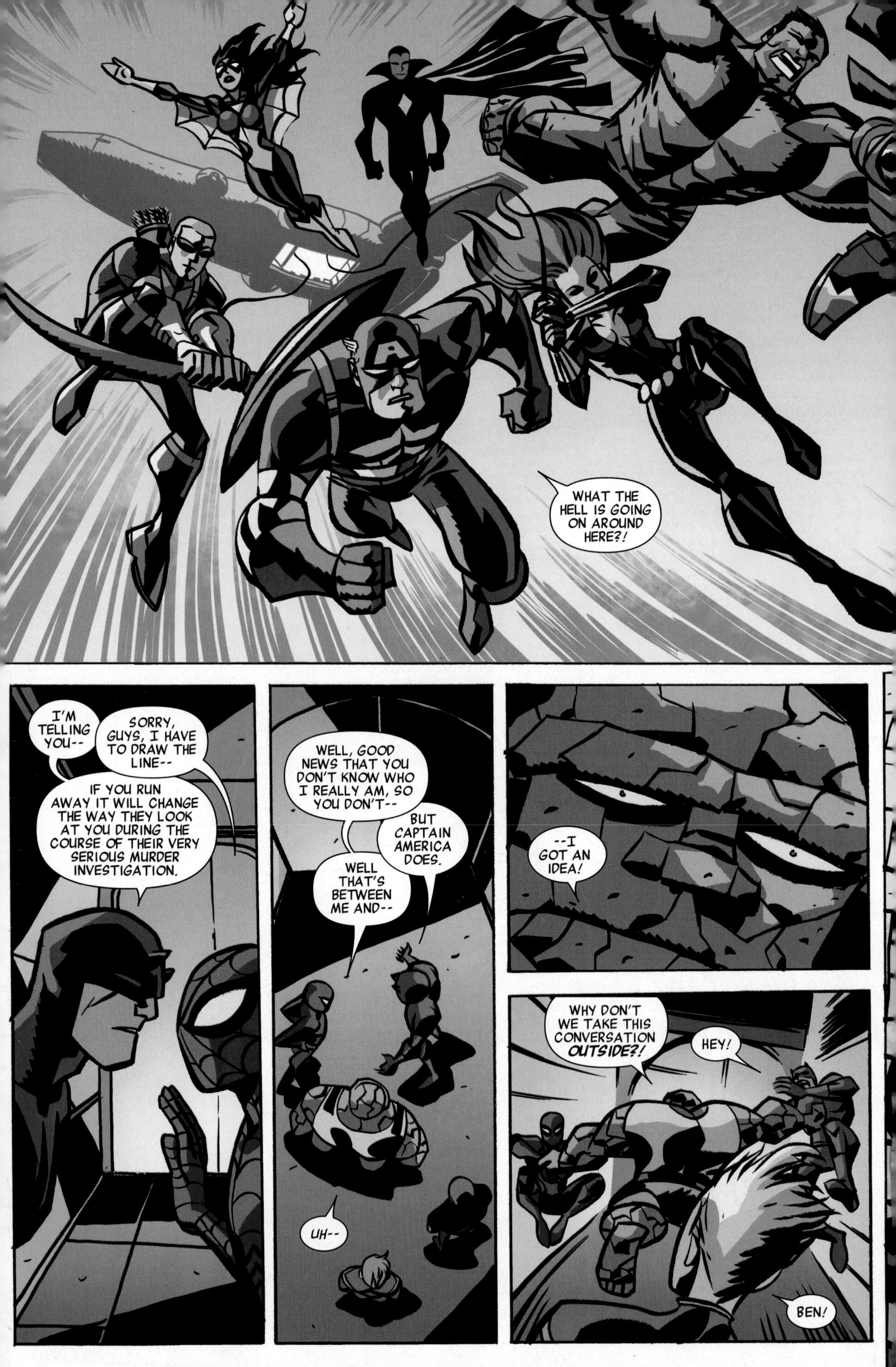
WHAT THE HELL IS GOING ON AROUND HERE?!
I'M TELLING YOU--
SORRY, GUYS, I HAVE TO DRAW THE LINE--
IF YOU RUN AWAY IT WILL CHANGE THE WAY THEY LOOK AT YOU DURING THE COURSE OF THEIR VERY SERIOUS MURDER INVESTIGATION.
WELL, GOOD NEWS THAT YOU DON'T KNOW WHO I REALLY AM, SO YOU DON'T--
BUT CAPTAIN AMERICA DOES.
WELL THAT'S BETWEEN ME AND--
UH--
--I GOT AN IDEA!
WHY DON'T WE TAKE THIS CONVERSATION OUTSIDE?!
HEY!
BEN!

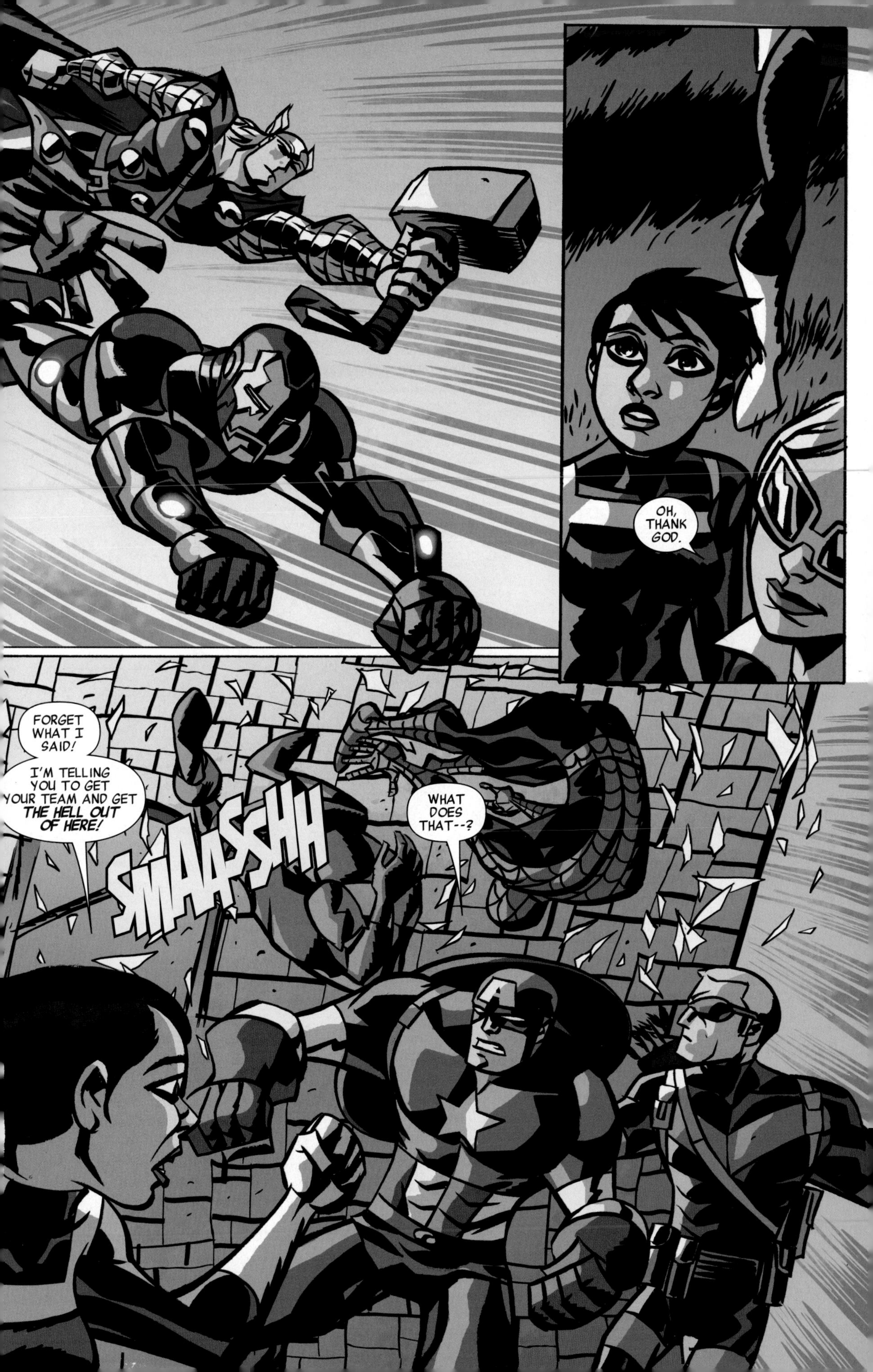

OH, THANK GOD.
FORGET WHAT I SAID!
I'M TELLING YOU TO GET YOUR TEAM AND GET THE HELL OUT OF HERE!
SMAASSHH
WHAT DOES THAT--?

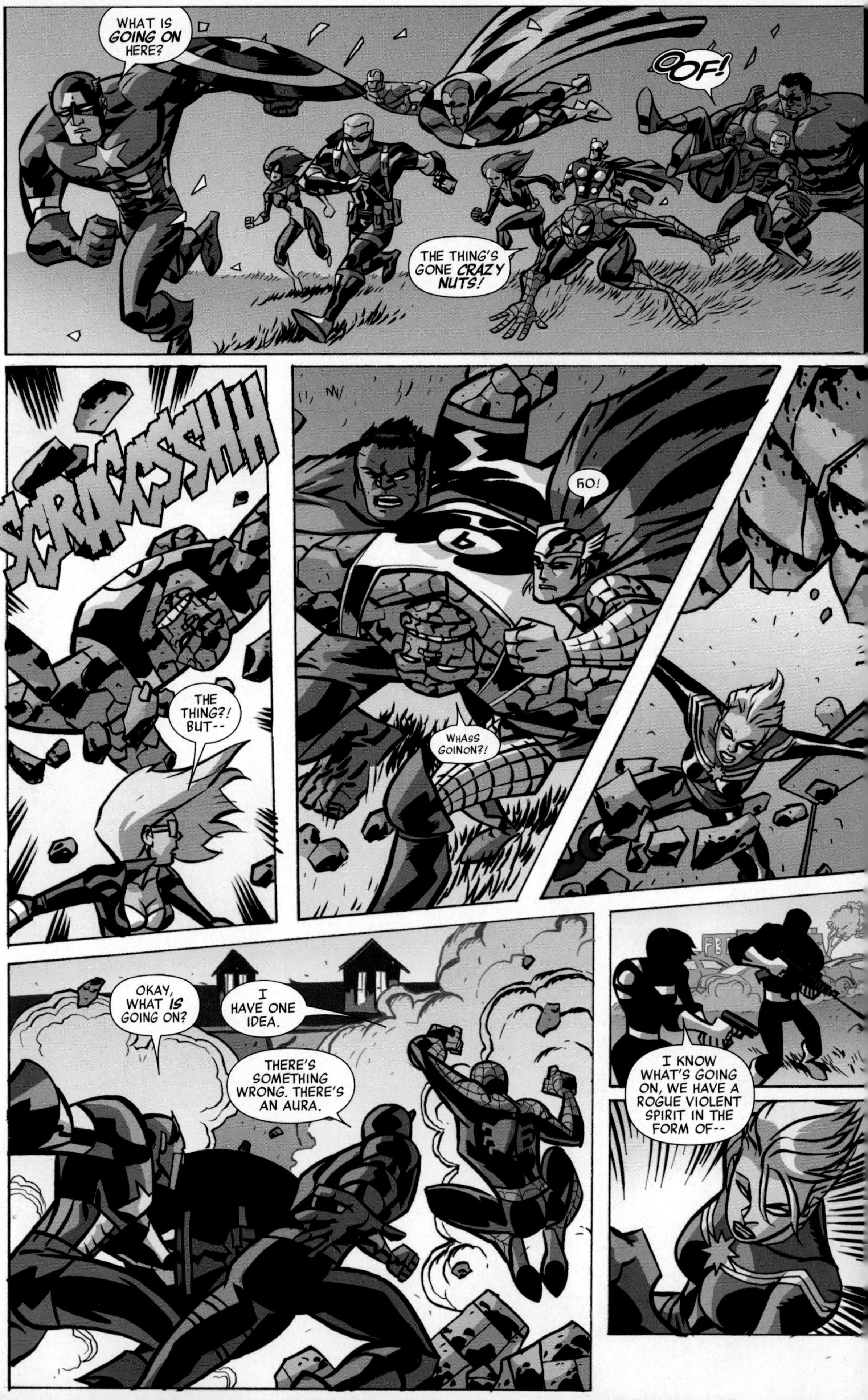
WHAT IS GOING ON HERE?
OOF!
THE THING'S GONE CRAZY NUTS!
SCRACCSSHH
THE THING?! BUT--
HO!
WHASS GOINON?!
OKAY, WHAT IS GOING ON?
I HAVE ONE IDEA.
THERE'S SOMETHING WRONG. THERE'S AN AURA.
FBI
I KNOW WHAT'S GOING ON, WE HAVE A ROGUE VIOLENT SPIRIT IN THE FORM OF--

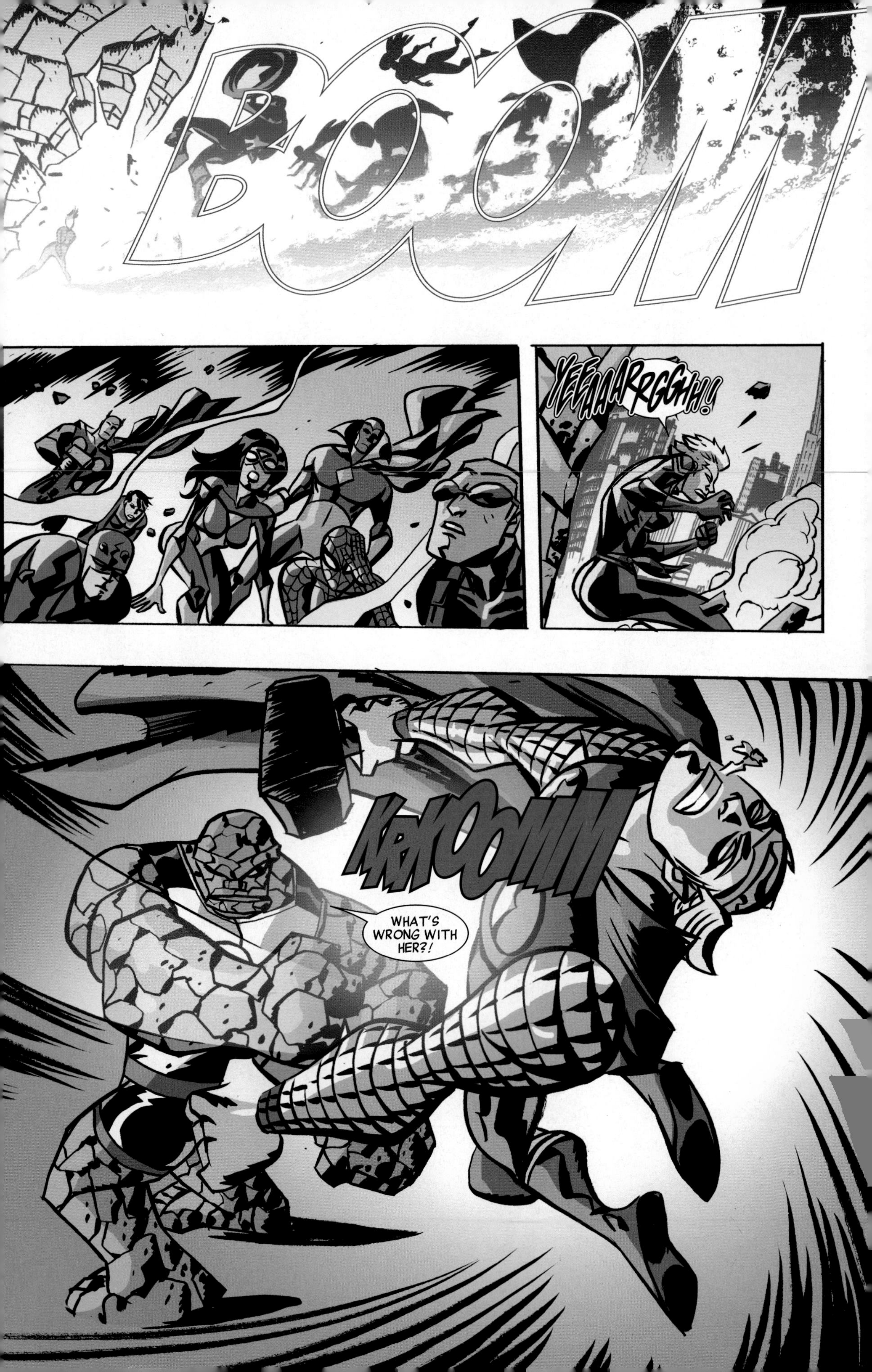
BOOM
YEEAAARRGGHH!
KRRKOOMM
WHAT'S WRONG WITH HER?!

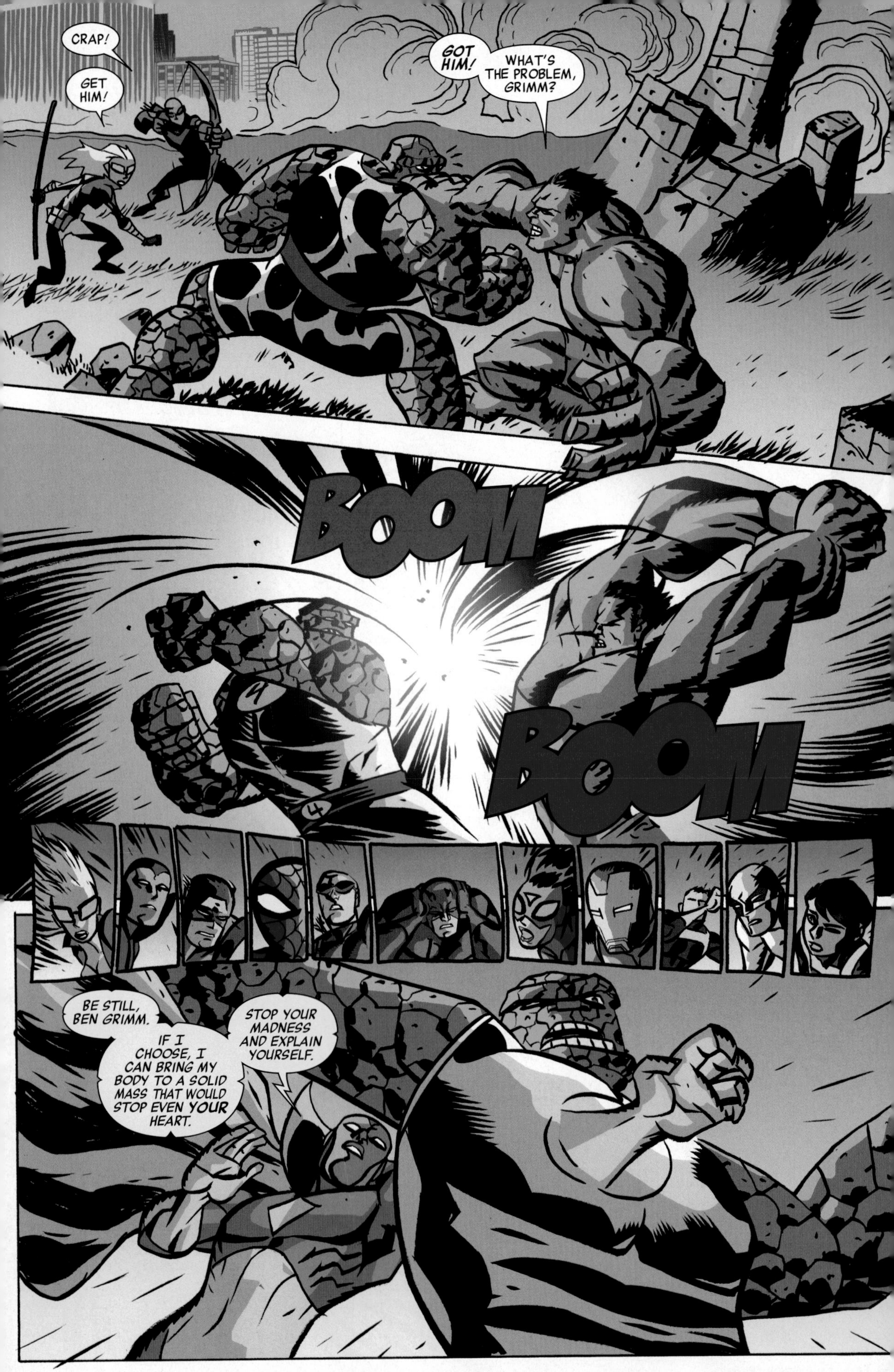
CRAP!
GET HIM!
GOT HIM!
WHAT'S THE PROBLEM, GRIMM?
BOOM
BOOM
BE STILL, BEN GRIMM.
IF I CHOOSE, I CAN BRING MY BODY TO A SOLID MASS THAT WOULD STOP EVEN YOUR HEART.
STOP YOUR MADNESS AND EXPLAIN YOURSELF.

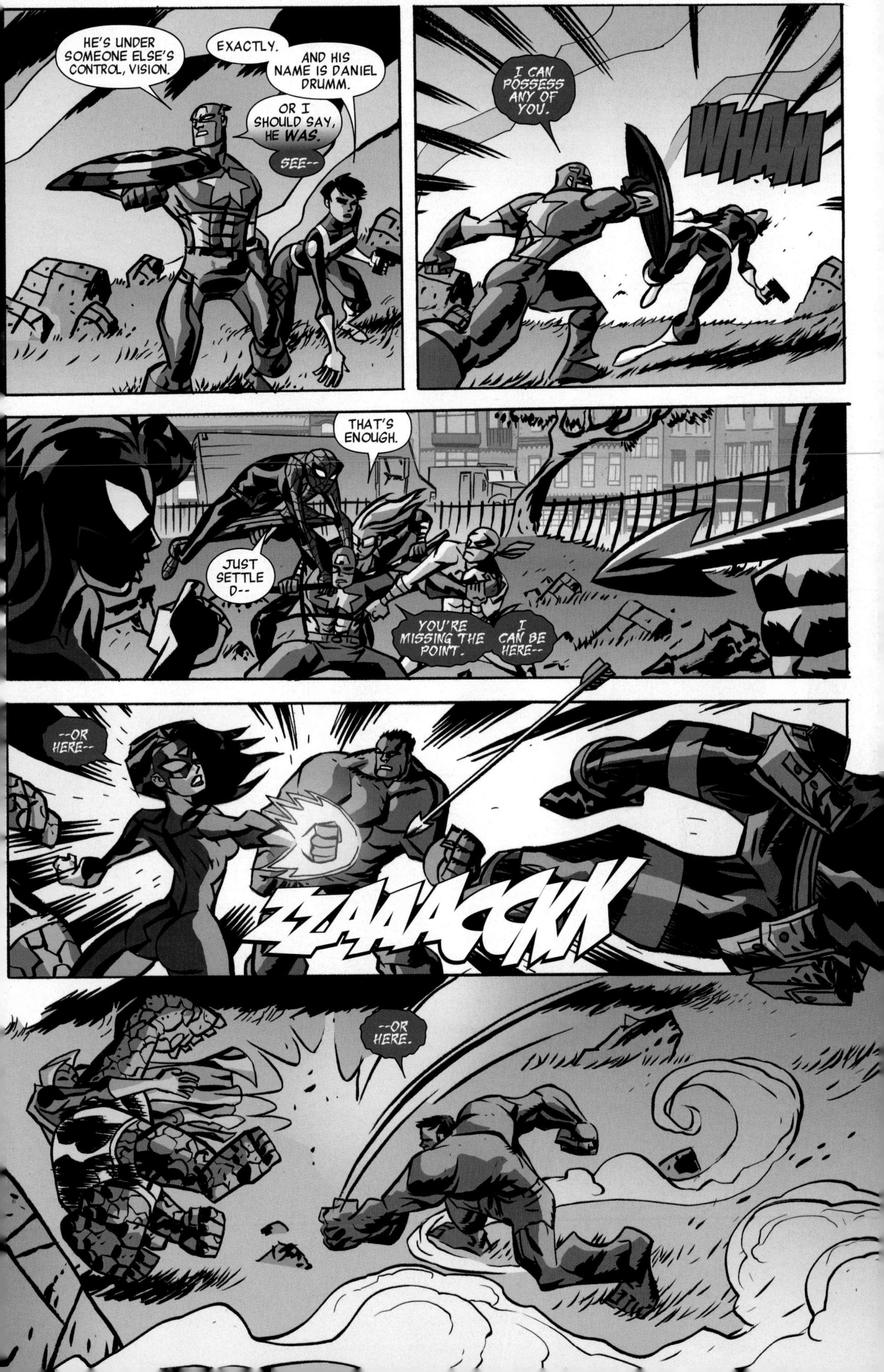
HE'S UNDER SOMEONE ELSE'S CONTROL, VISION.
EXACTLY.
AND HIS NAME IS DANIEL DRUMM.
OR I SHOULD SAY, HE WAS.
SEE--
I CAN POSSESS ANY OF YOU.
WHAM
THAT'S ENOUGH.
JUST SETTLE D--
YOU'RE MISSING THE POINT.
I CAN BE HERE--
--OR HERE--
ZZAAACCKK
--OR HERE.

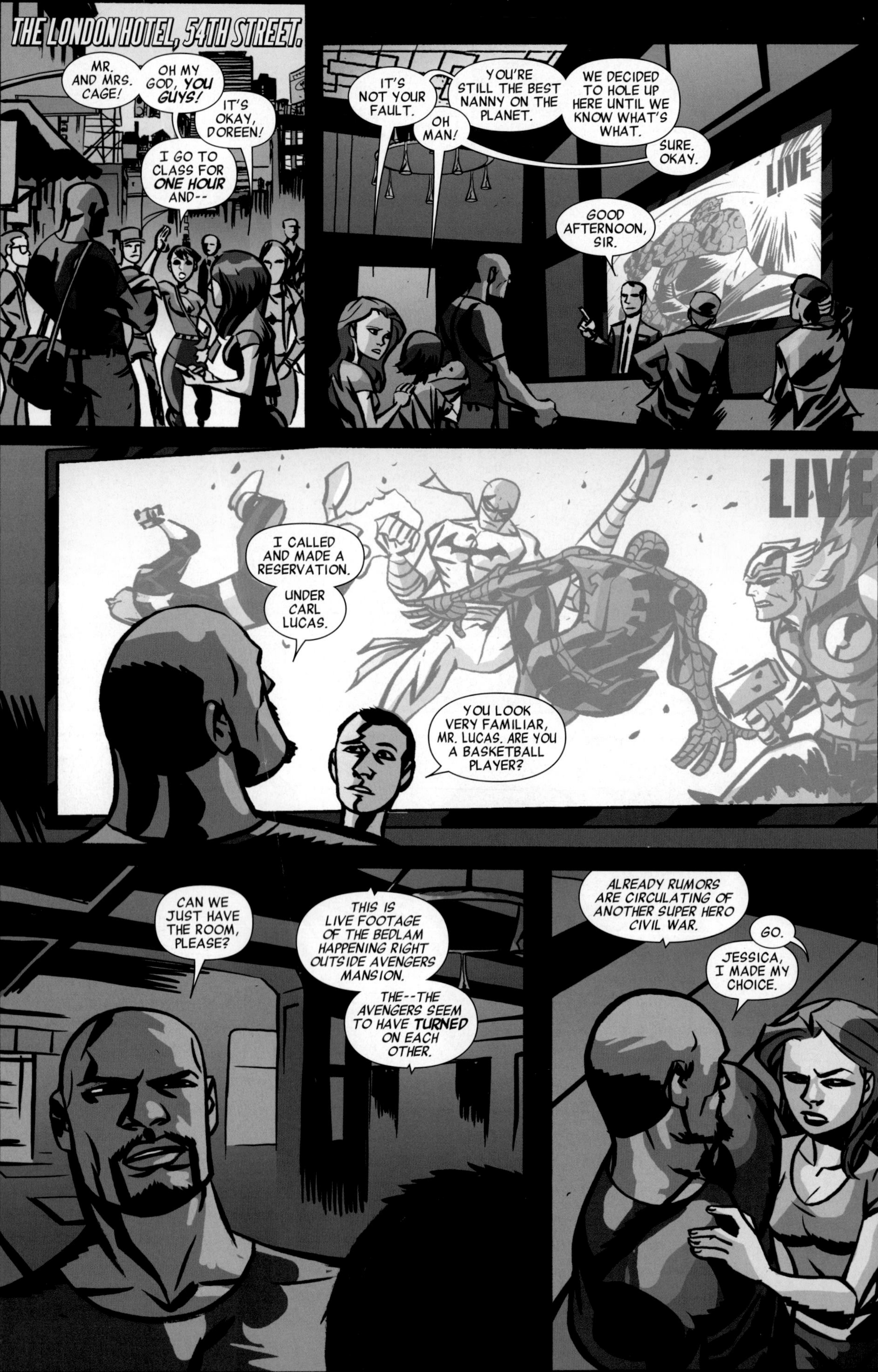
THE LONDON HOTEL, 54TH STREET.
MR. AND MRS. CAGE!
OH MY GOD, YOU GUYS!
IT'S OKAY, DOREEN!
I GO TO CLASS FOR ONE HOUR AND--
IT'S NOT YOUR FAULT.
OH MAN!
YOU'RE STILL THE BEST NANNY ON THE PLANET.
WE DECIDED TO HOLE UP HERE UNTIL WE KNOW WHAT'S WHAT.
SURE. OKAY.
LIVE
GOOD AFTERNOON, SIR.
LIVE
I CALLED AND MADE A RESERVATION.
UNDER CARL LUCAS.
YOU LOOK VERY FAMILIAR, MR. LUCAS. ARE YOU A BASKETBALL PLAYER?
CAN WE JUST HAVE THE ROOM, PLEASE?
THIS IS LIVE FOOTAGE OF THE BEDLAM HAPPENING RIGHT OUTSIDE AVENGERS MANSION.
THE--THE AVENGERS SEEM TO HAVE TURNED ON EACH OTHER.
ALREADY RUMORS ARE CIRCULATING OF ANOTHER SUPER HERO CIVIL WAR.
GO.
JESSICA, I MADE MY CHOICE.

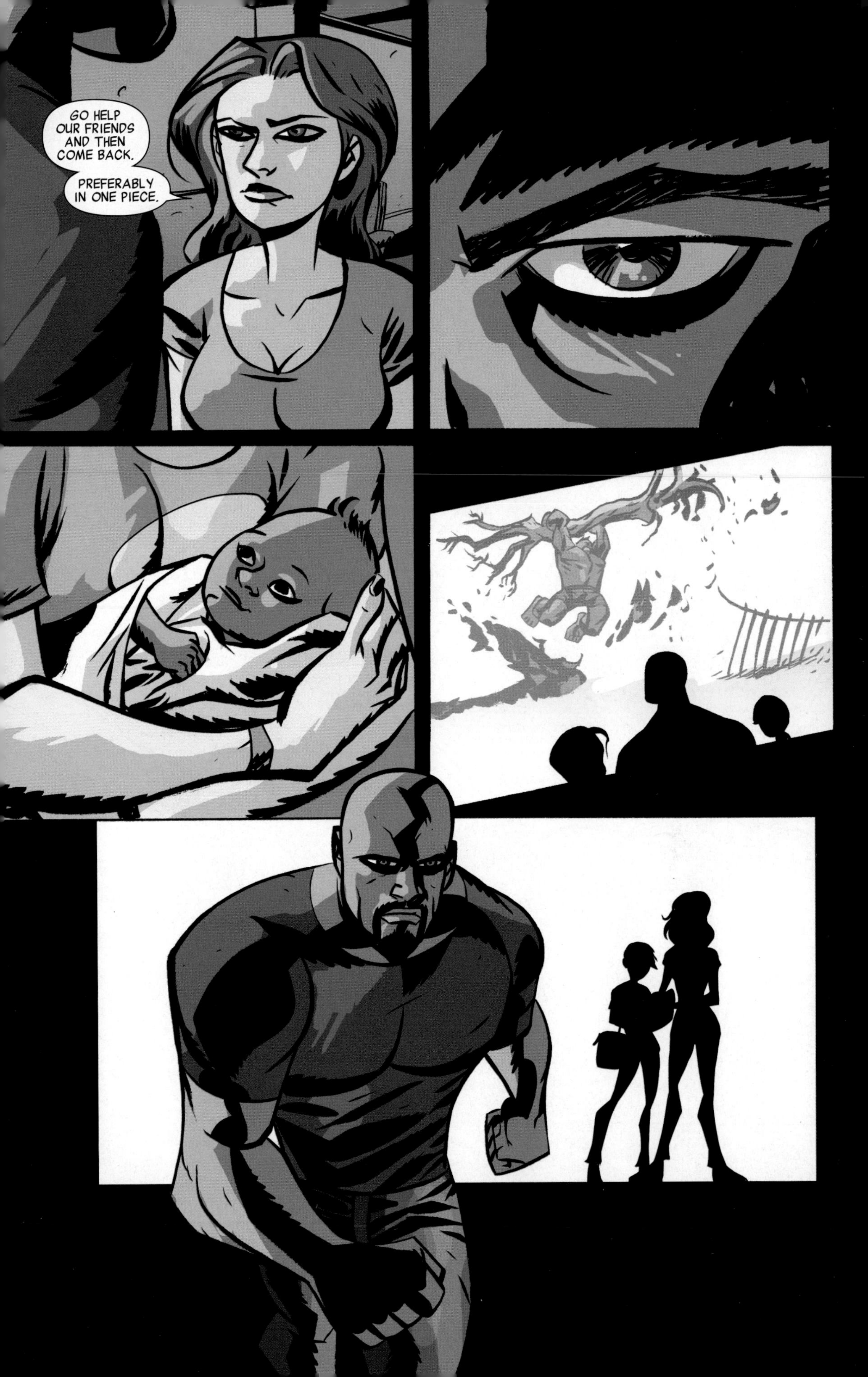
GO HELP OUR FRIENDS AND THEN COME BACK.
PREFERABLY IN ONE PIECE.

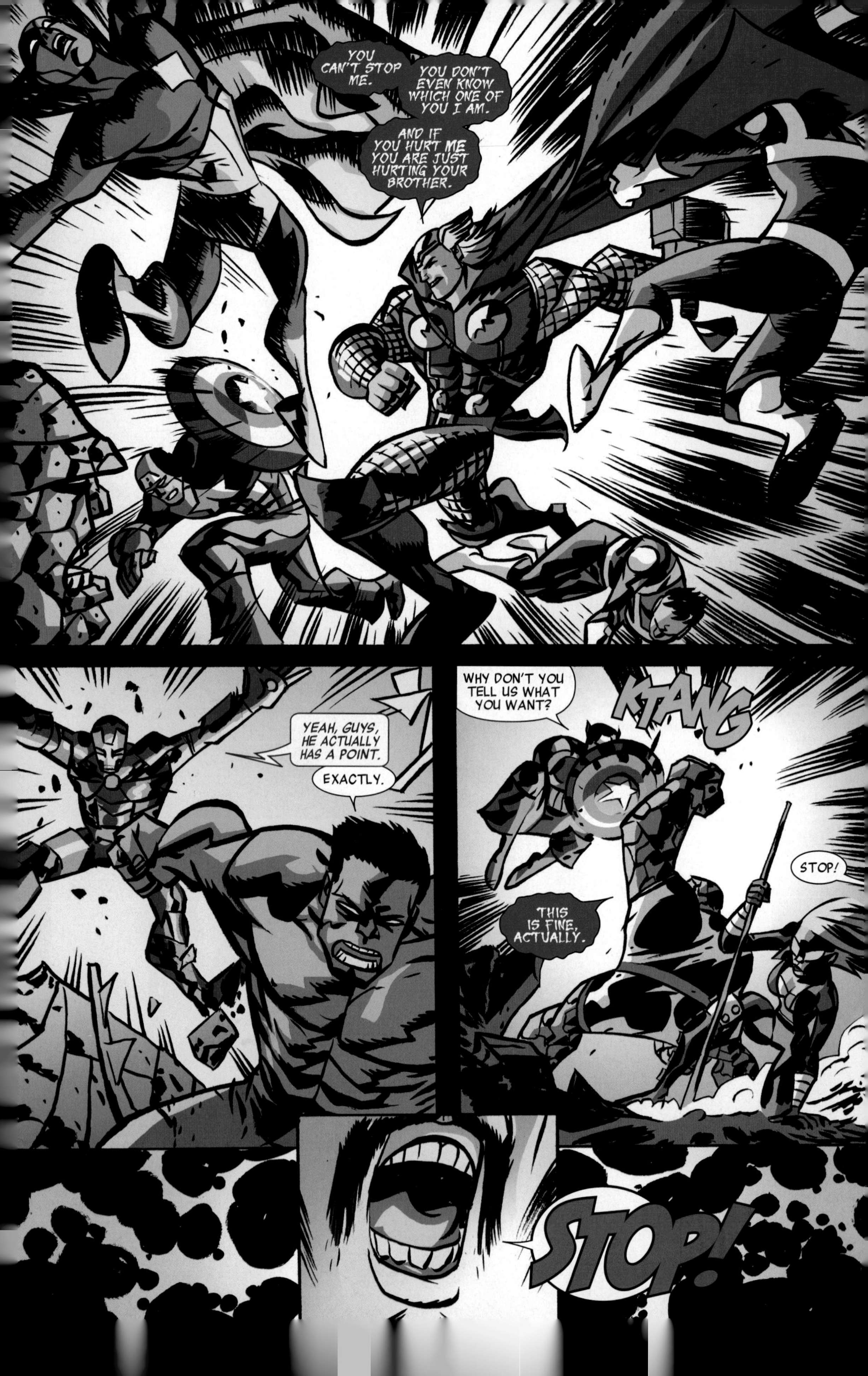
YOU CAN'T STOP ME.
YOU DON'T EVEN KNOW WHICH ONE OF YOU I AM.
AND IF YOU HURT ME YOU ARE JUST HURTING YOUR BROTHER.
YEAH, GUYS, HE ACTUALLY HAS A POINT.
EXACTLY.
WHY DON'T YOU TELL US WHAT YOU WANT?
KTANG
THIS IS FINE, ACTUALLY.
STOP!
STOP!

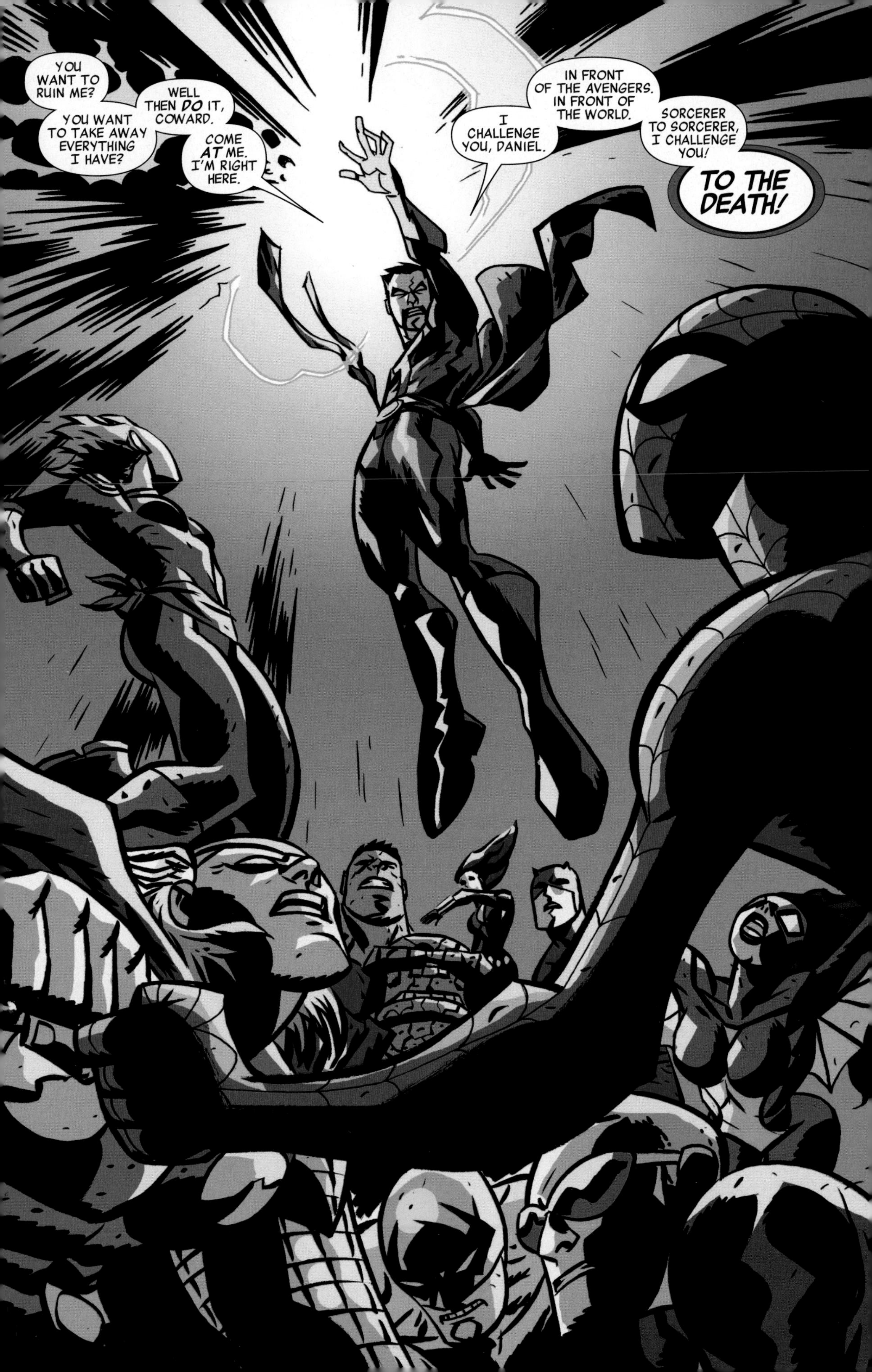
YOU WANT TO RUIN ME?
YOU WANT TO TAKE AWAY EVERYTHING I HAVE?
WELL THEN DO IT, COWARD.
COME AT ME. I'M RIGHT HERE.
I CHALLENGE YOU, DANIEL.
IN FRONT OF THE AVENGERS. IN FRONT OF THE WORLD.
SORCERER TO SORCERER, I CHALLENGE YOU!
TO THE DEATH!

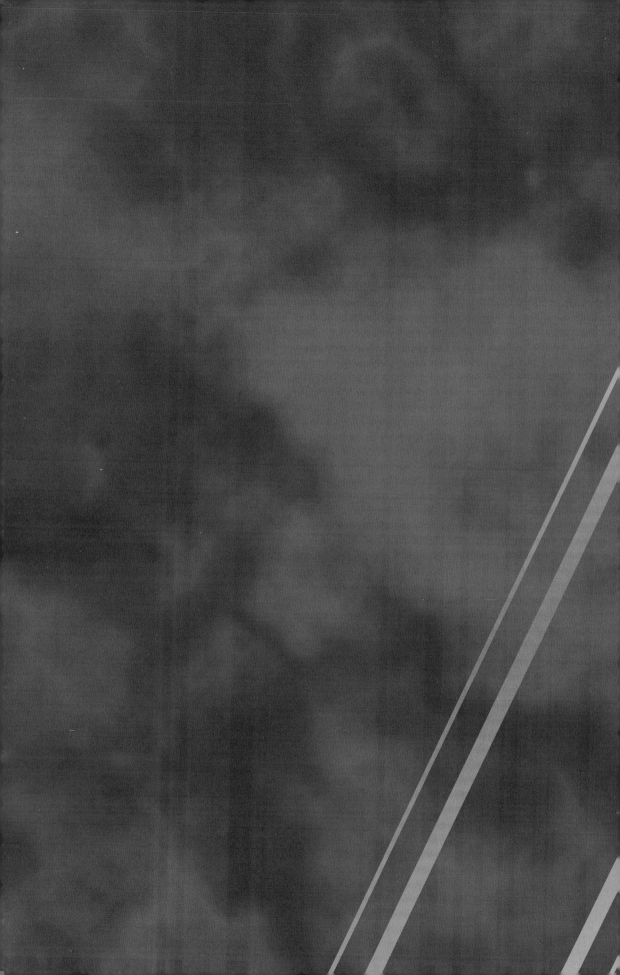

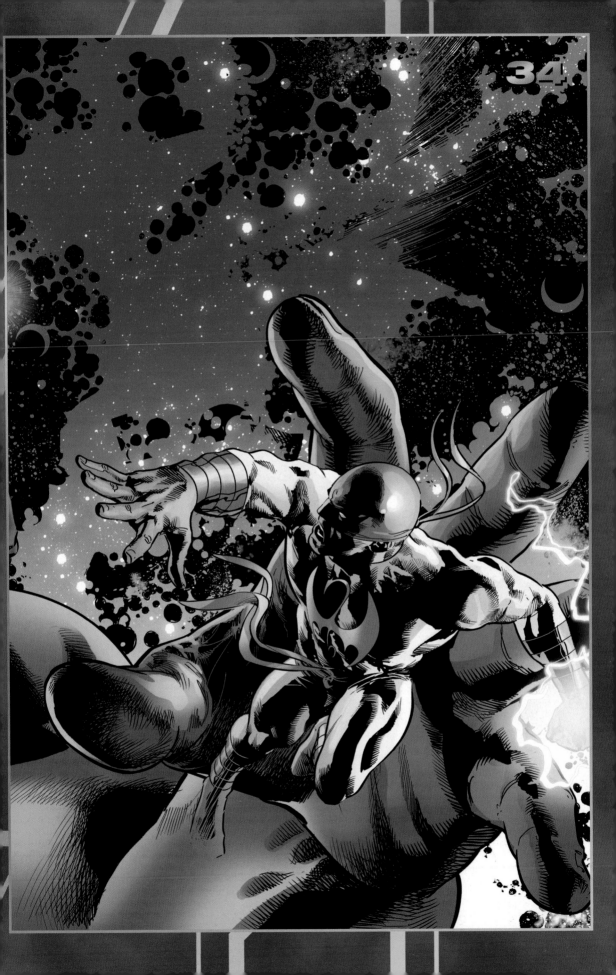

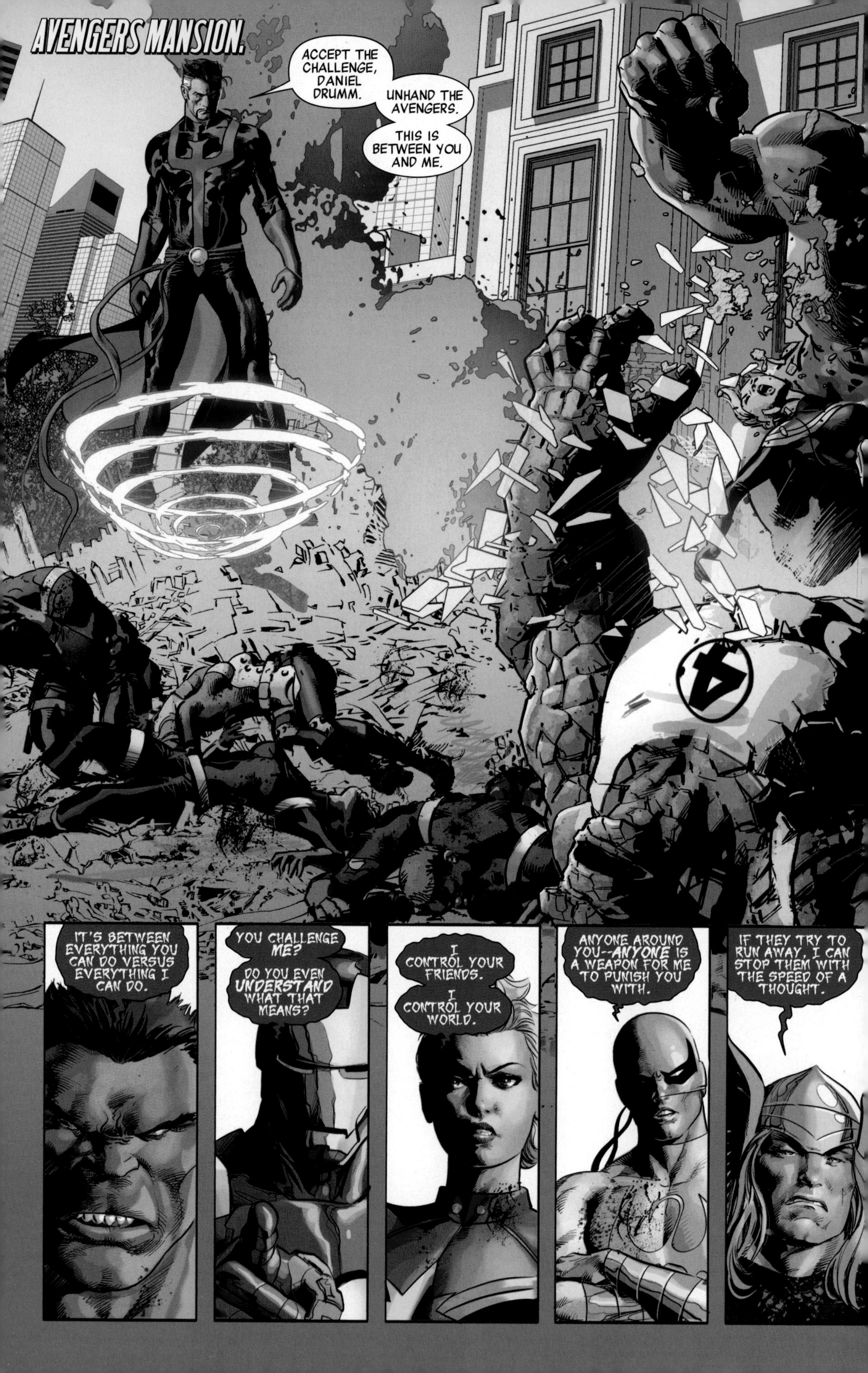
AVENGERS MANSION.
ACCEPT THE CHALLENGE, DANIEL DRUMM.
UNHAND THE AVENGERS.
THIS IS BETWEEN YOU AND ME.
IT'S BETWEEN EVERYTHING YOU CAN DO VERSUS EVERYTHING I CAN DO.
YOU CHALLENGE ME?
DO YOU EVEN UNDERSTAND WHAT THAT MEANS?
I CONTROL YOUR FRIENDS.
I CONTROL YOUR WORLD.
ANYONE AROUND YOU--ANYONE IS A WEAPON FOR ME TO PUNISH YOU WITH.
IF THEY TRY TO RUN AWAY, I CAN STOP THEM WITH THE SPEED OF A THOUGHT.

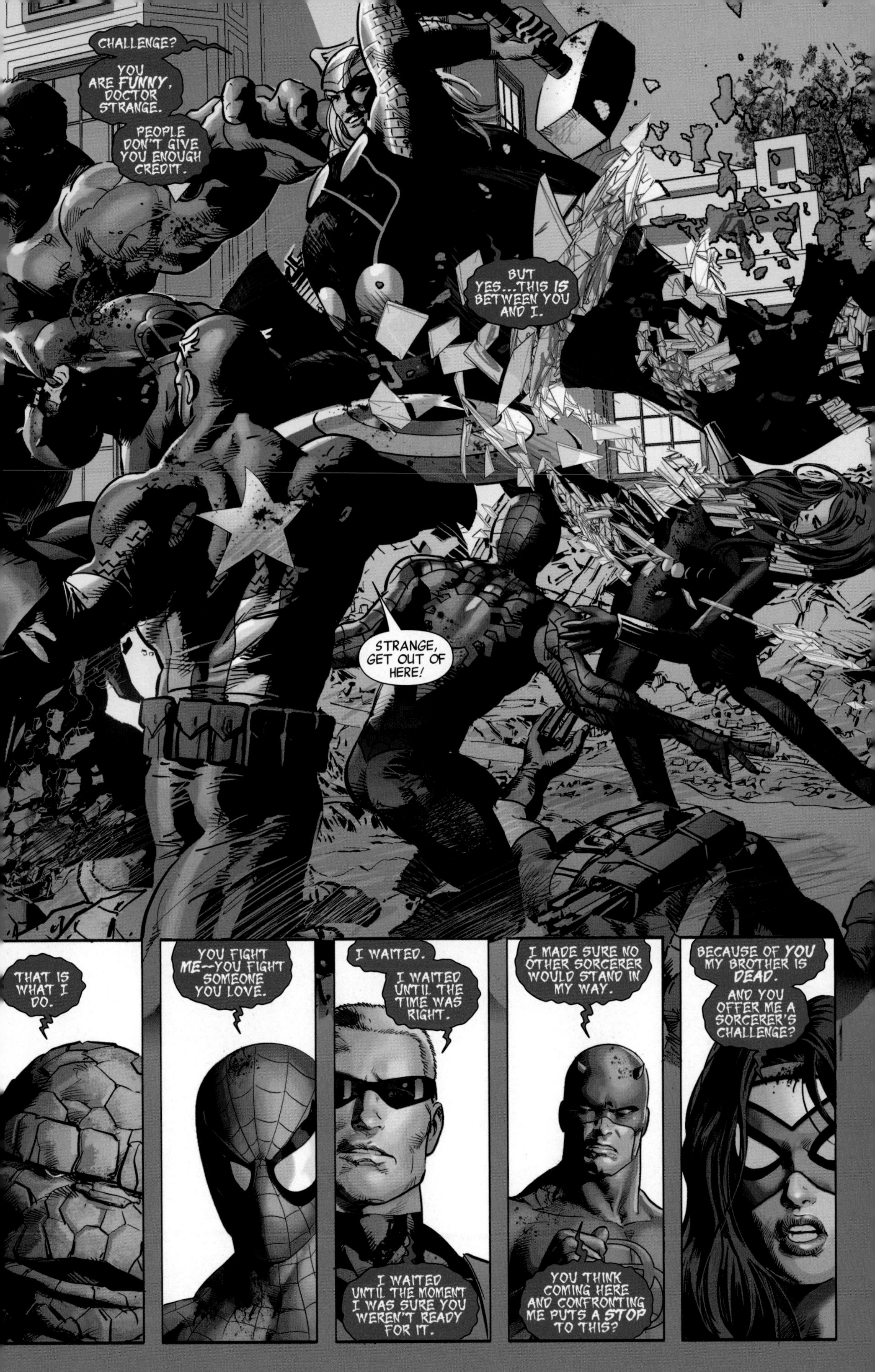
CHALLENGE?
YOU ARE FUNNY, DOCTOR STRANGE.
PEOPLE DON'T GIVE YOU ENOUGH CREDIT.
BUT YES...THIS IS BETWEEN YOU AND I.
STRANGE, GET OUT OF HERE!
THAT IS WHAT I DO.
YOU FIGHT ME--YOU FIGHT SOMEONE YOU LOVE.
I WAITED.
I WAITED UNTIL THE TIME WAS RIGHT.
I WAITED UNTIL THE MOMENT I WAS SURE YOU WEREN'T READY FOR IT.
I MADE SURE NO OTHER SORCERER WOULD STAND IN MY WAY.
YOU THINK COMING HERE AND CONFRONTING ME PUTS A STOP TO THIS?
BECAUSE OF YOU MY BROTHER IS DEAD.
AND YOU OFFER ME A SORCERER'S CHALLENGE?

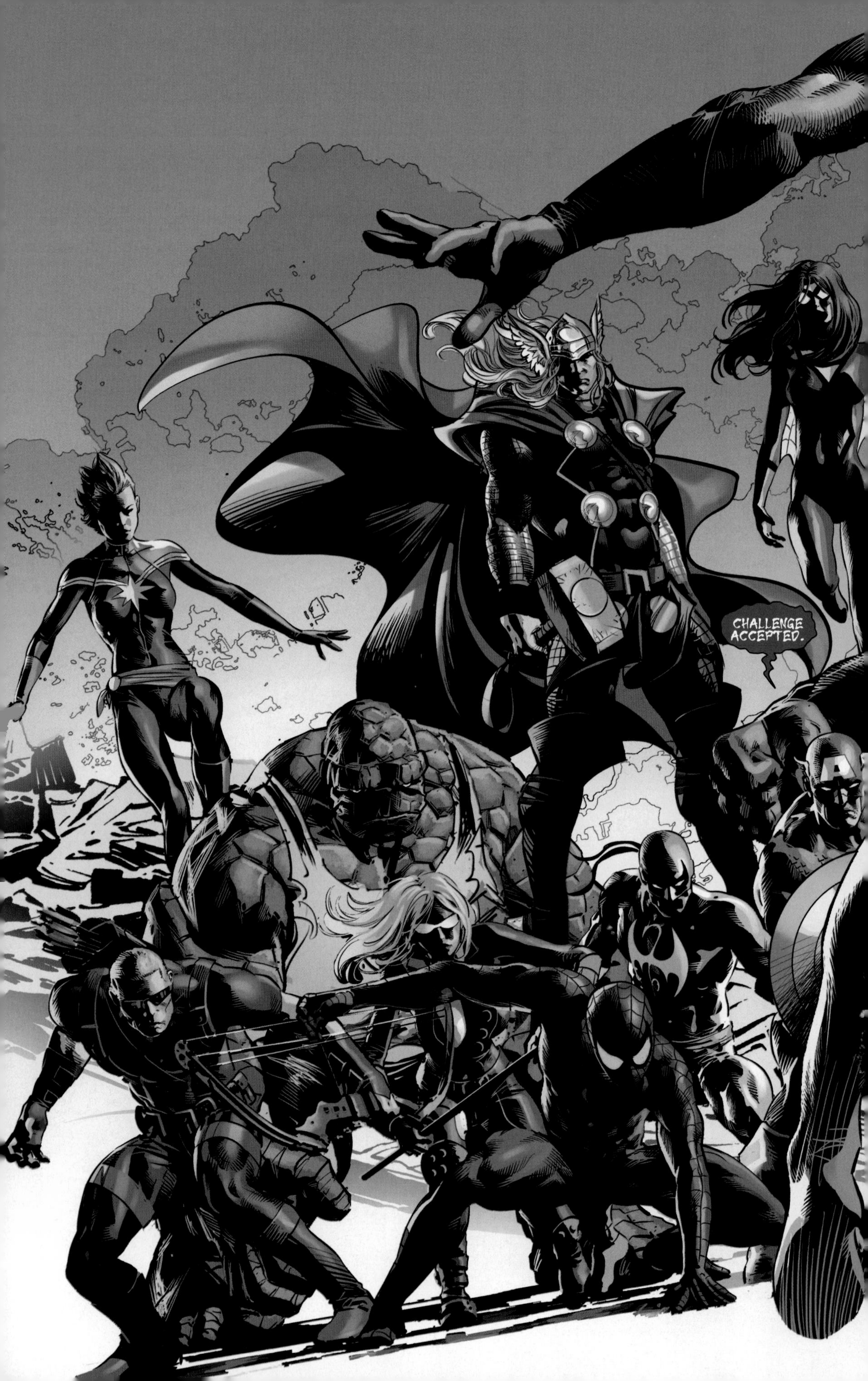
CHALLENGE ACCEPTED.

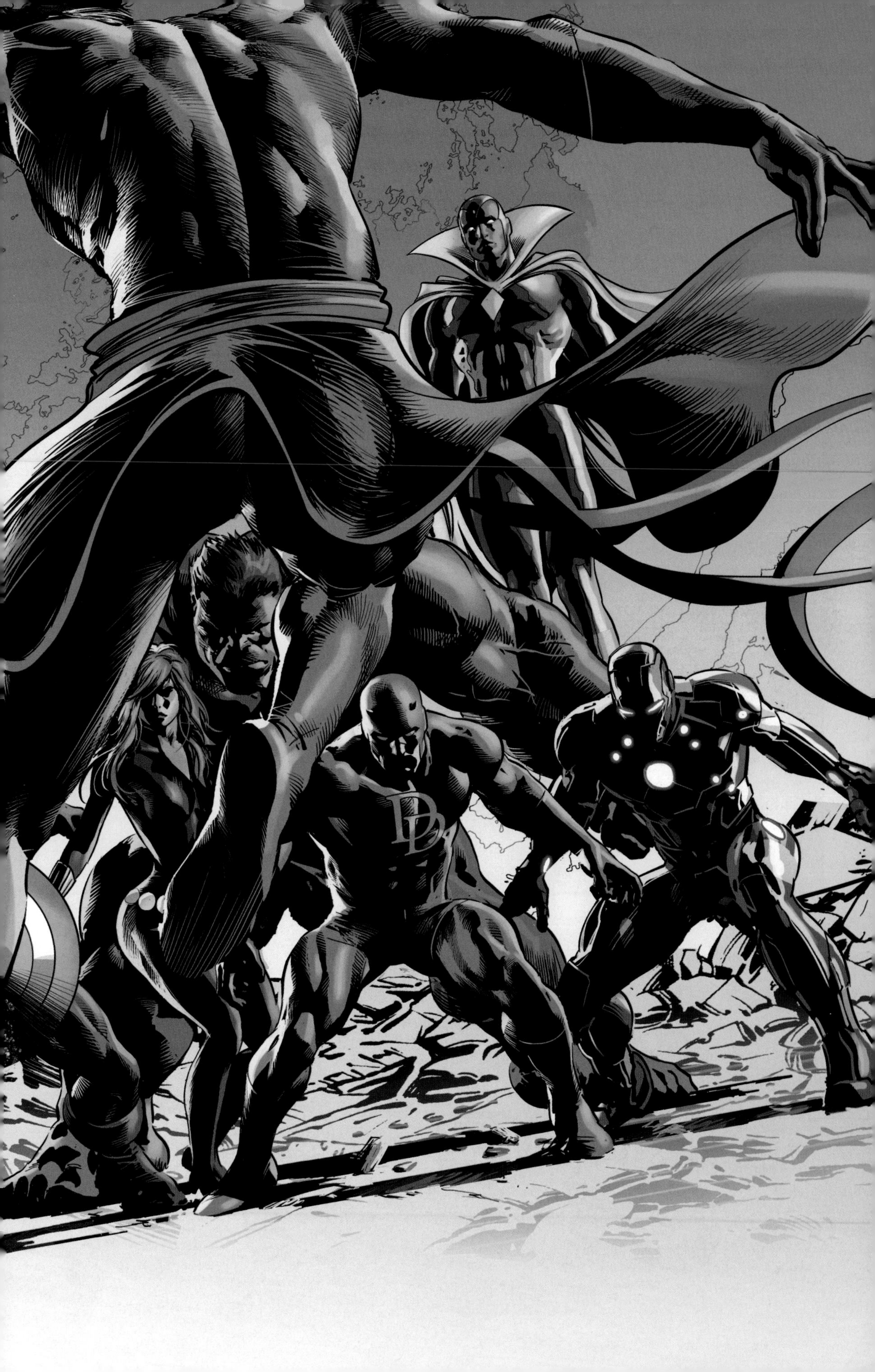

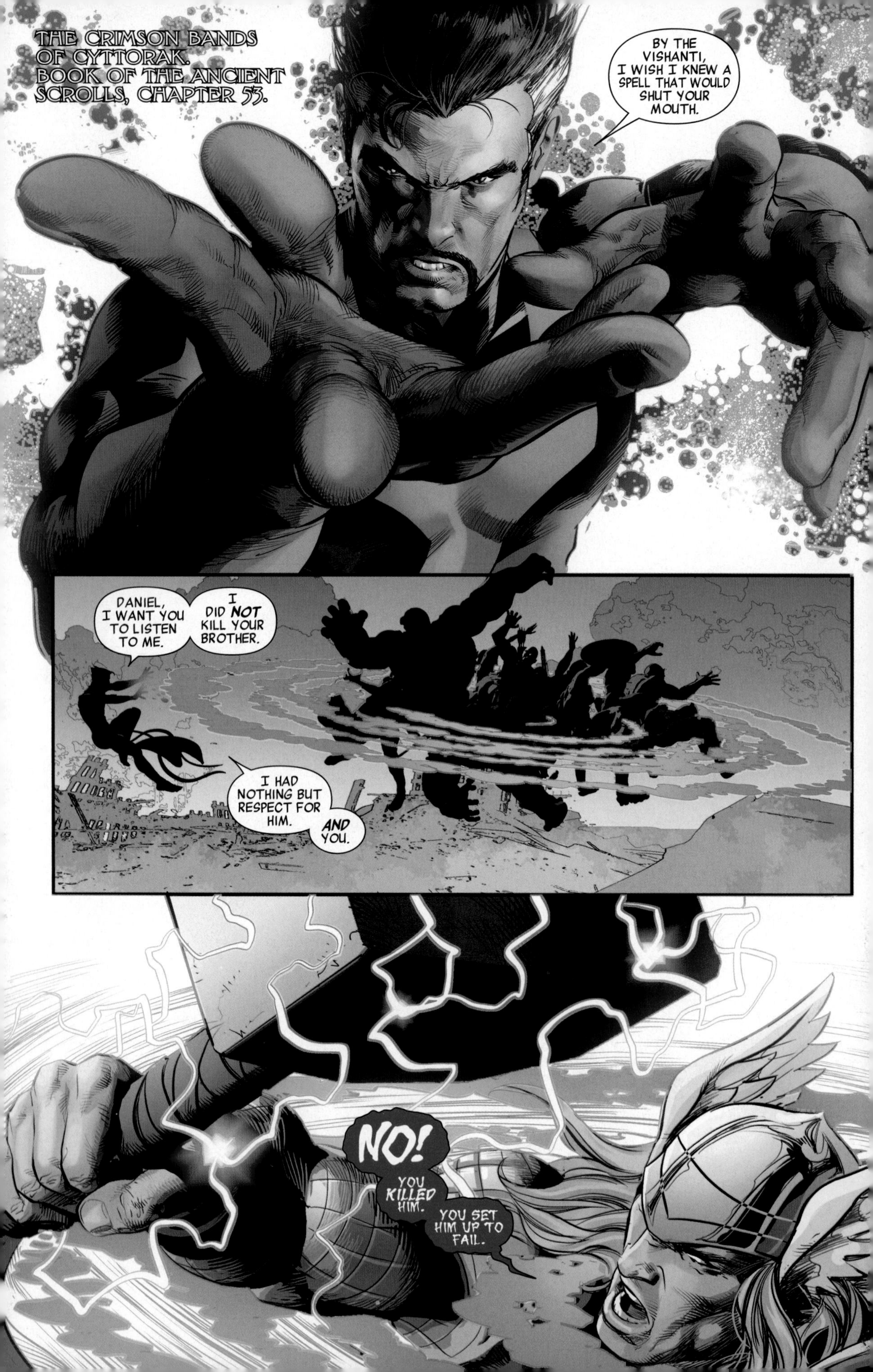
THE CRIMSON BANDS OF CYTTORAK. BOOK OF THE ANCIENT SCROLLS, CHAPTER 53.
BY THE VISHANTI, I WISH I KNEW A SPELL THAT WOULD SHUT YOUR MOUTH.
DANIEL, I WANT YOU TO LISTEN TO ME.
I DID NOT KILL YOUR BROTHER.
I HAD NOTHING BUT RESPECT FOR HIM.
AND YOU.
NO!
YOU KILLED HIM.
YOU SET HIM UP TO FAIL.

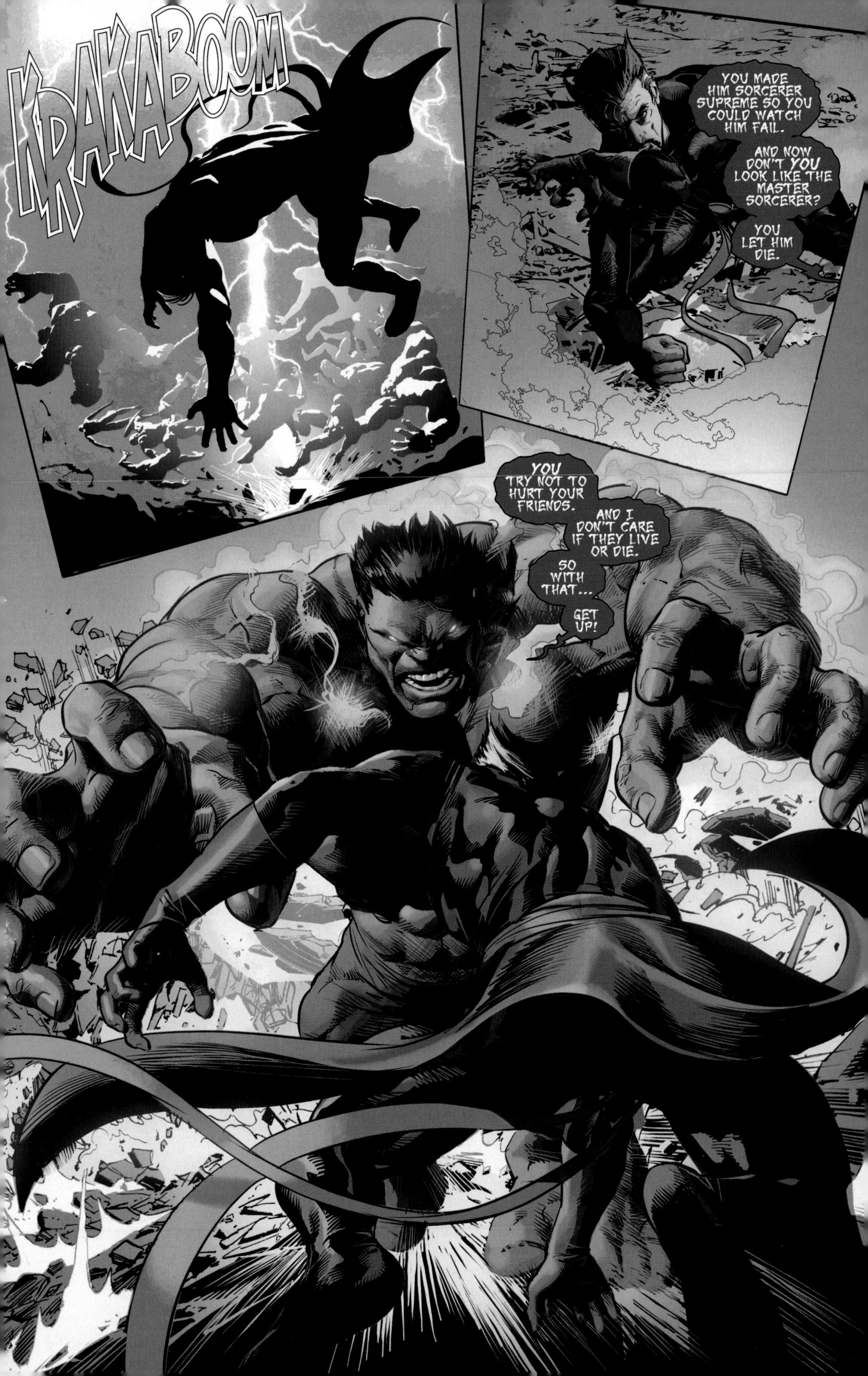
KRAKABOOM
YOU MADE HIM SORCERER SUPREME SO YOU COULD WATCH HIM FAIL.
AND NOW DON'T YOU LOOK LIKE THE MASTER SORCERER?
YOU LET HIM DIE.
YOU TRY NOT TO HURT YOUR FRIENDS.
AND I DON'T CARE IF THEY LIVE OR DIE.
SO WITH THAT...
GET UP!

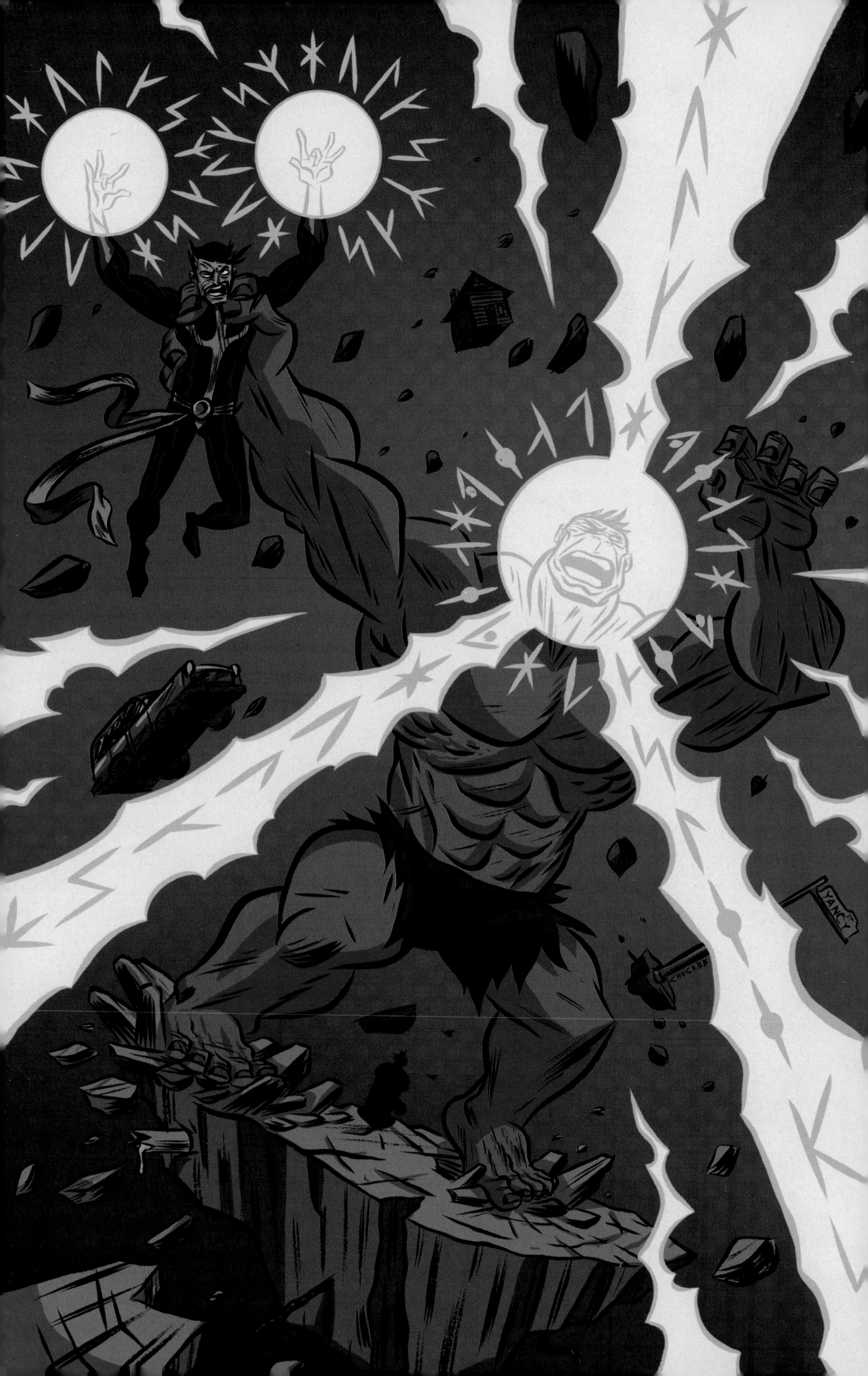
YANCY
CHUCKBB

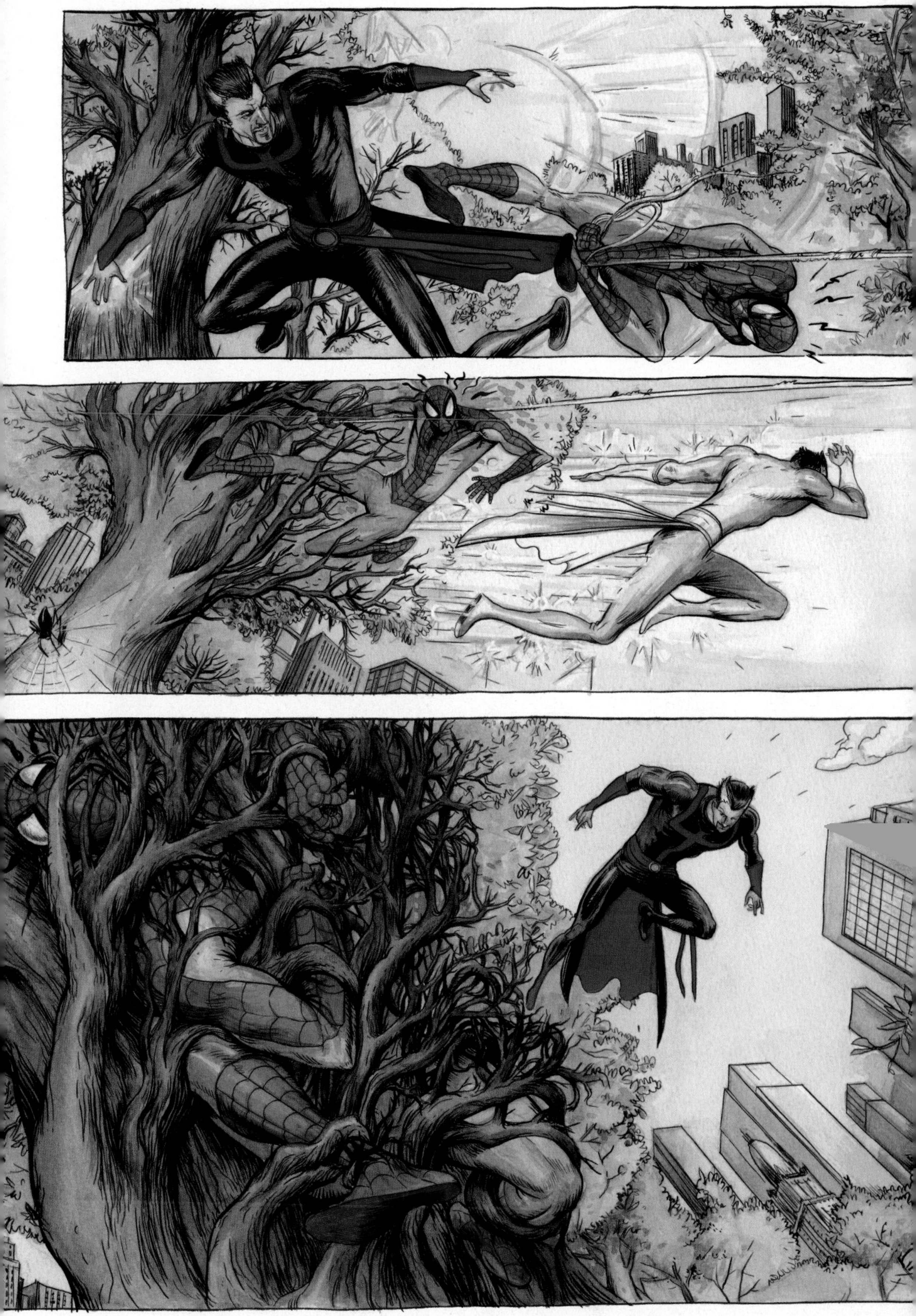

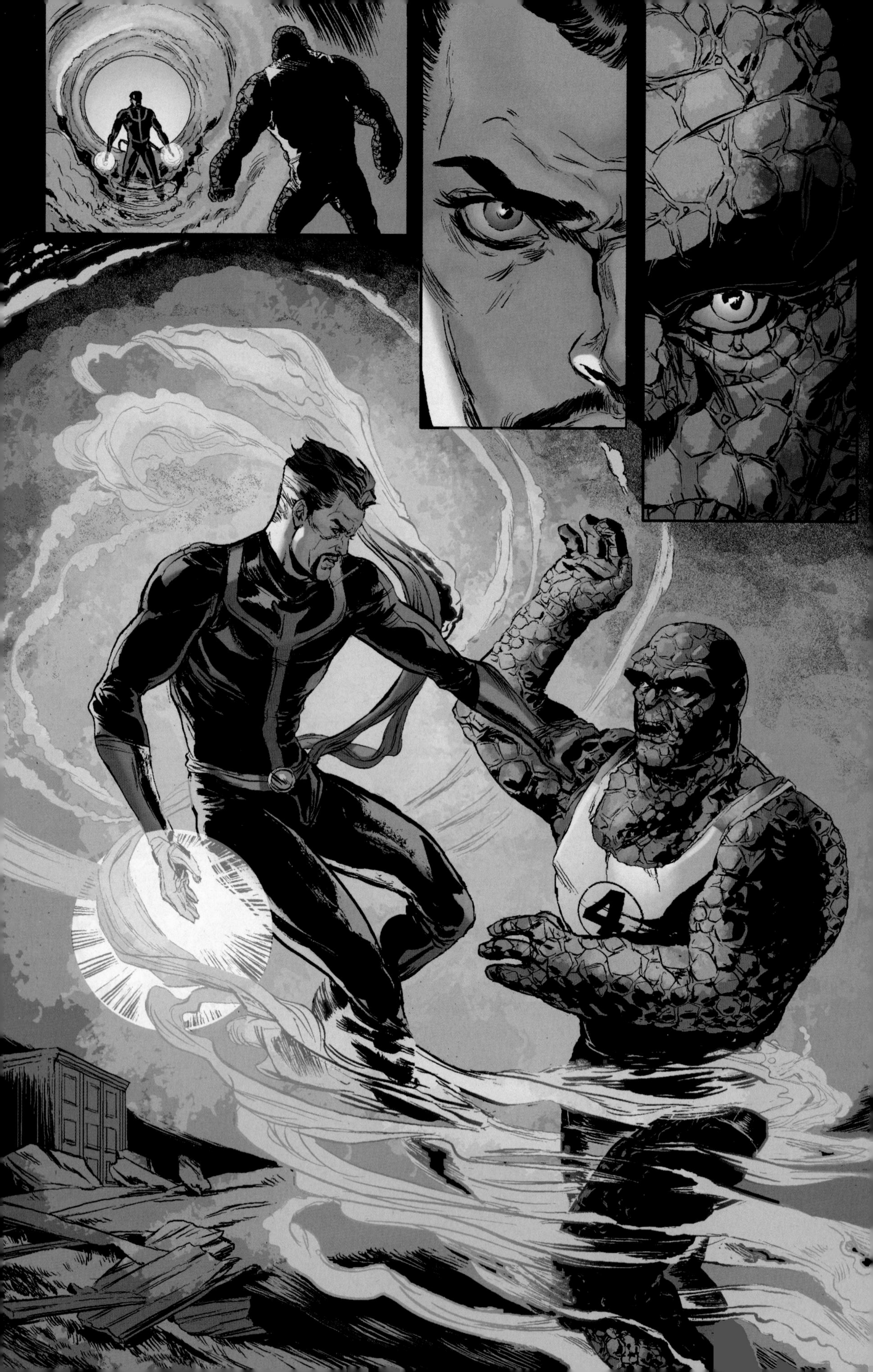

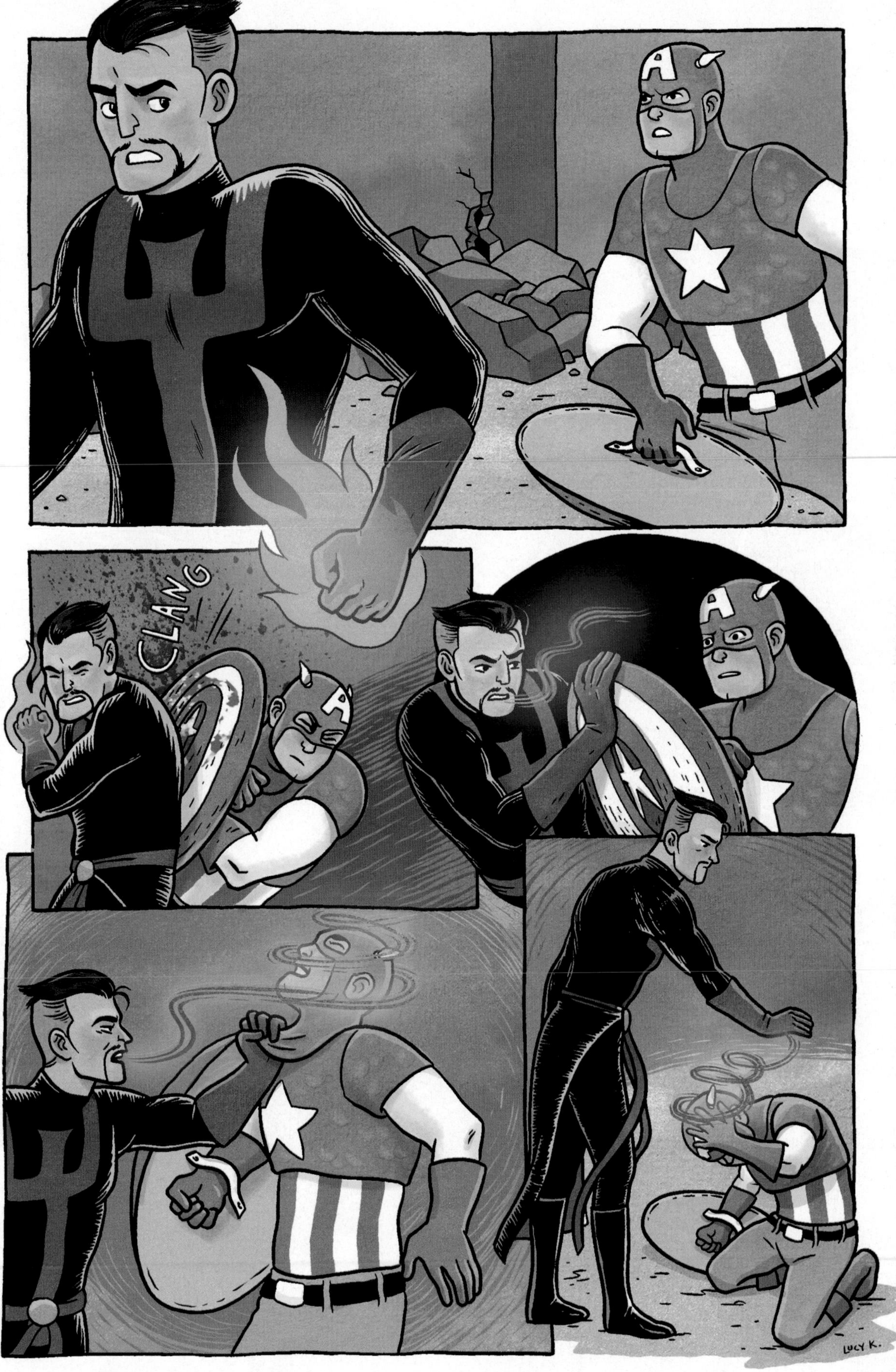
CLANG
LUCY K.

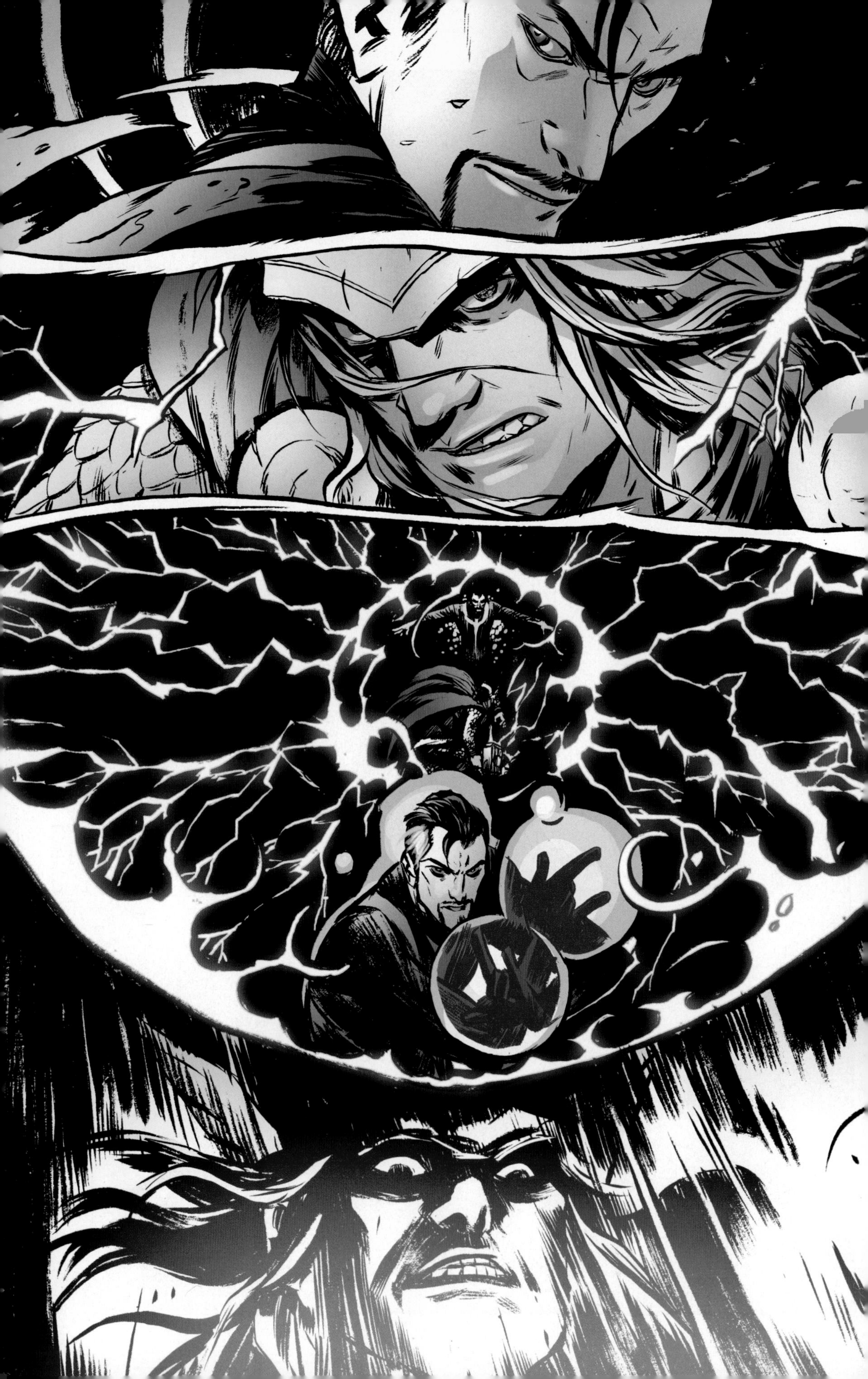

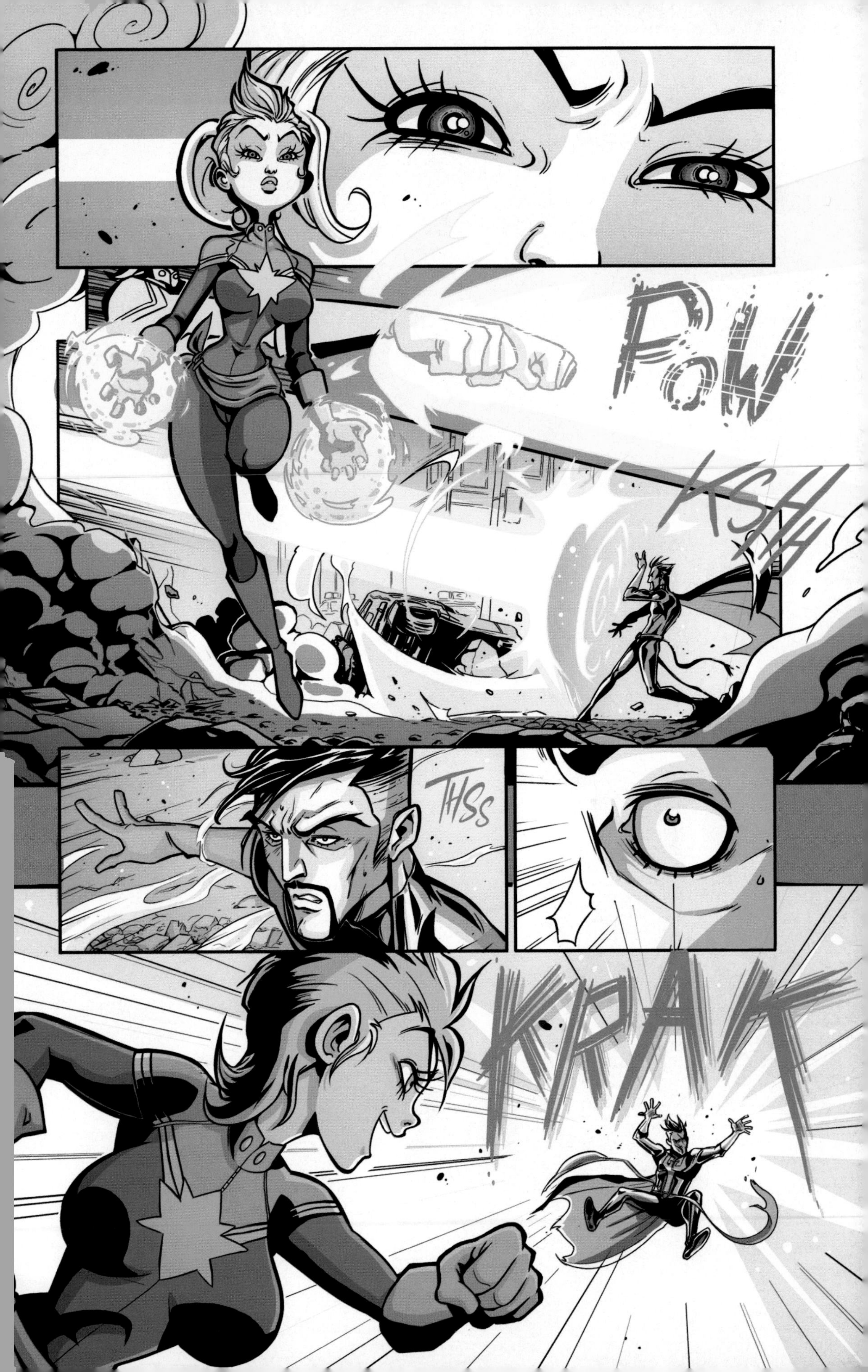
POW
KSHH
THSS
KRAK

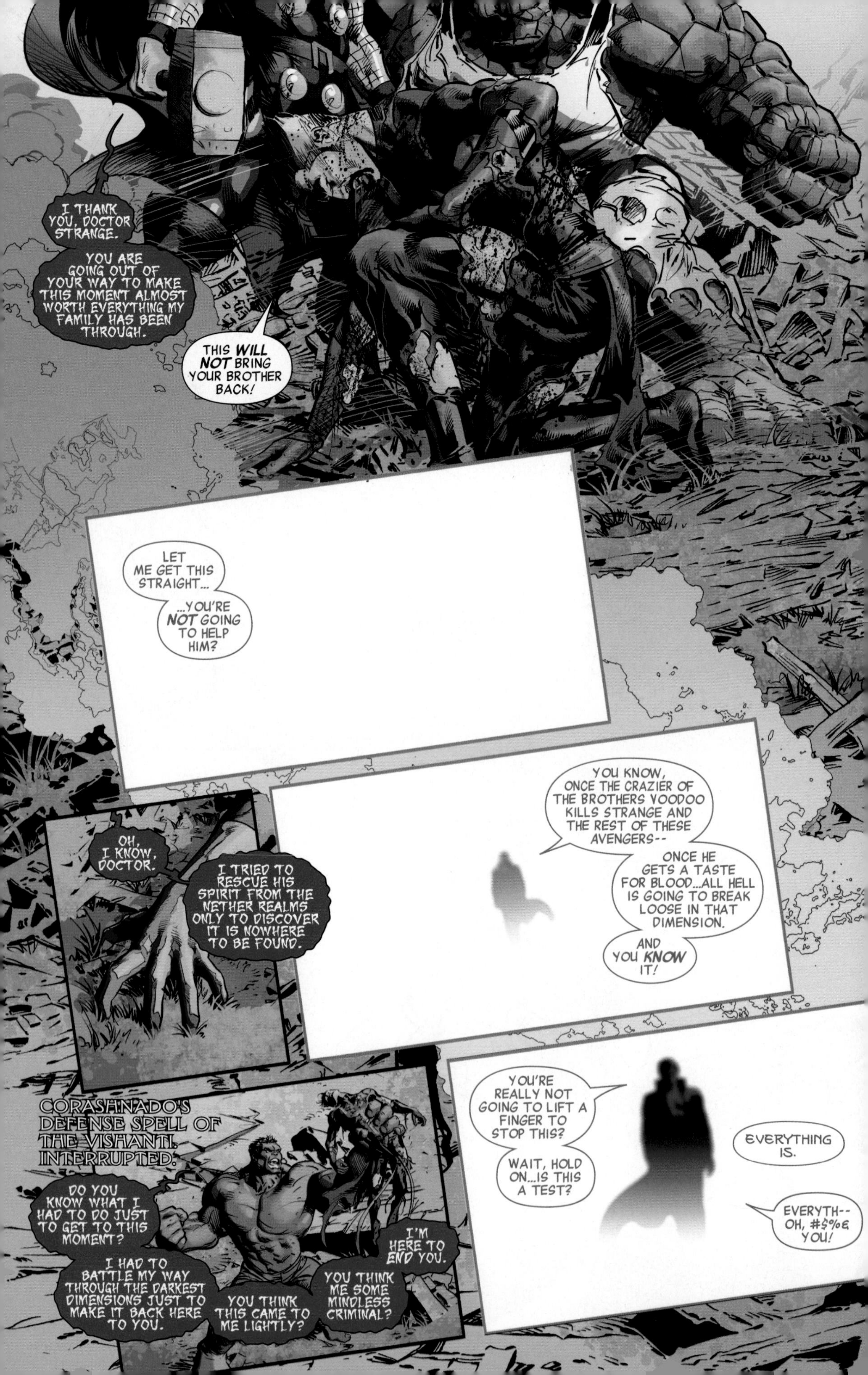
I THANK YOU, DOCTOR STRANGE.
YOU ARE GOING OUT OF YOUR WAY TO MAKE THIS MOMENT ALMOST WORTH EVERYTHING MY FAMILY HAS BEEN THROUGH.
THIS WILL NOT BRING YOUR BROTHER BACK!
LET ME GET THIS STRAIGHT...
...YOU'RE NOT GOING TO HELP HIM?
OH, I KNOW, DOCTOR.
I TRIED TO RESCUE HIS SPIRIT FROM THE NETHER REALMS ONLY TO DISCOVER IT IS NOWHERE TO BE FOUND.
YOU KNOW, ONCE THE CRAZIER OF THE BROTHERS VOODOO KILLS STRANGE AND THE REST OF THESE AVENGERS--
ONCE HE GETS A TASTE FOR BLOOD...ALL HELL IS GOING TO BREAK LOOSE IN THAT DIMENSION.
AND YOU KNOW IT!
CORASHNADO'S DEFENSE SPELL OF THE VISHANTI. INTERRUPTED.
DO YOU KNOW WHAT I HAD TO DO JUST TO GET TO THIS MOMENT?
I HAD TO BATTLE MY WAY THROUGH THE DARKEST DIMENSIONS JUST TO MAKE IT BACK HERE TO YOU.
YOU THINK THIS CAME TO ME LIGHTLY?
YOU THINK ME SOME MINDLESS CRIMINAL?
I'M HERE TO END YOU.
YOU'RE REALLY NOT GOING TO LIFT A FINGER TO STOP THIS?
WAIT, HOLD ON...IS THIS A TEST?
EVERYTHING IS.
EVERYTH-- OH, #$%& YOU!

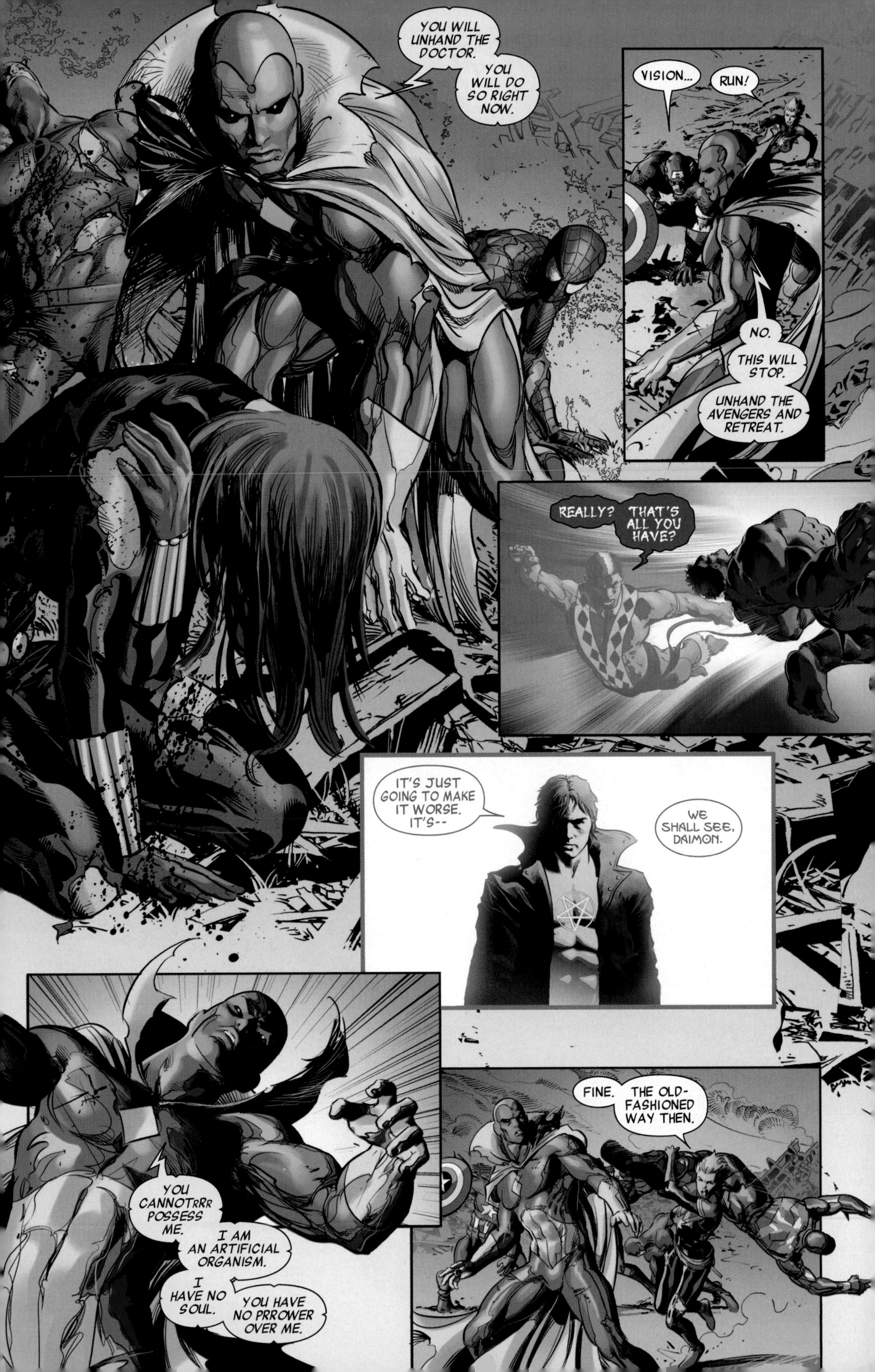
YOU WILL UNHAND THE DOCTOR.
YOU WILL DO SO RIGHT NOW.
VISION...
RUN!
NO.
THIS WILL STOP.
UNHAND THE AVENGERS AND RETREAT.
REALLY?
THAT'S ALL YOU HAVE?
IT'S JUST GOING TO MAKE IT WORSE. IT'S--
WE SHALL SEE, DAIMON.
YOU CANNOTRRR POSSESS ME.
I AM AN ARTIFICIAL ORGANISM.
I HAVE NO SOUL.
YOU HAVE NO PRROWER OVER ME.
FINE.
THE OLD-FASHIONED WAY THEN.

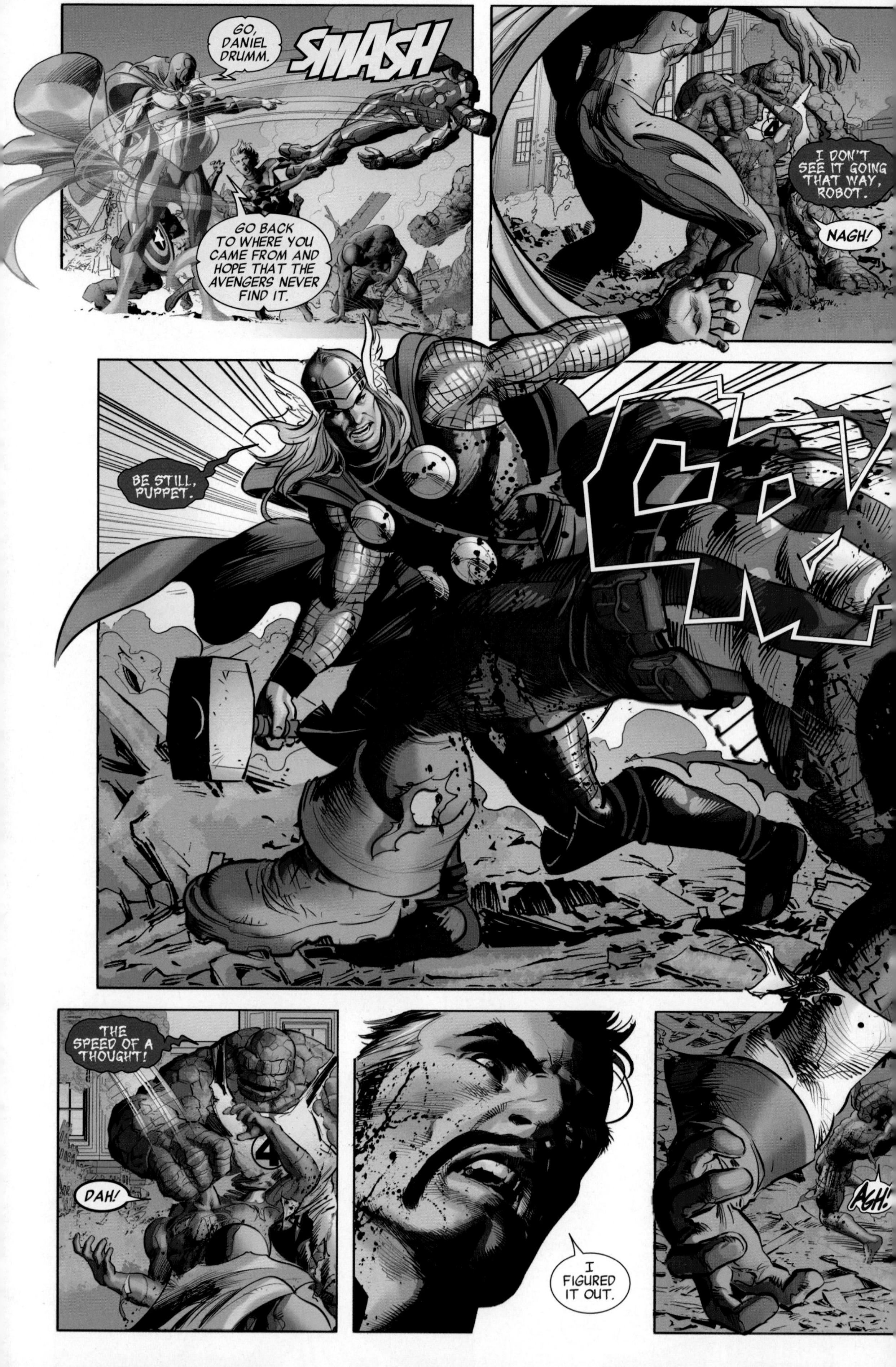
GO, DANIEL DRUMM.
SMASH
GO BACK TO WHERE YOU CAME FROM AND HOPE THAT THE AVENGERS NEVER FIND IT.
I DON'T SEE IT GOING THAT WAY, ROBOT.
NAGH!
BE STILL, PUPPET.
THE SPEED OF A THOUGHT!
DAH!
I FIGURED IT OUT.
AGH!

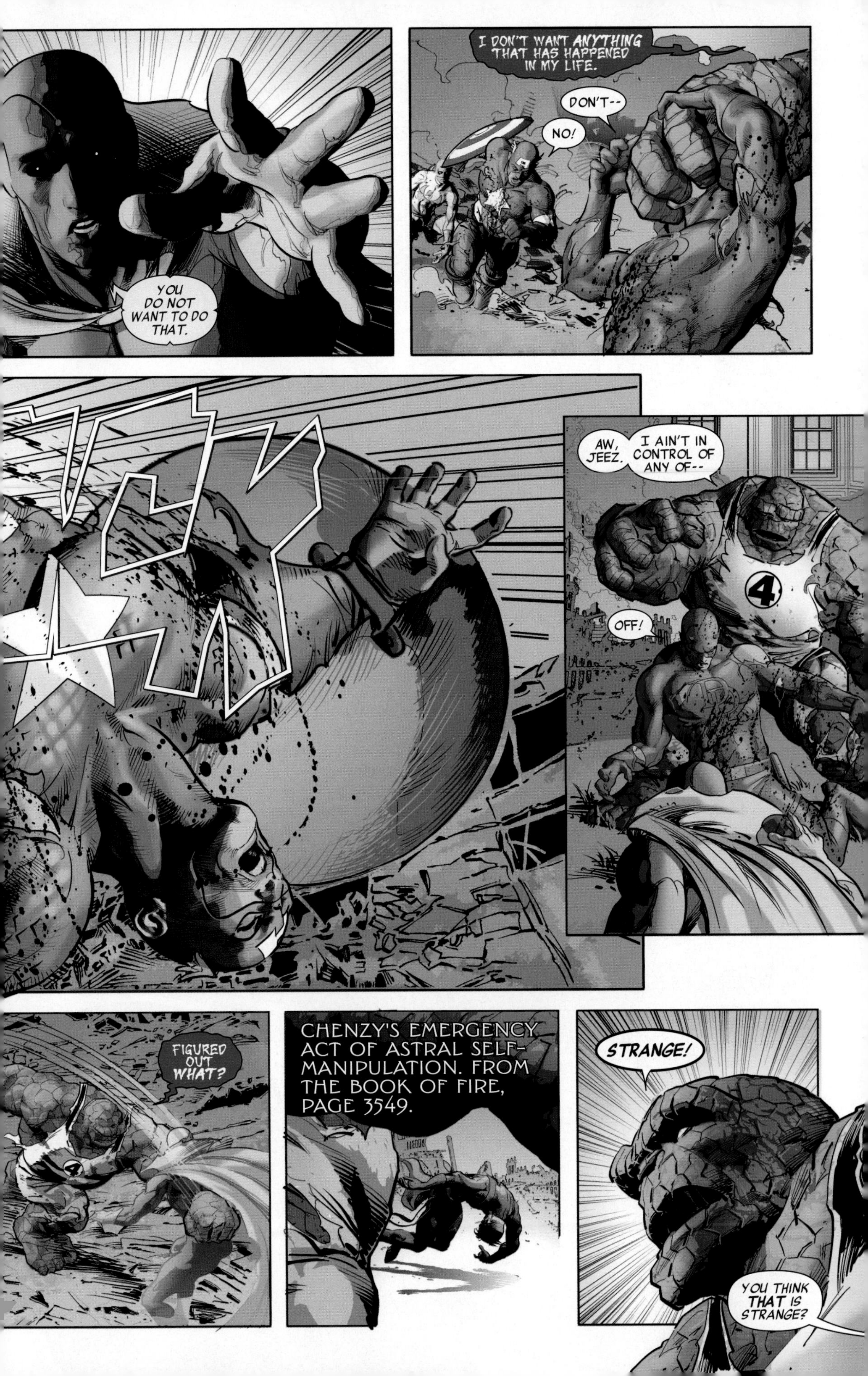
YOU DO NOT WANT TO DO THAT.
I DON'T WANT ANYTHING THAT HAS HAPPENED IN MY LIFE.
DON'T--
NO!
AW, JEEZ.
I AIN'T IN CONTROL OF ANY OF--
OFF!
FIGURED OUT WHAT?
CHENZY'S EMERGENCY ACT OF ASTRAL SELF-MANIPULATION. FROM THE BOOK OF FIRE, PAGE 3549.
STRANGE!
YOU THINK THAT IS STRANGE?

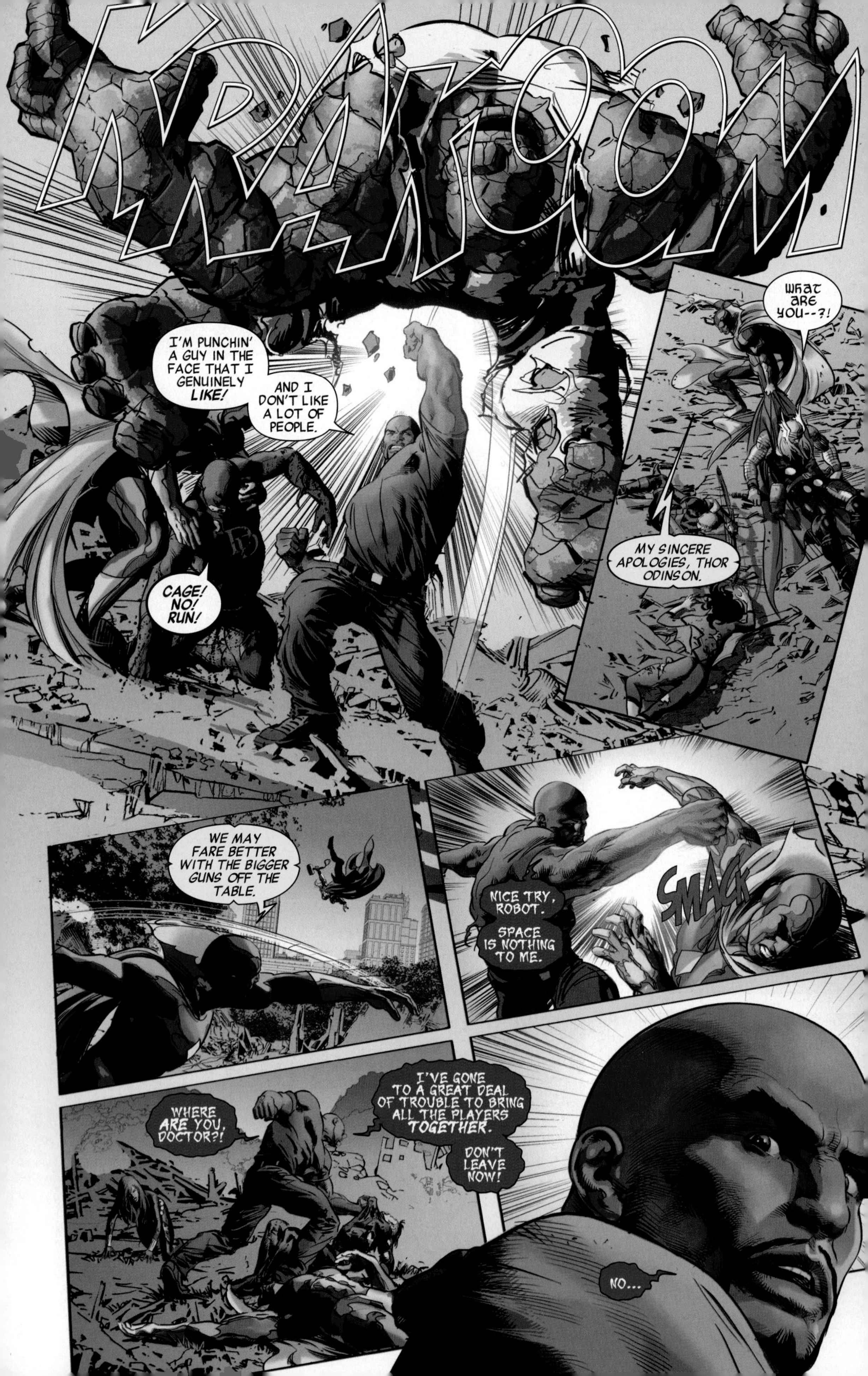
KRAKOOM
I'M PUNCHIN' A GUY IN THE FACE THAT I GENUINELY LIKE!
AND I DON'T LIKE A LOT OF PEOPLE.
CAGE! NO! RUN!
WHAT ARE YOU--?!
MY SINCERE APOLOGIES, THOR ODINSON.
WE MAY FARE BETTER WITH THE BIGGER GUNS OFF THE TABLE.
NICE TRY, ROBOT.
SPACE IS NOTHING TO ME.
SMACK
WHERE ARE YOU, DOCTOR?!
I'VE GONE TO A GREAT DEAL OF TROUBLE TO BRING ALL THE PLAYERS TOGETHER.
DON'T LEAVE NOW!
NO...

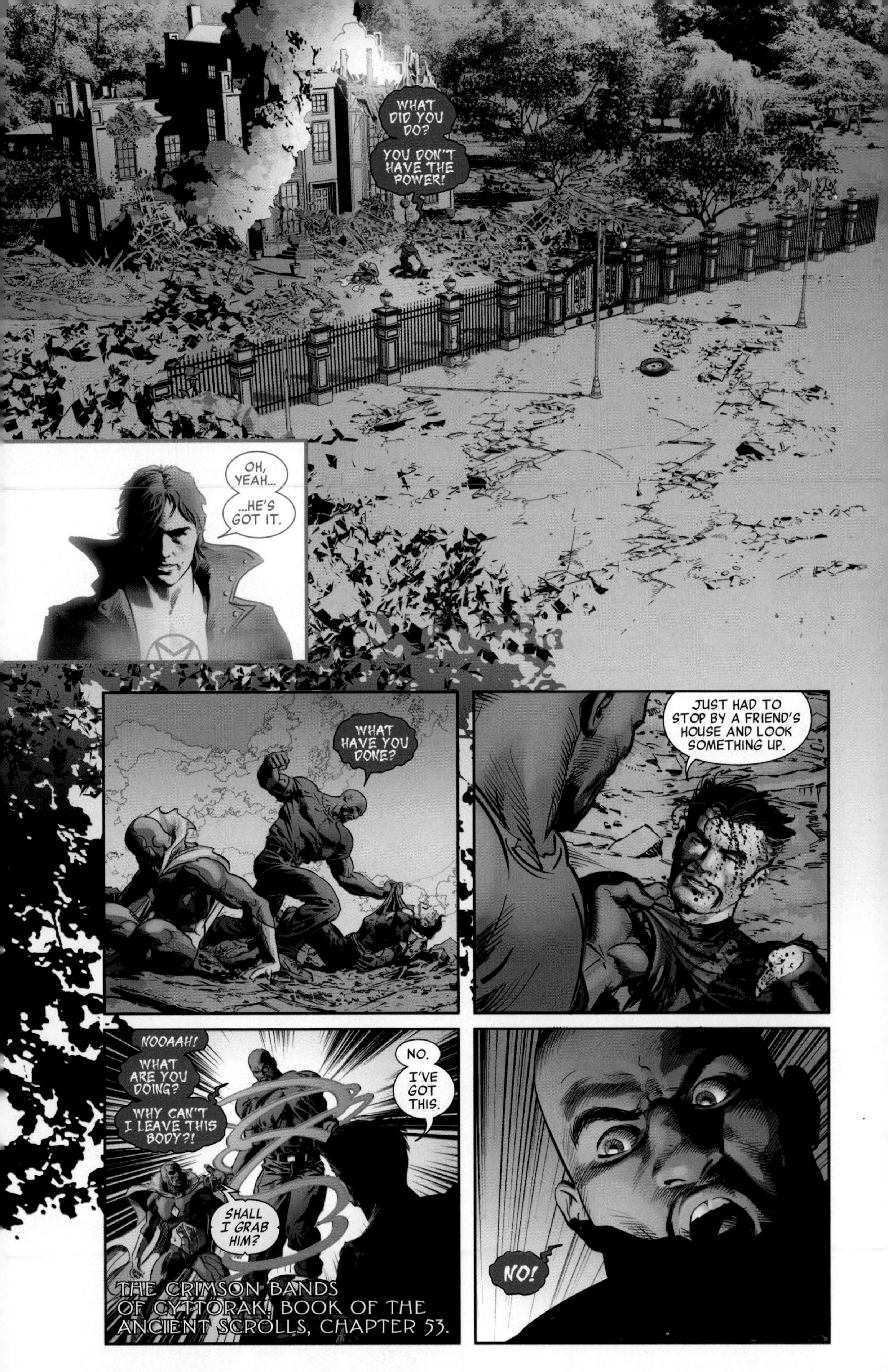
WHAT DID YOU DO?
YOU DON'T HAVE THE POWER!
OH, YEAH...
...HE'S GOT IT.
WHAT HAVE YOU DONE?
JUST HAD TO STOP BY A FRIEND'S HOUSE AND LOOK SOMETHING UP.
NOOAAH!
WHAT ARE YOU DOING?
WHY CAN'T I LEAVE THIS BODY?!
NO.
I'VE GOT THIS.
SHALL I GRAB HIM?
THE CRIMSON BANDS OF CYTTORAK! BOOK OF THE ANCIENT SCROLLS, CHAPTER 53.
NO!

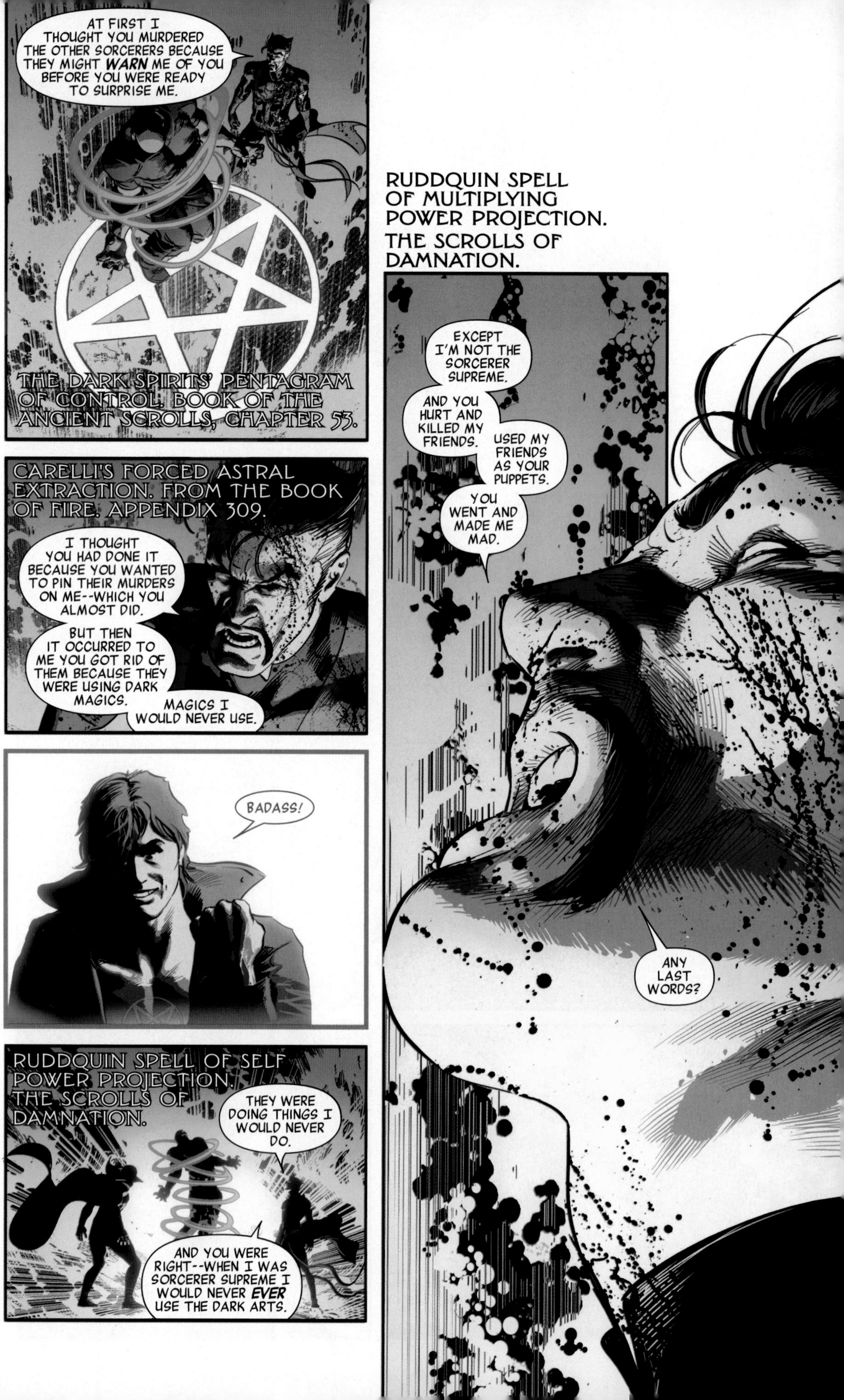
AT FIRST I THOUGHT YOU MURDERED THE OTHER SORCERERS BECAUSE THEY MIGHT WARN ME OF YOU BEFORE YOU WERE READY TO SURPRISE ME.
THE DARK SPIRITS' PENTAGRAM OF CONTROL. BOOK OF THE ANCIENT SCROLLS, CHAPTER 53.
CARELLI'S FORCED ASTRAL EXTRACTION. FROM THE BOOK OF FIRE. APPENDIX 309.
I THOUGHT YOU HAD DONE IT BECAUSE YOU WANTED TO PIN THEIR MURDERS ON ME--WHICH YOU ALMOST DID.
BUT THEN IT OCCURRED TO ME YOU GOT RID OF THEM BECAUSE THEY WERE USING DARK MAGICS.
MAGICS I WOULD NEVER USE.
BADASS!
RUDDQUIN SPELL OF SELF POWER PROJECTION. THE SCROLLS OF DAMNATION.
THEY WERE DOING THINGS I WOULD NEVER DO.
AND YOU WERE RIGHT--WHEN I WAS SORCERER SUPREME I WOULD NEVER EVER USE THE DARK ARTS.
RUDDQUIN SPELL OF MULTIPLYING POWER PROJECTION. THE SCROLLS OF DAMNATION.
EXCEPT I'M NOT THE SORCERER SUPREME.
AND YOU HURT AND KILLED MY FRIENDS.
USED MY FRIENDS AS YOUR PUPPETS.
YOU WENT AND MADE ME MAD.
ANY LAST WORDS?

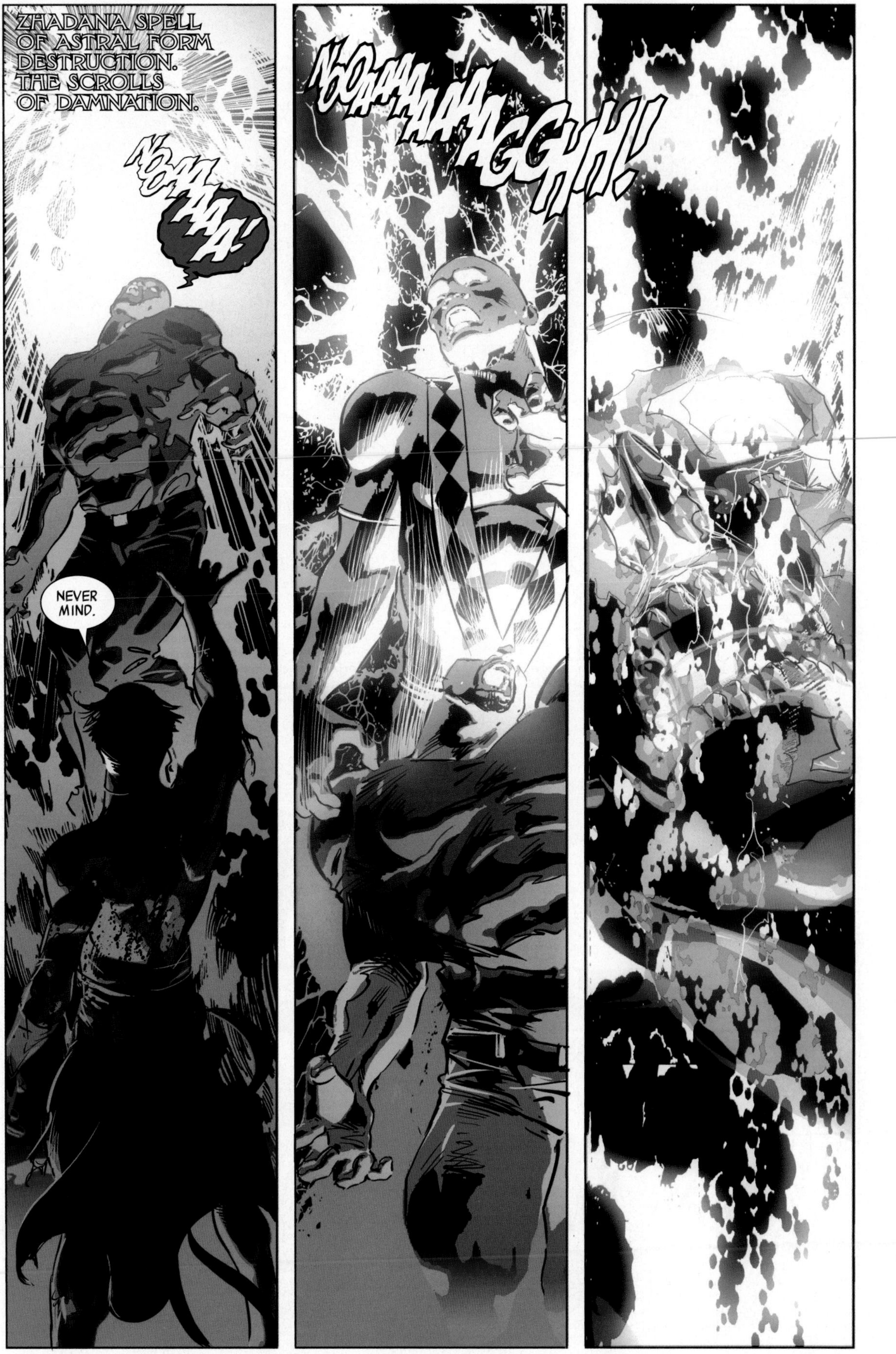
ZHADANA SPELL OF ASTRAL FORM DESTRUCTION. THE SCROLLS OF DAMNATION.
NOOAAAAAA!
NEVER MIND.
NOOAAAAAAAAAAAGGHH!

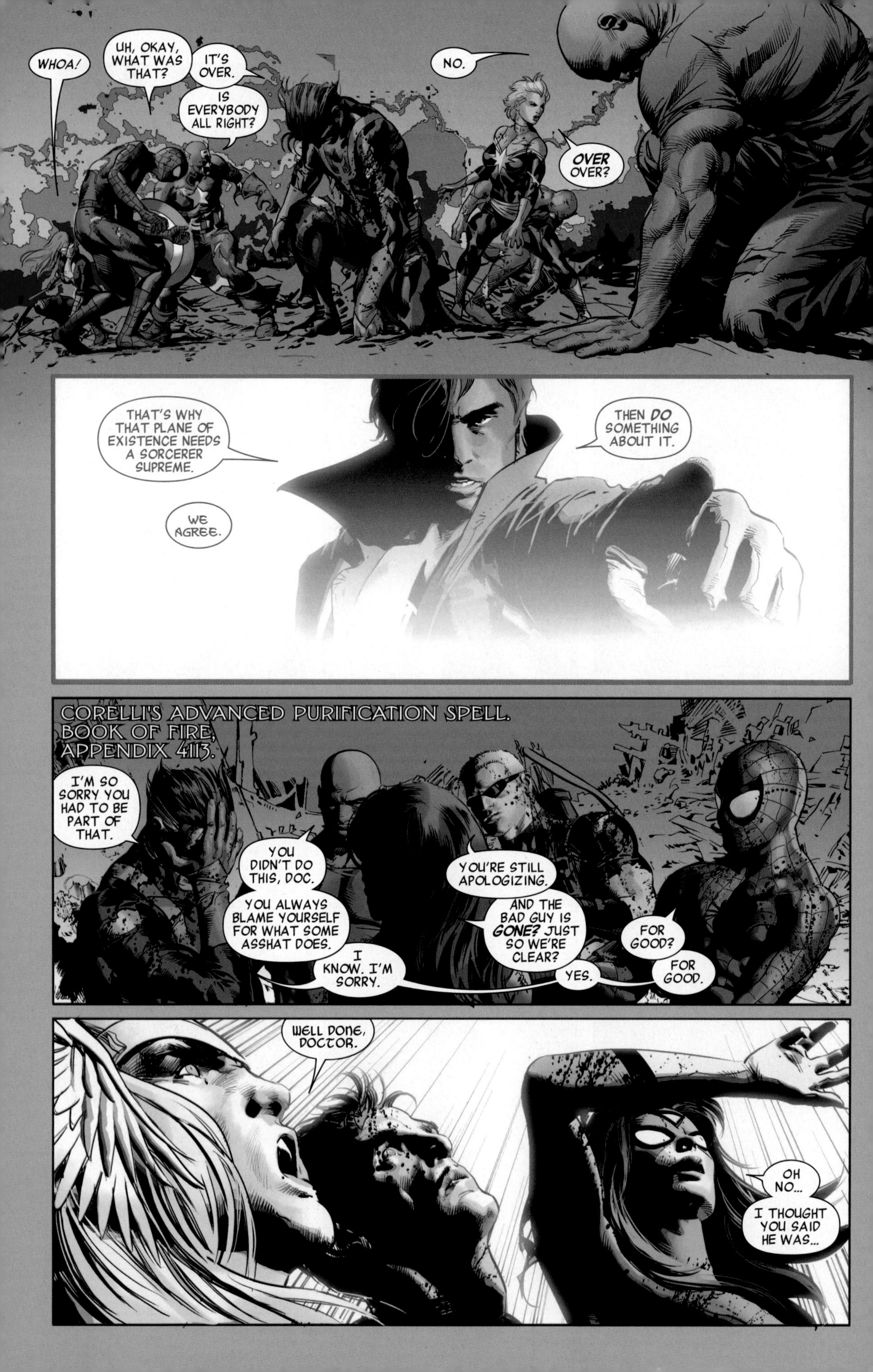
WHOA!
UH, OKAY, WHAT WAS THAT?
IT'S OVER.
IS EVERYBODY ALL RIGHT?
NO.
OVER OVER?
THAT'S WHY THAT PLANE OF EXISTENCE NEEDS A SORCERER SUPREME.
THEN DO SOMETHING ABOUT IT.
WE AGREE.
CORELLI'S ADVANCED PURIFICATION SPELL. BOOK OF FIRE, APPENDIX 4113.
I'M SO SORRY YOU HAD TO BE PART OF THAT.
YOU DIDN'T DO THIS, DOC.
YOU ALWAYS BLAME YOURSELF FOR WHAT SOME ASSHAT DOES.
I KNOW. I'M SORRY.
YOU'RE STILL APOLOGIZING.
AND THE BAD GUY IS GONE? JUST SO WE'RE CLEAR?
YES.
FOR GOOD?
FOR GOOD.
WELL DONE, DOCTOR.
OH NO...
I THOUGHT YOU SAID HE WAS...

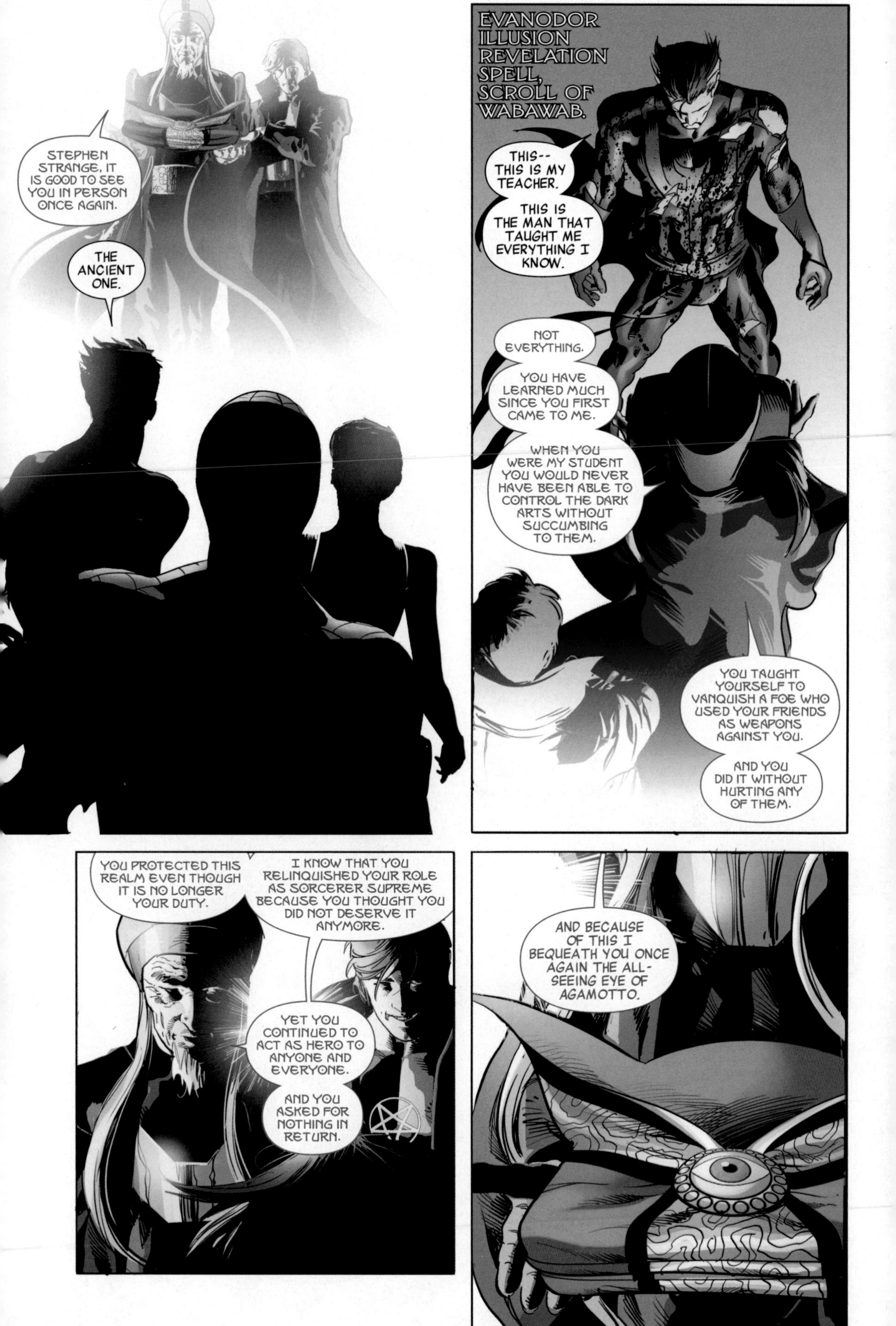
STEPHEN STRANGE, IT IS GOOD TO SEE YOU IN PERSON ONCE AGAIN.
THE ANCIENT ONE.
EVANODOR ILLUSION REVELATION SPELL, SCROLL OF WABAWAB.
THIS-- THIS IS MY TEACHER.
THIS IS THE MAN THAT TAUGHT ME EVERYTHING I KNOW.
NOT EVERYTHING.
YOU HAVE LEARNED MUCH SINCE YOU FIRST CAME TO ME.
WHEN YOU WERE MY STUDENT YOU WOULD NEVER HAVE BEEN ABLE TO CONTROL THE DARK ARTS WITHOUT SUCCUMBING TO THEM.
YOU TAUGHT YOURSELF TO VANQUISH A FOE WHO USED YOUR FRIENDS AS WEAPONS AGAINST YOU.
AND YOU DID IT WITHOUT HURTING ANY OF THEM.
YOU PROTECTED THIS REALM EVEN THOUGH IT IS NO LONGER YOUR DUTY.
I KNOW THAT YOU RELINQUISHED YOUR ROLE AS SORCERER SUPREME BECAUSE YOU THOUGHT YOU DID NOT DESERVE IT ANYMORE.
YET YOU CONTINUED TO ACT AS HERO TO ANYONE AND EVERYONE.
AND YOU ASKED FOR NOTHING IN RETURN.
AND BECAUSE OF THIS I BEQUEATH YOU ONCE AGAIN THE ALL-SEEING EYE OF AGAMOTTO.

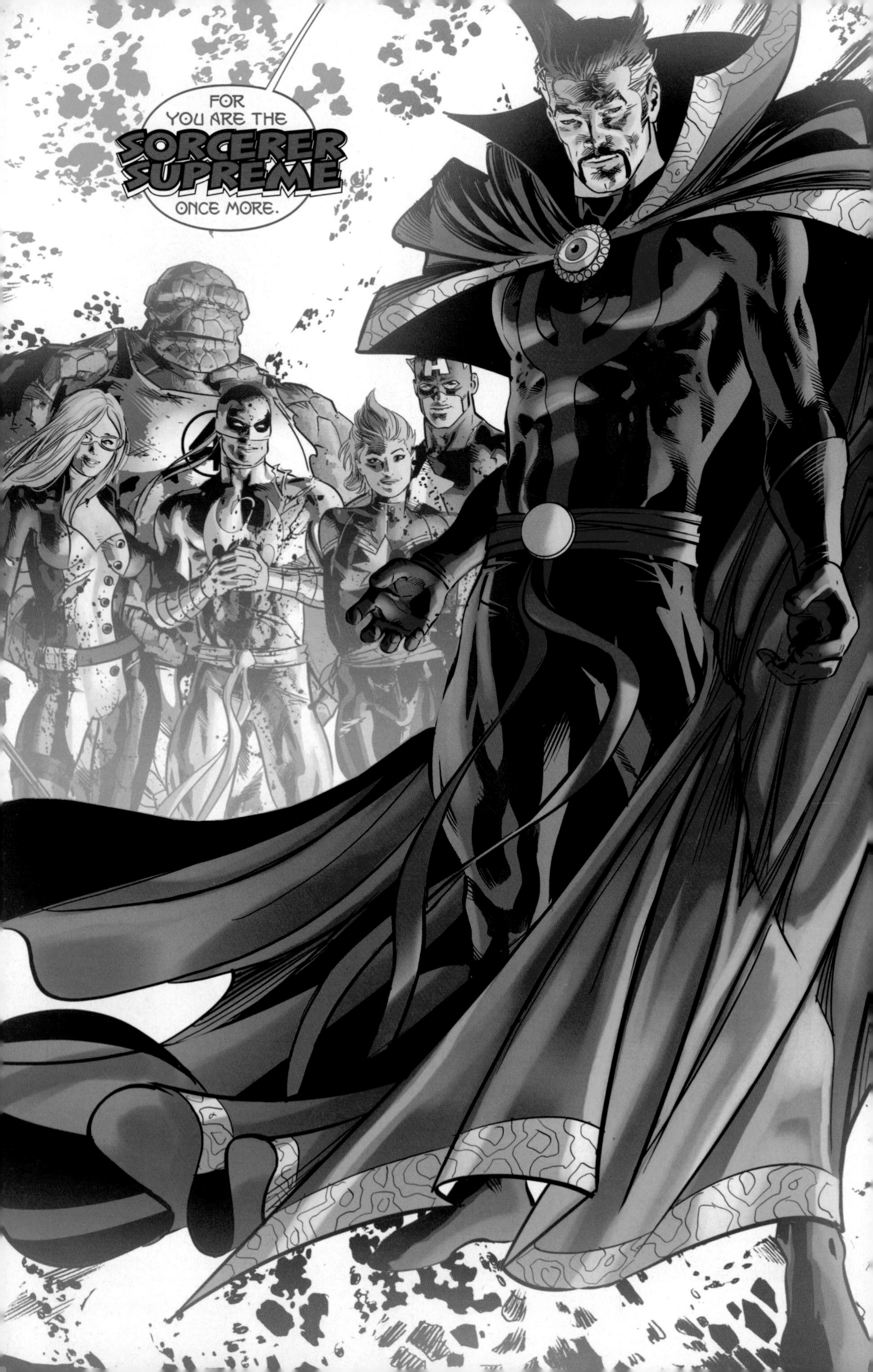
FOR YOU ARE THE SORCERER SUPREME ONCE MORE.

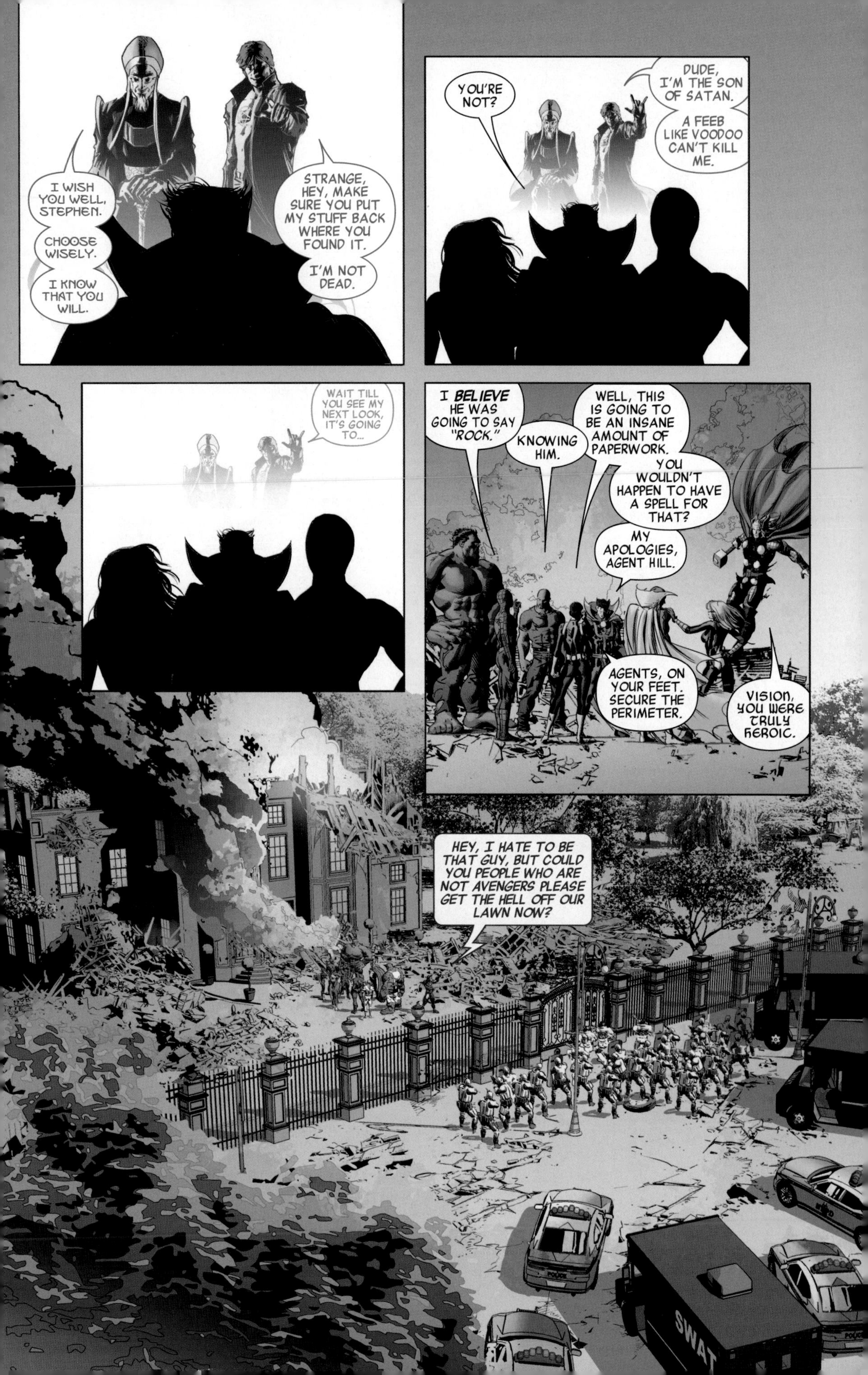
I WISH YOU WELL, STEPHEN.
CHOOSE WISELY.
I KNOW THAT YOU WILL.
STRANGE, HEY, MAKE SURE YOU PUT MY STUFF BACK WHERE YOU FOUND IT.
I'M NOT DEAD.
YOU'RE NOT?
DUDE, I'M THE SON OF SATAN.
A FEEB LIKE VOODOO CAN'T KILL ME.
WAIT TILL YOU SEE MY NEXT LOOK, IT'S GOING TO...
I BELIEVE HE WAS GOING TO SAY "ROCK."
KNOWING HIM.
WELL, THIS IS GOING TO BE AN INSANE AMOUNT OF PAPERWORK.
YOU WOULDN'T HAPPEN TO HAVE A SPELL FOR THAT?
MY APOLOGIES, AGENT HILL.
AGENTS, ON YOUR FEET. SECURE THE PERIMETER.
VISION, YOU WERE TRULY HEROIC.
HEY, I HATE TO BE THAT GUY, BUT COULD YOU PEOPLE WHO ARE NOT AVENGERS PLEASE GET THE HELL OFF OUR LAWN NOW?
SWAT

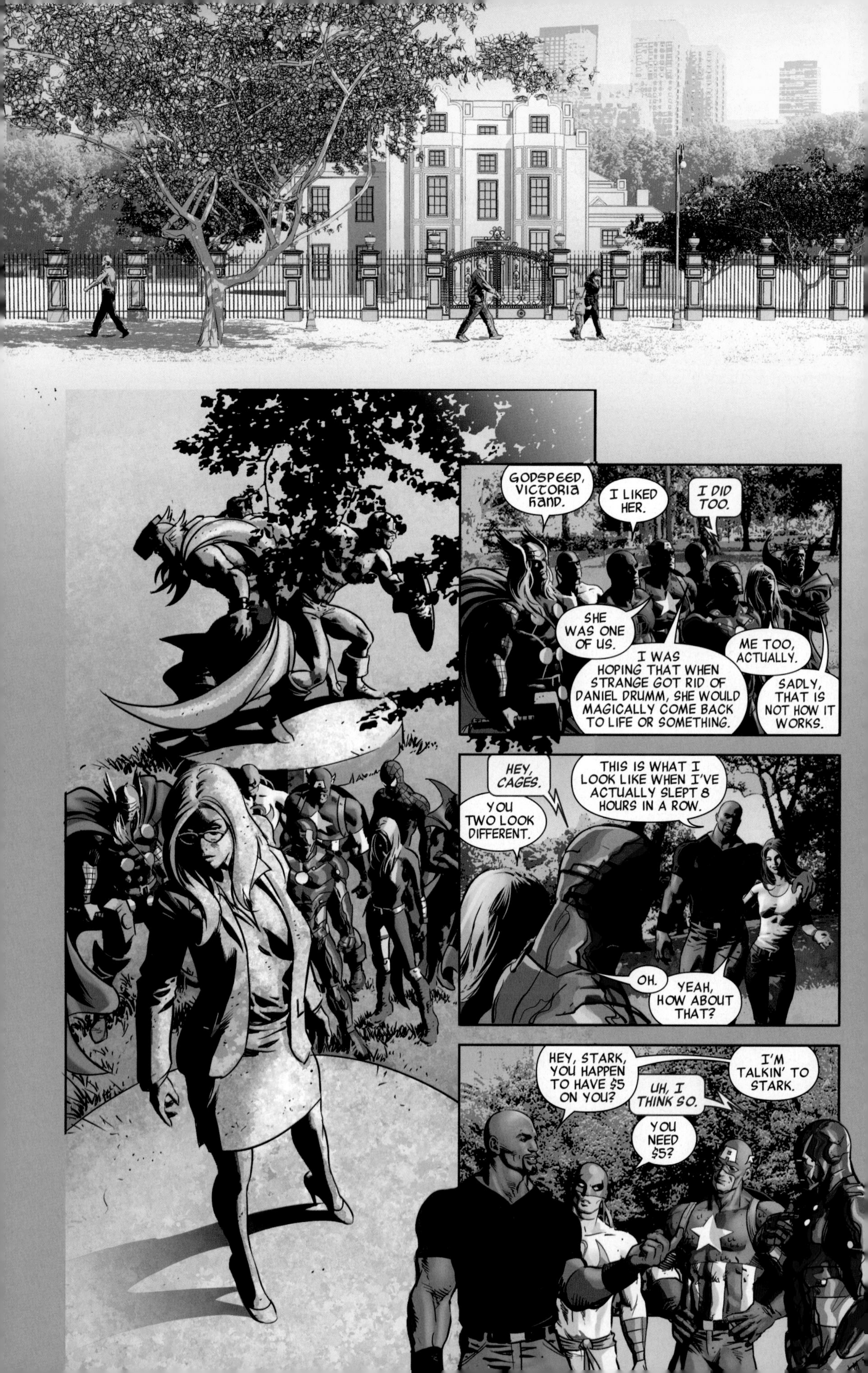
GODSPEED, VICTORIA HAND.
I LIKED HER.
I DID TOO.
SHE WAS ONE OF US.
I WAS HOPING THAT WHEN STRANGE GOT RID OF DANIEL DRUMM, SHE WOULD MAGICALLY COME BACK TO LIFE OR SOMETHING.
ME TOO, ACTUALLY.
SADLY, THAT IS NOT HOW IT WORKS.
HEY, CAGES.
YOU TWO LOOK DIFFERENT.
THIS IS WHAT I LOOK LIKE WHEN I'VE ACTUALLY SLEPT 8 HOURS IN A ROW.
OH.
YEAH, HOW ABOUT THAT?
HEY, STARK, YOU HAPPEN TO HAVE $5 ON YOU?
UH, I THINK SO.
YOU NEED $5?
I'M TALKIN' TO STARK.

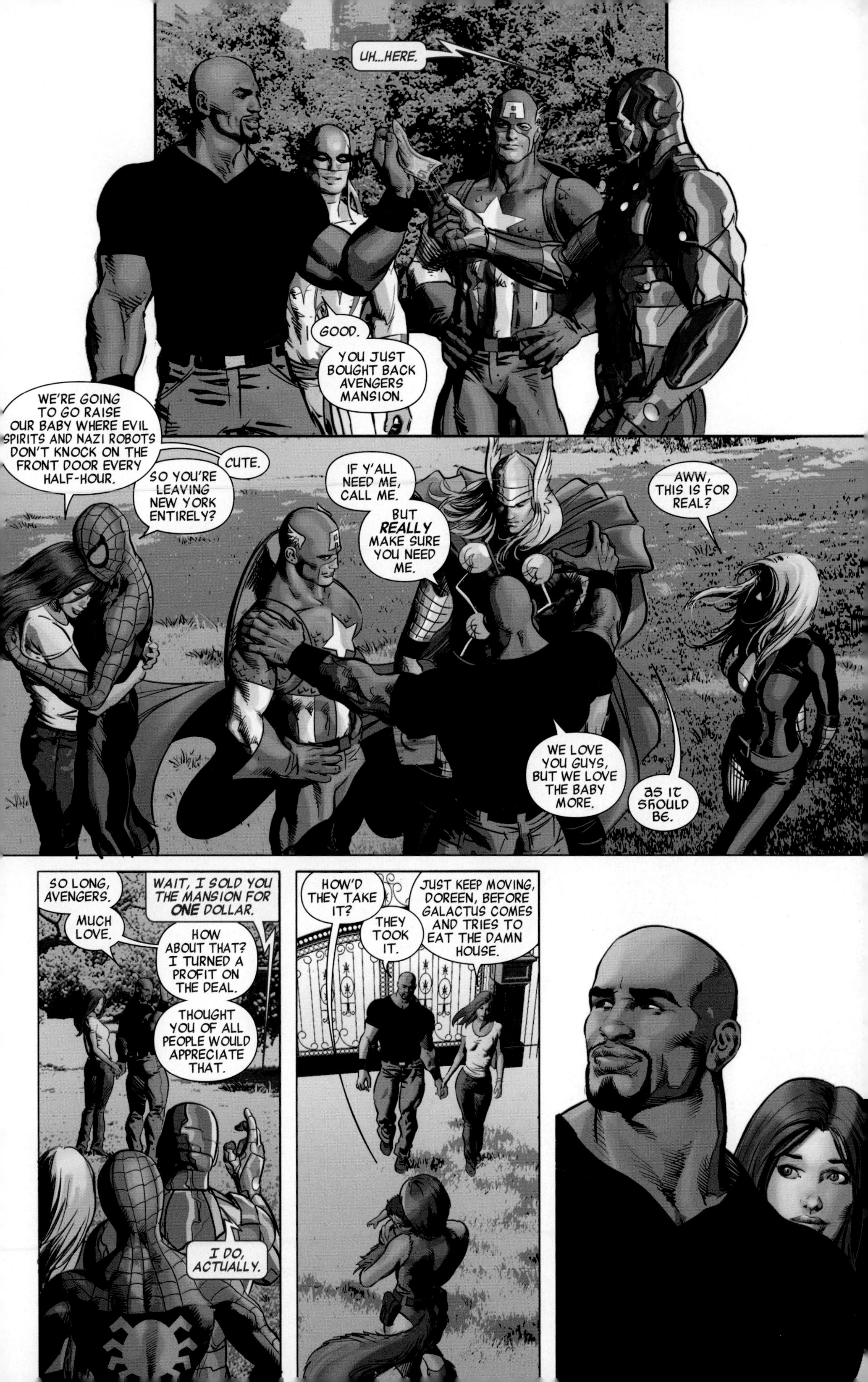
UH...HERE.
GOOD.
YOU JUST BOUGHT BACK AVENGERS MANSION.
WE'RE GOING TO GO RAISE OUR BABY WHERE EVIL SPIRITS AND NAZI ROBOTS DON'T KNOCK ON THE FRONT DOOR EVERY HALF-HOUR.
CUTE.
SO YOU'RE LEAVING NEW YORK ENTIRELY?
IF Y'ALL NEED ME, CALL ME.
BUT REALLY MAKE SURE YOU NEED ME.
AWW, THIS IS FOR REAL?
WE LOVE YOU GUYS, BUT WE LOVE THE BABY MORE.
AS IT SHOULD BE.
SO LONG, AVENGERS.
WAIT, I SOLD YOU THE MANSION FOR ONE DOLLAR.
MUCH LOVE.
HOW ABOUT THAT? I TURNED A PROFIT ON THE DEAL.
THOUGHT YOU OF ALL PEOPLE WOULD APPRECIATE THAT.
I DO, ACTUALLY.
HOW'D THEY TAKE IT?
THEY TOOK IT.
JUST KEEP MOVING, DOREEN, BEFORE GALACTUS COMES AND TRIES TO EAT THE DAMN HOUSE.

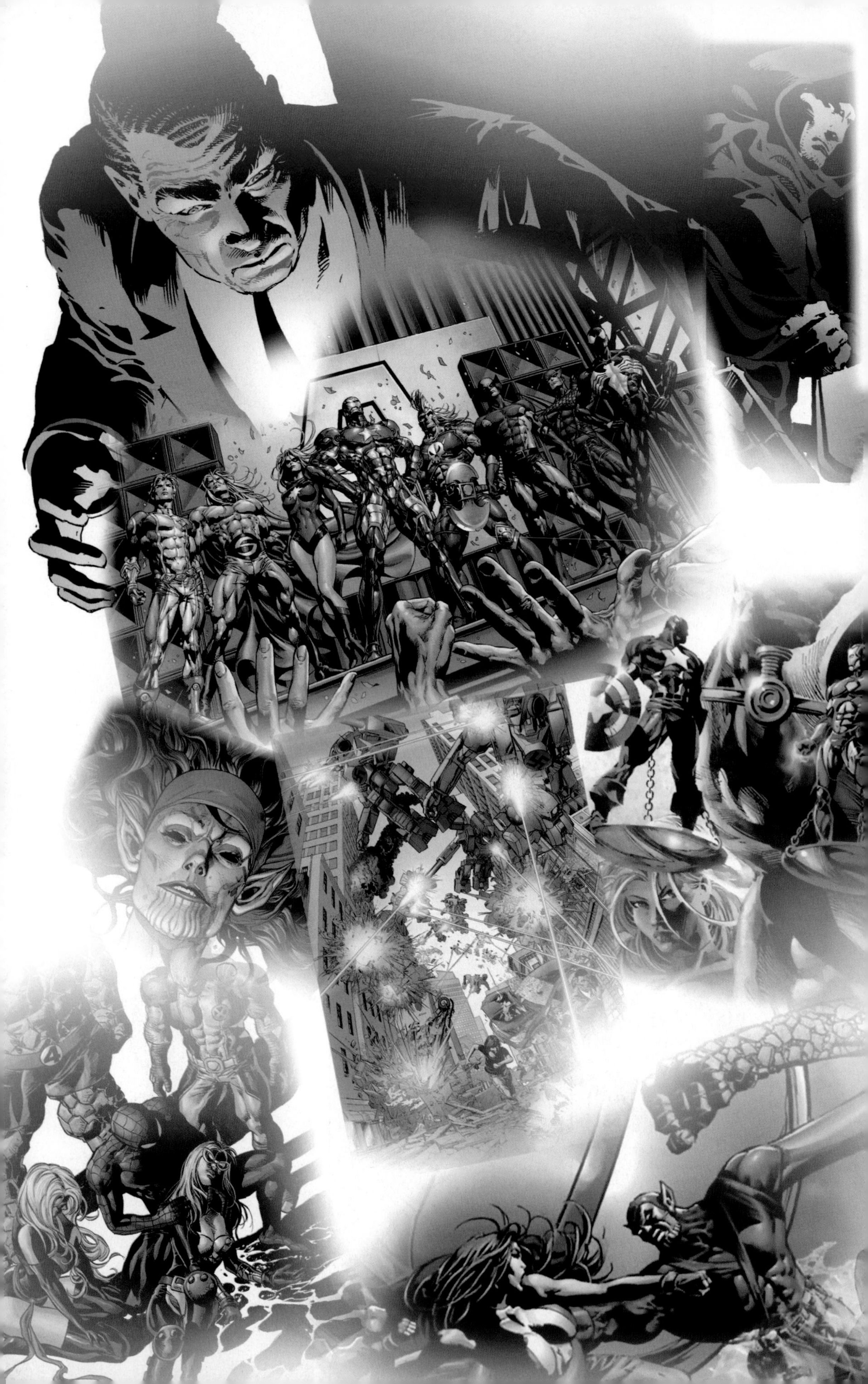

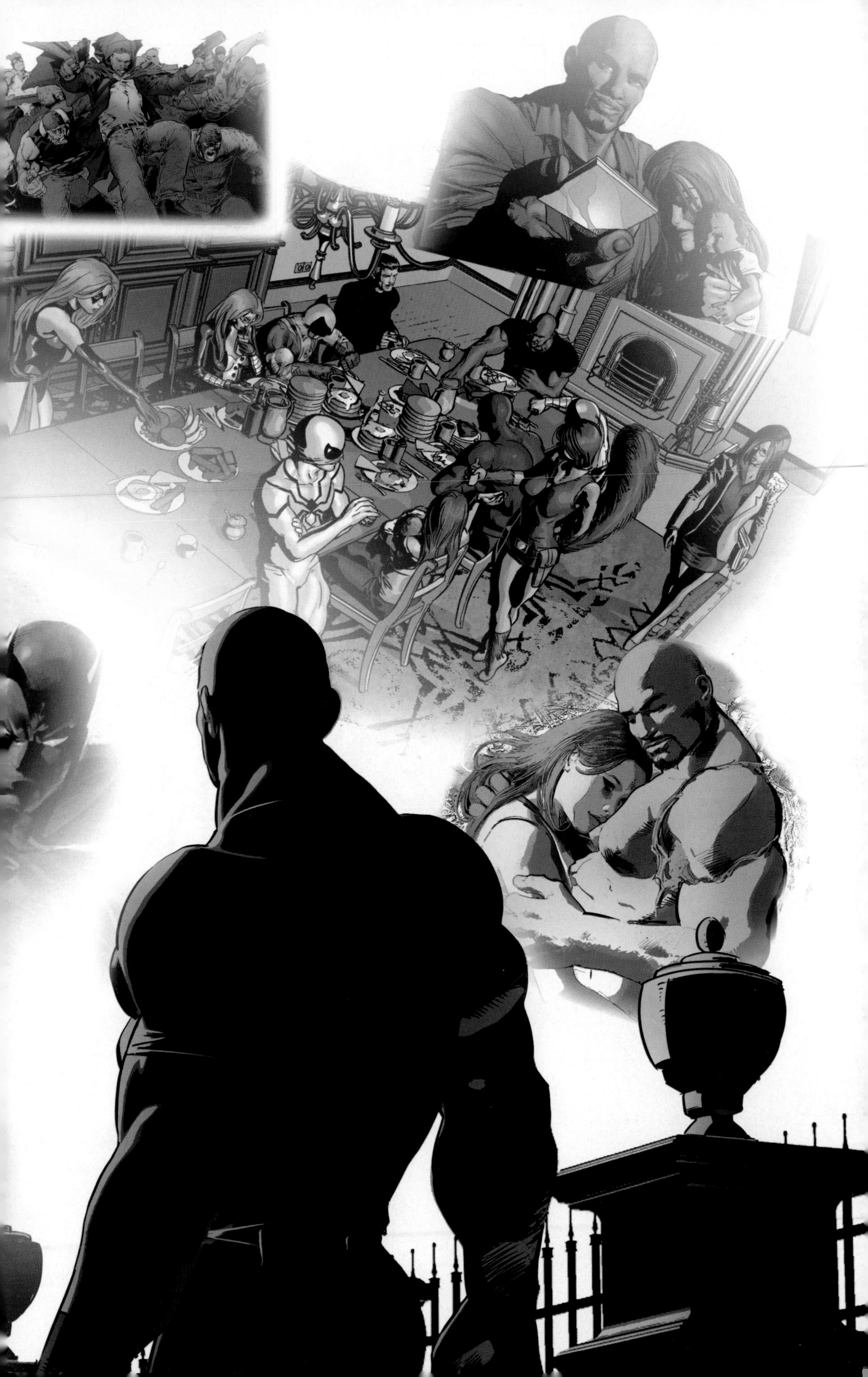

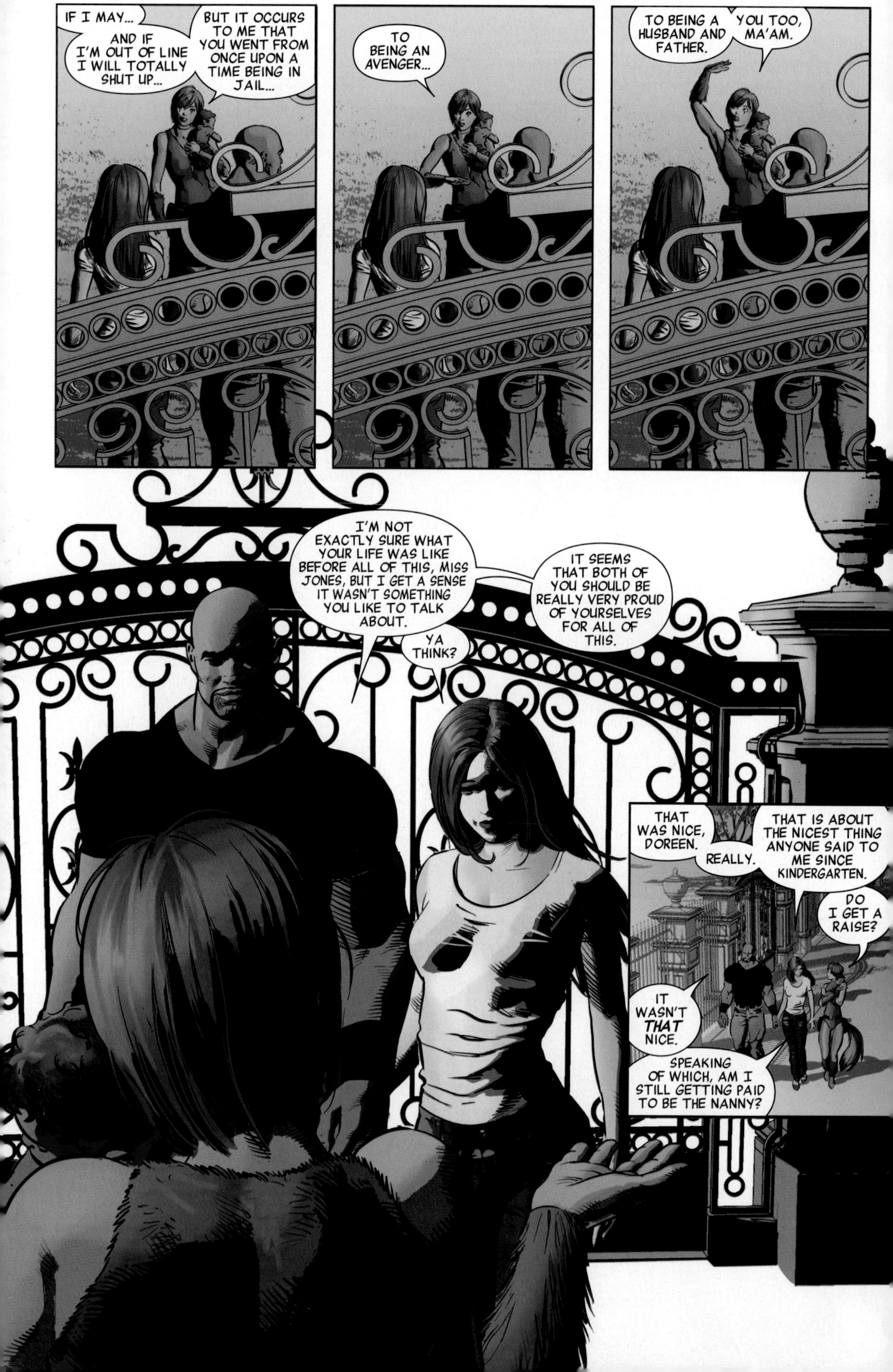
IF I MAY...
AND IF I'M OUT OF LINE I WILL TOTALLY SHUT UP...
BUT IT OCCURS TO ME THAT YOU WENT FROM ONCE UPON A TIME BEING IN JAIL...
TO BEING AN AVENGER...
TO BEING A HUSBAND AND FATHER.
YOU TOO, MA'AM.
I'M NOT EXACTLY SURE WHAT YOUR LIFE WAS LIKE BEFORE ALL OF THIS, MISS JONES, BUT I GET A SENSE IT WASN'T SOMETHING YOU LIKE TO TALK ABOUT.
IT SEEMS THAT BOTH OF YOU SHOULD BE REALLY VERY PROUD OF YOURSELVES FOR ALL OF THIS.
YA THINK?
THAT WAS NICE, DOREEN.
REALLY.
THAT IS ABOUT THE NICEST THING ANYONE SAID TO ME SINCE KINDERGARTEN.
DO I GET A RAISE?
IT WASN'T *THAT* NICE.
SPEAKING OF WHICH, AM I STILL GETTING PAID TO BE THE NANNY?

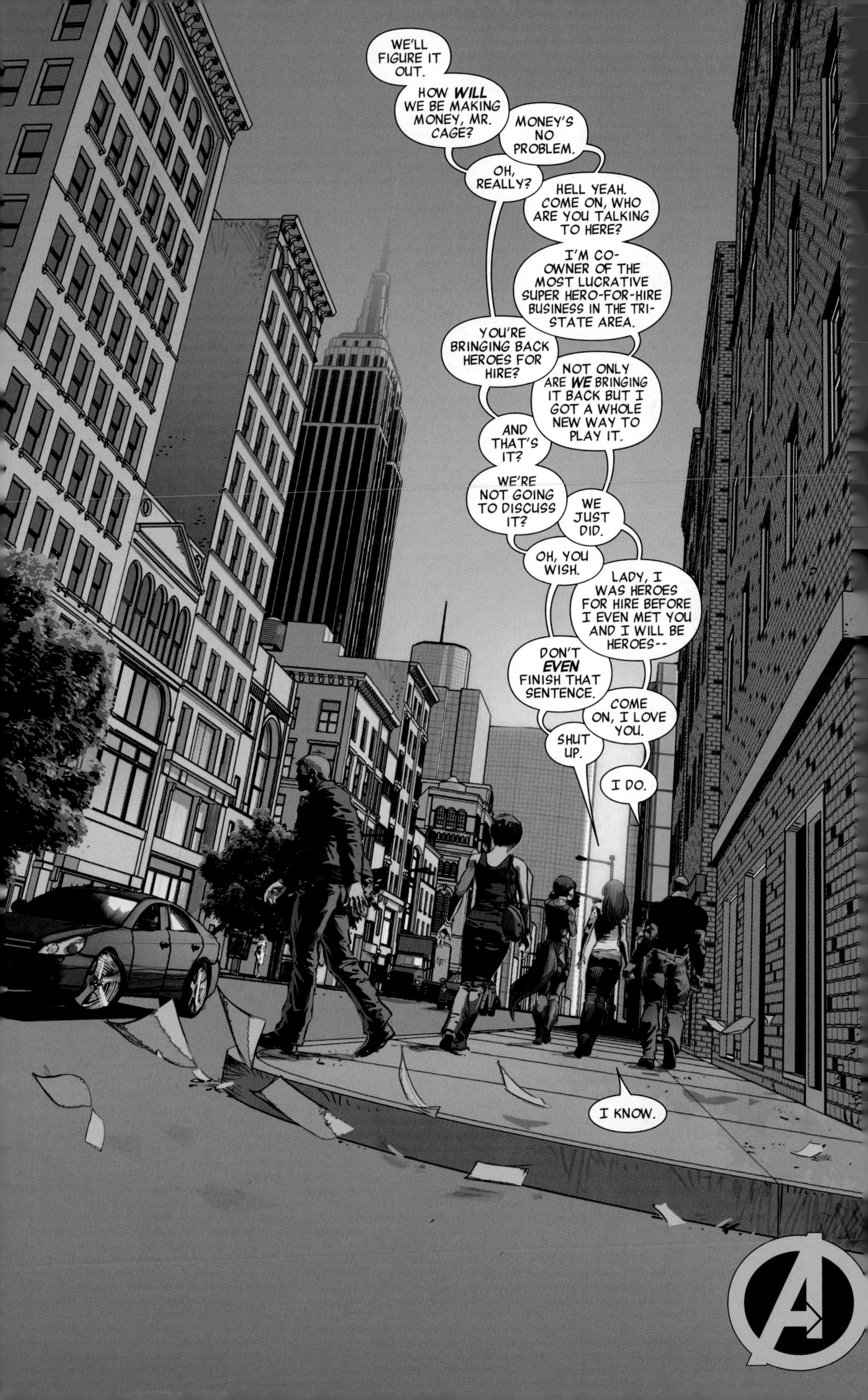

WE'LL FIGURE IT OUT.
HOW WILL WE BE MAKING MONEY, MR. CAGE?
MONEY'S NO PROBLEM.
OH, REALLY?
HELL YEAH. COME ON, WHO ARE YOU TALKING TO HERE?
I'M CO-OWNER OF THE MOST LUCRATIVE SUPER HERO-FOR-HIRE BUSINESS IN THE TRI-STATE AREA.
YOU'RE BRINGING BACK HEROES FOR HIRE?
NOT ONLY ARE WE BRINGING IT BACK BUT I GOT A WHOLE NEW WAY TO PLAY IT.
AND THAT'S IT?
WE'RE NOT GOING TO DISCUSS IT?
WE JUST DID.
OH, YOU WISH.
LADY, I WAS HEROES FOR HIRE BEFORE I EVEN MET YOU AND I WILL BE HEROES--
DON'T EVEN FINISH THAT SENTENCE.
COME ON, I LOVE YOU.
SHUT UP.
I DO.
I KNOW.

BRIAN MICHAEL BENDIS-ERA COVER GALLERY

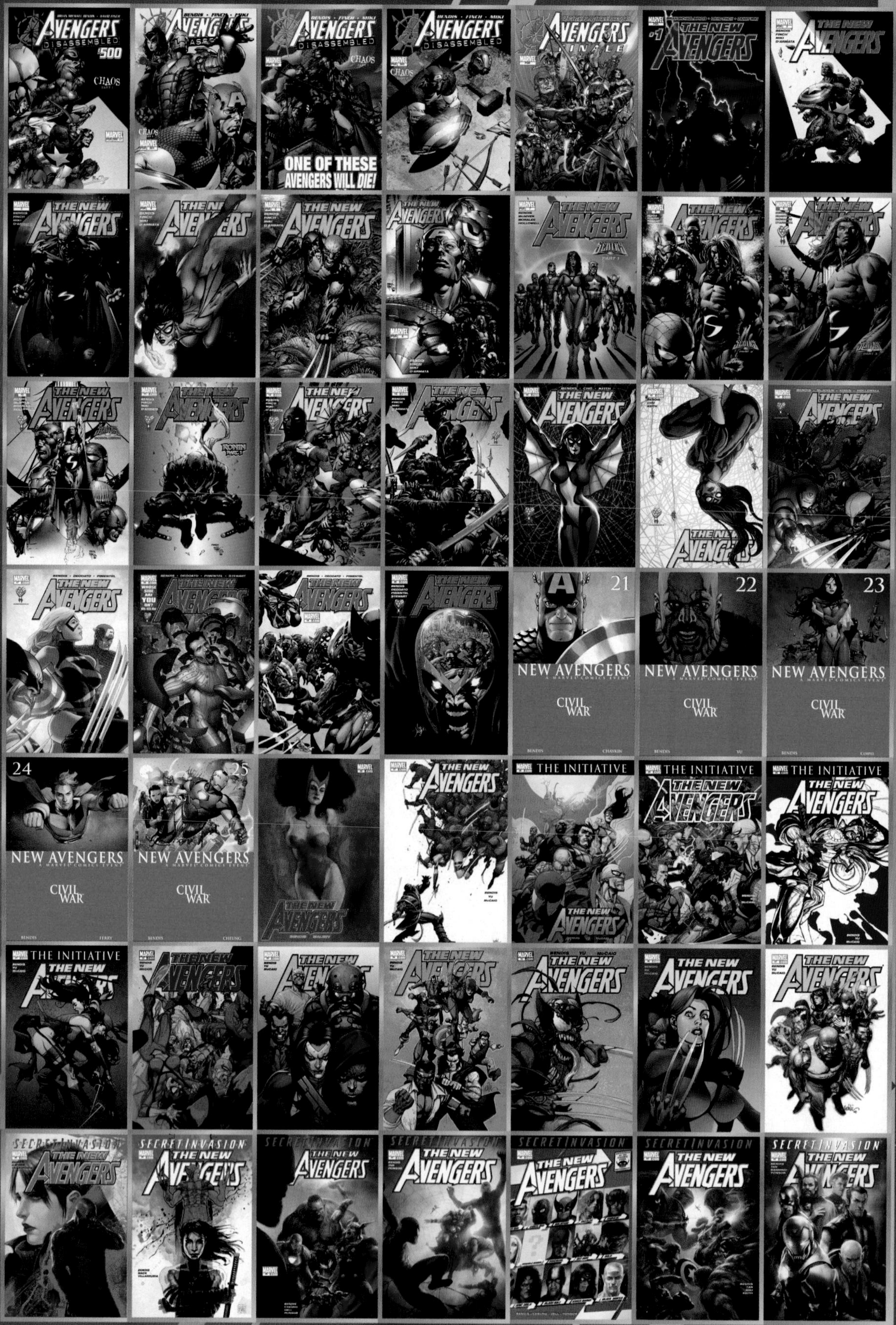
AVENGERS DISASSEMBLED
#500
CHAOS
ONE OF THESE AVENGERS WILL DIE!
AVENGERS FINALE
THE NEW AVENGERS
#1
RONIN
21
22
23
24
25
NEW AVENGERS
A MARVEL COMICS EVENT
CIVIL WAR
THE INITIATIVE
SECRET INVASION

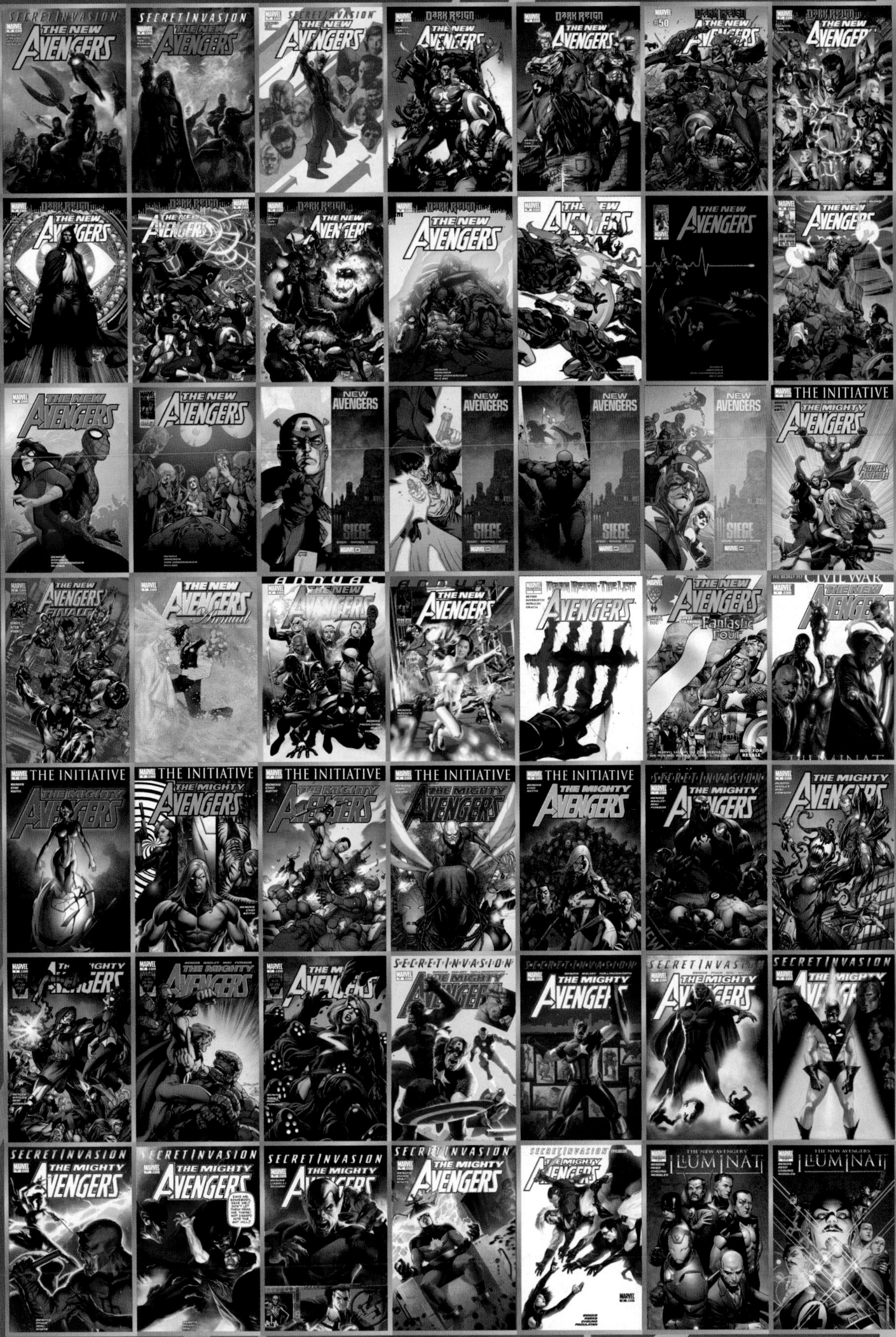

SECRET INVASION THE NEW AVENGERS
SECRET INVASION THE NEW AVENGERS
SECRET INVASION THE NEW AVENGERS
DARK REIGN THE NEW AVENGERS
DARK REIGN THE NEW AVENGERS
#50 DARK REIGN THE NEW AVENGERS
DARK REIGN THE NEW AVENGERS
DARK REIGN THE NEW AVENGERS
DARK REIGN THE NEW AVENGERS
DARK REIGN THE NEW AVENGERS
DARK REIGN THE NEW AVENGERS
THE NEW AVENGERS
THE NEW AVENGERS
THE NEW AVENGERS
THE NEW AVENGERS
THE NEW AVENGERS
NEW AVENGERS SIEGE
NEW AVENGERS SIEGE
NEW AVENGERS SIEGE
NEW AVENGERS SIEGE
THE INITIATIVE THE MIGHTY AVENGERS
AVENGERS ASSEMBLE!
THE NEW AVENGERS FINALE
THE NEW AVENGERS Annual
ANNUAL THE NEW AVENGERS
ANNUAL THE NEW AVENGERS
DARK REIGN: THE LIST AVENGERS
THE NEW AVENGERS Fantastic Four
THE ROAD TO CIVIL WAR THE NEW AVENGERS
THE INITIATIVE THE MIGHTY AVENGERS
THE INITIATIVE THE MIGHTY AVENGERS
THE INITIATIVE THE MIGHTY AVENGERS
THE INITIATIVE THE MIGHTY AVENGERS
THE INITIATIVE THE MIGHTY AVENGERS
SECRET INVASION THE MIGHTY AVENGERS
THE MIGHTY AVENGERS
THE MIGHTY AVENGERS
THE MIGHTY AVENGERS
THE MIGHTY AVENGERS
SECRET INVASION THE MIGHTY AVENGERS
SECRET INVASION THE MIGHTY AVENGERS
SECRET INVASION THE MIGHTY AVENGERS
SECRET INVASION THE MIGHTY AVENGERS
SECRET INVASION THE MIGHTY AVENGERS
SECRET INVASION THE MIGHTY AVENGERS
SECRET INVASION THE MIGHTY AVENGERS
SECRET INVASION THE MIGHTY AVENGERS
SECRET INVASION EPILOGUE THE MIGHTY AVENGERS
THE NEW AVENGERS ILLUMINATI
THE NEW AVENGERS ILLUMINATI

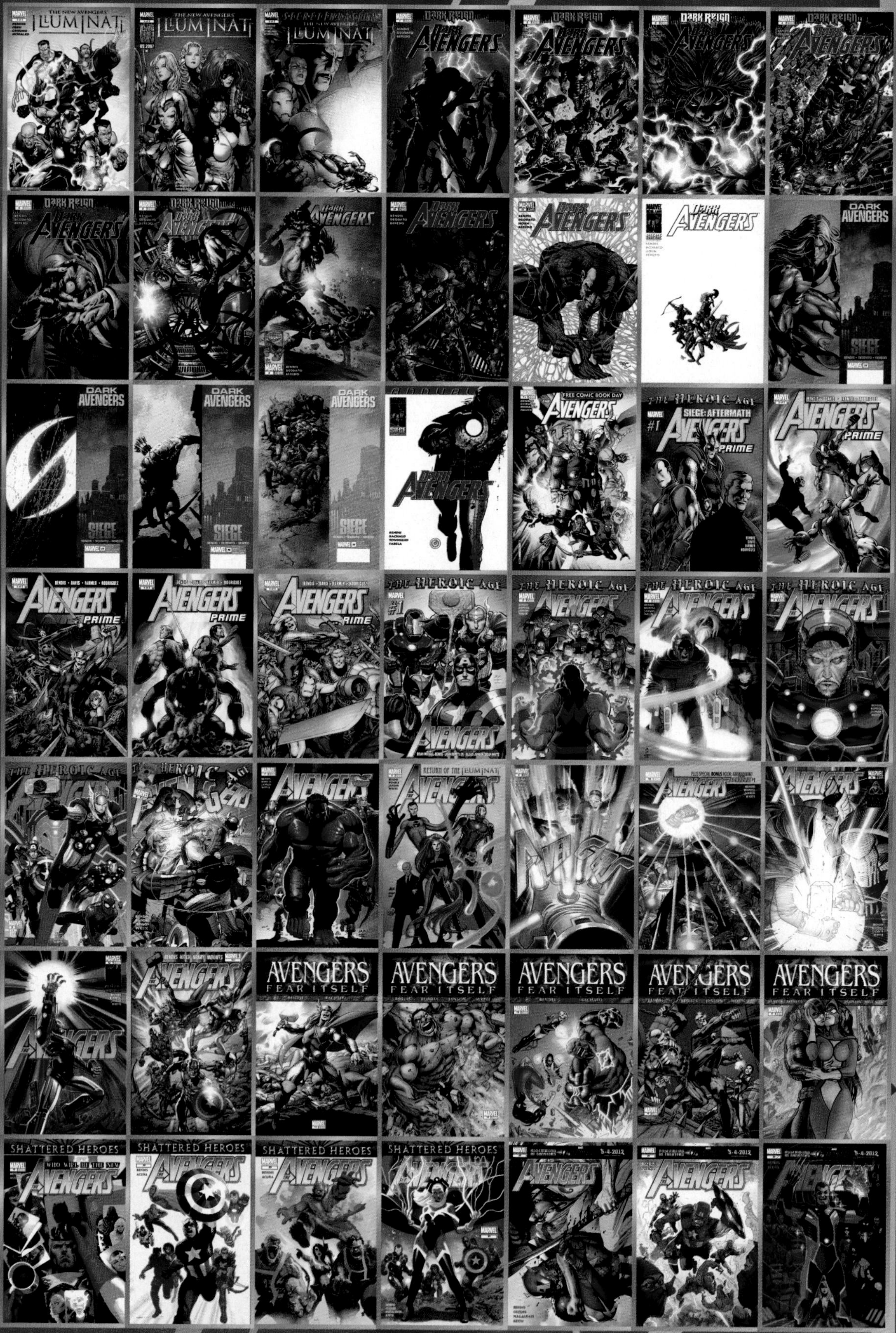
THE NEW AVENGERS
ILLUMINATI
ILLUMINATI
SECRET INVASION
THE NEW AVENGERS
ILLUMINATI
DARK REIGN
DARK AVENGERS
DARK REIGN
DARK AVENGERS
DARK REIGN
DARK AVENGERS
DARK REIGN
DARK AVENGERS
DARK REIGN
DARK AVENGERS
DARK REIGN
DARK AVENGERS
DARK AVENGERS
DARK AVENGERS
DARK AVENGERS
DARK AVENGERS
DARK AVENGERS
SIEGE
DARK AVENGERS
SIEGE
DARK AVENGERS
SIEGE
DARK AVENGERS
SIEGE
ANNUAL
DARK AVENGERS
FREE COMIC BOOK DAY
AVENGERS
THE HEROIC AGE
SIEGE: AFTERMATH
#1
AVENGERS
PRIME
AVENGERS
PRIME
AVENGERS
PRIME
AVENGERS
PRIME
AVENGERS
PRIME
THE HEROIC AGE
#1
AVENGERS
THE HEROIC AGE
AVENGERS
THE HEROIC AGE
AVENGERS
THE HEROIC AGE
AVENGERS
THE HEROIC AGE
AVENGERS
THE HEROIC AGE
AVENGERS
AVENGERS
RETURN OF THE ILLUMINATI
AVENGERS
AVENGERS
AVENGERS
AVENGERS
AVENGERS
AVENGERS
AVENGERS
FEAR ITSELF
AVENGERS
FEAR ITSELF
AVENGERS
FEAR ITSELF
AVENGERS
FEAR ITSELF
AVENGERS
FEAR ITSELF
SHATTERED HEROES
WHO WILL BE THE NEW
AVENGERS
SHATTERED HEROES
AVENGERS
SHATTERED HEROES
AVENGERS
SHATTERED HEROES
AVENGERS
5-4-2012
AVENGERS
5-4-2012
AVENGERS
5-4-2012
AVENGERS

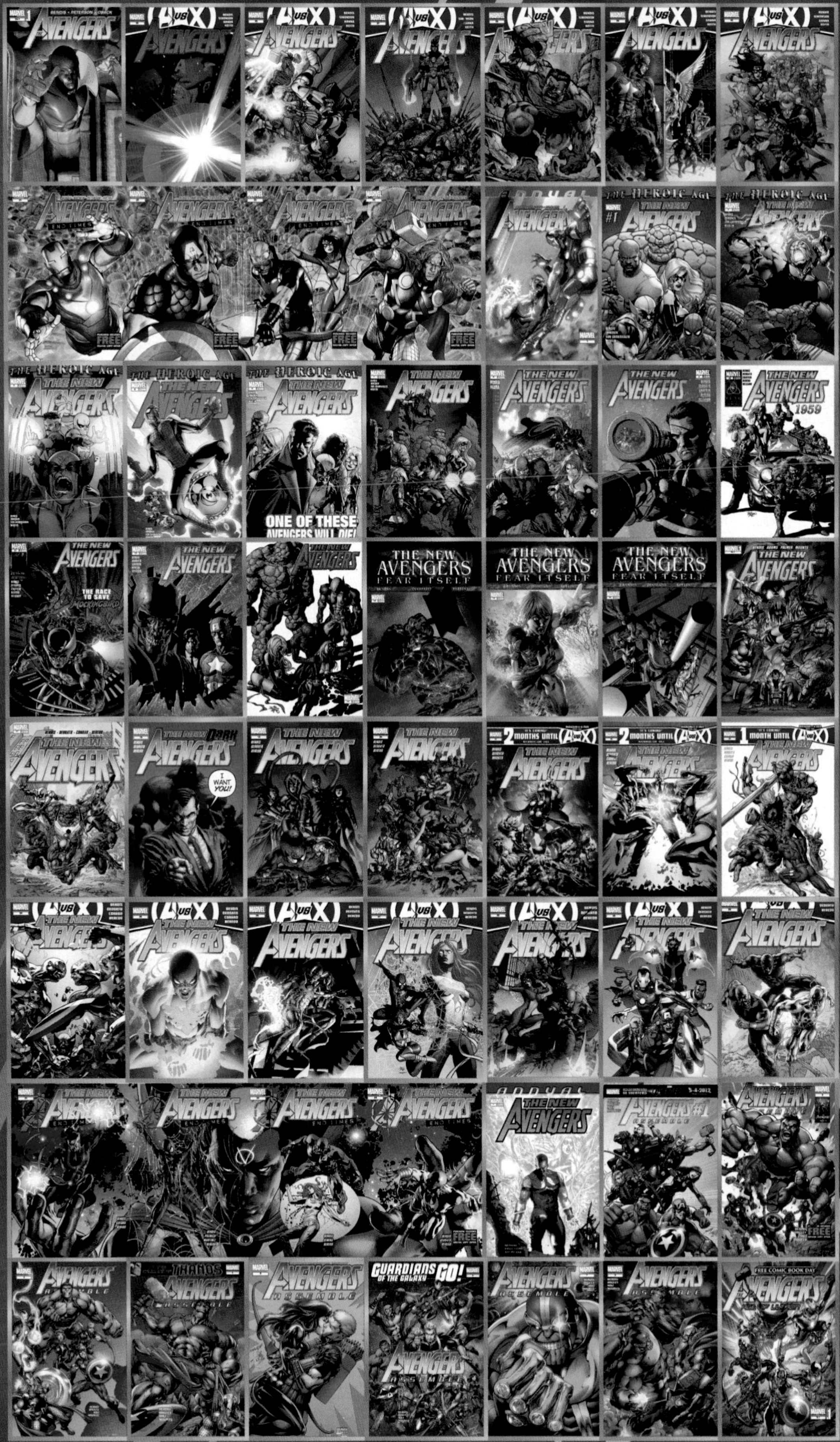

AVENGERS
THE HEROIC AGE
THE NEW AVENGERS
ONE OF THESE AVENGERS WILL DIE!
1959
THE RACE TO SAVE MOCKINGBIRD
THE NEW AVENGERS FEAR ITSELF
I WANT YOU!
2 MONTHS UNTIL
1 MONTH UNTIL
AVENGERS ASSEMBLE
GUARDIANS OF THE GALAXY GO!
FREE COMIC BOOK DAY

#31-34 COMBINED COVERS BY MIKE DEODATO & RAIN BEREDO

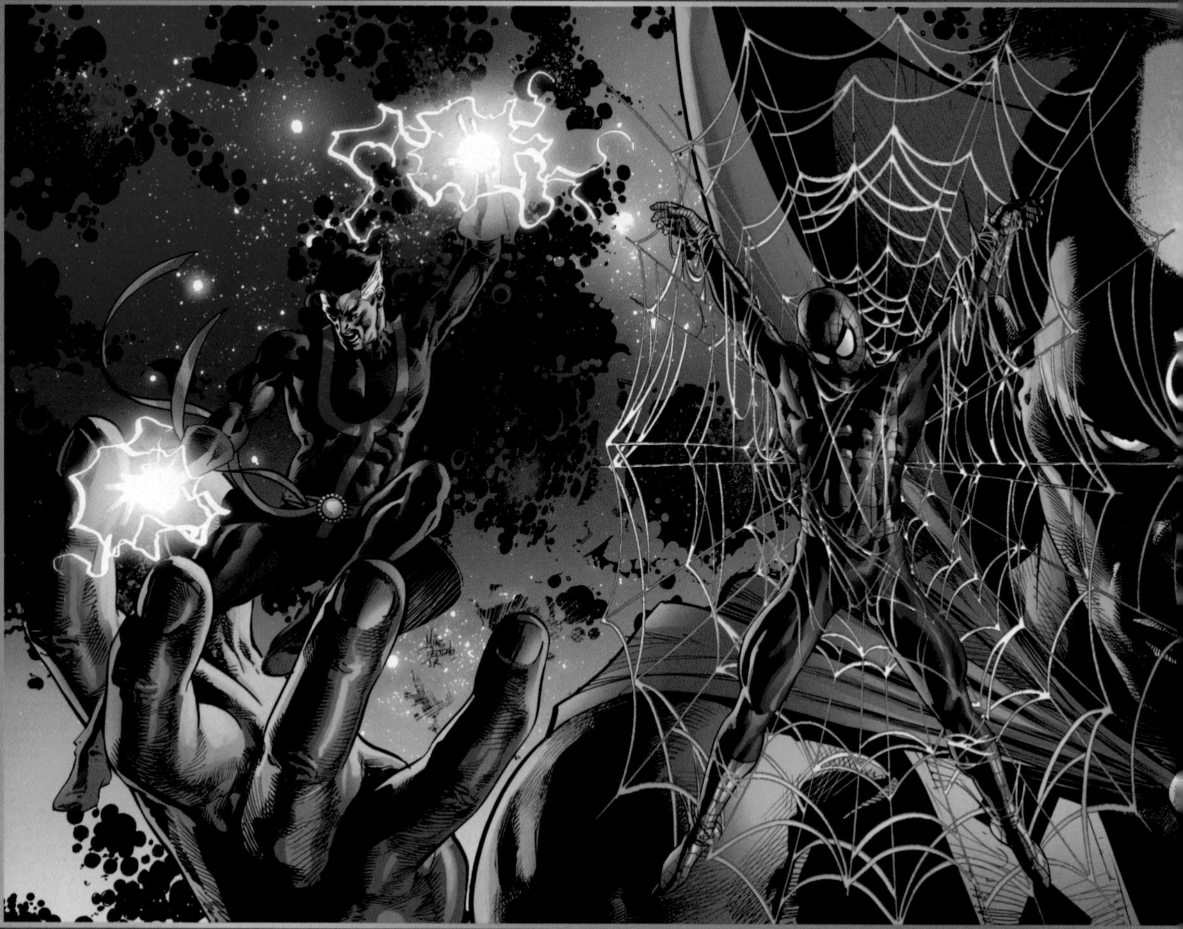

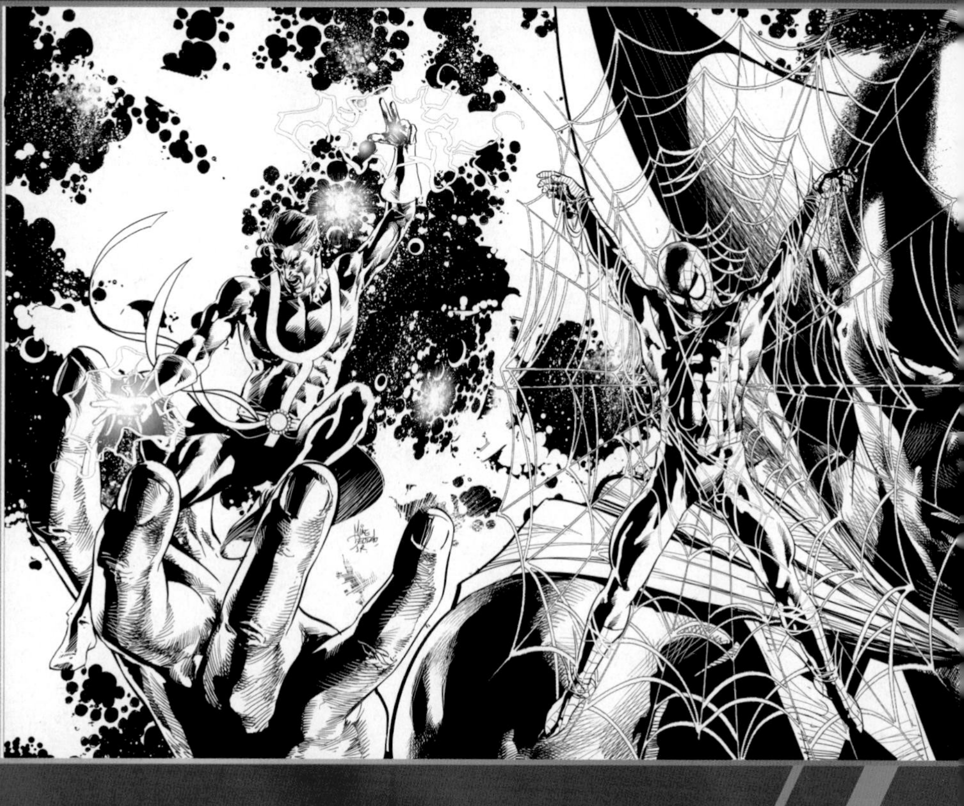

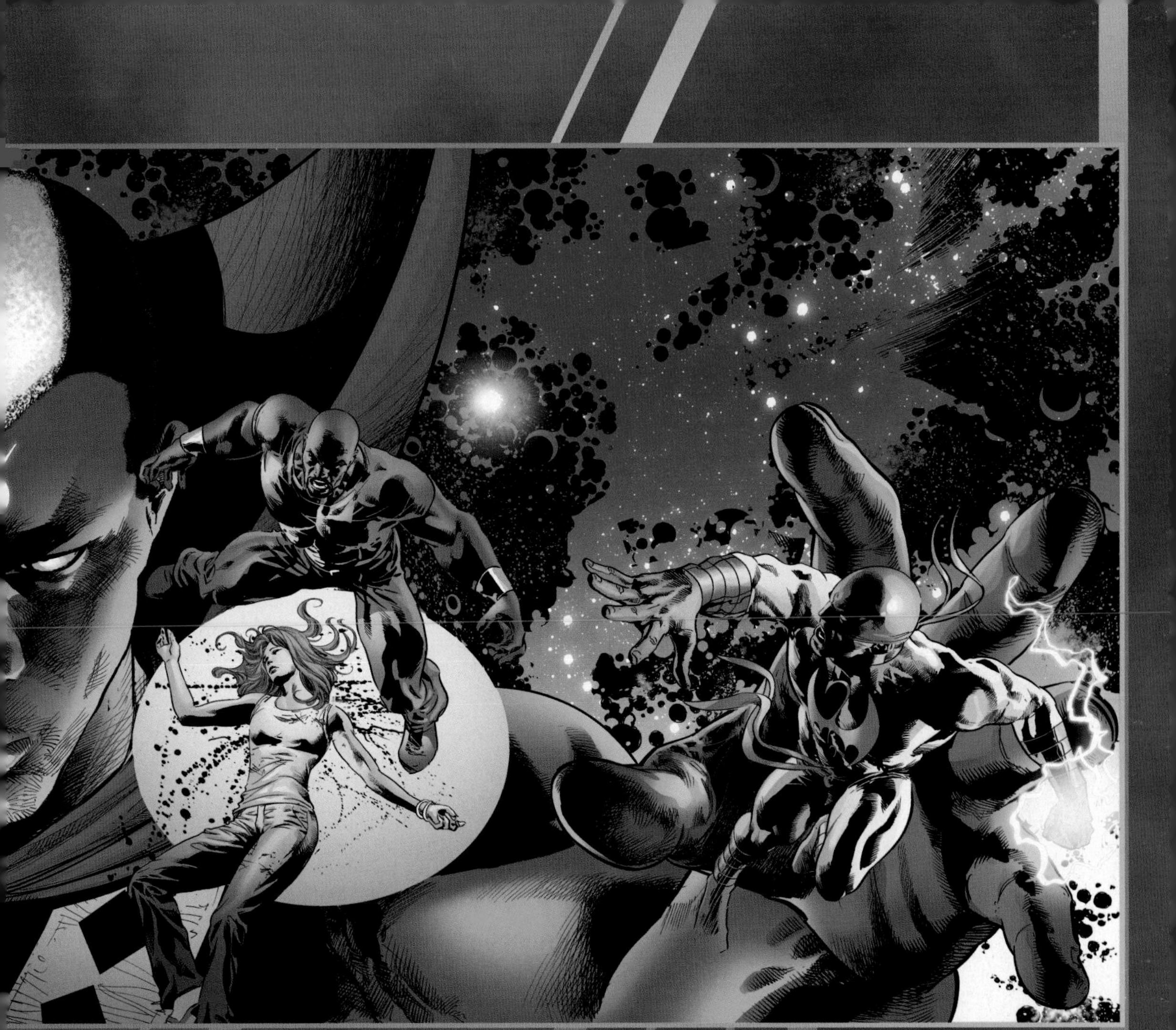

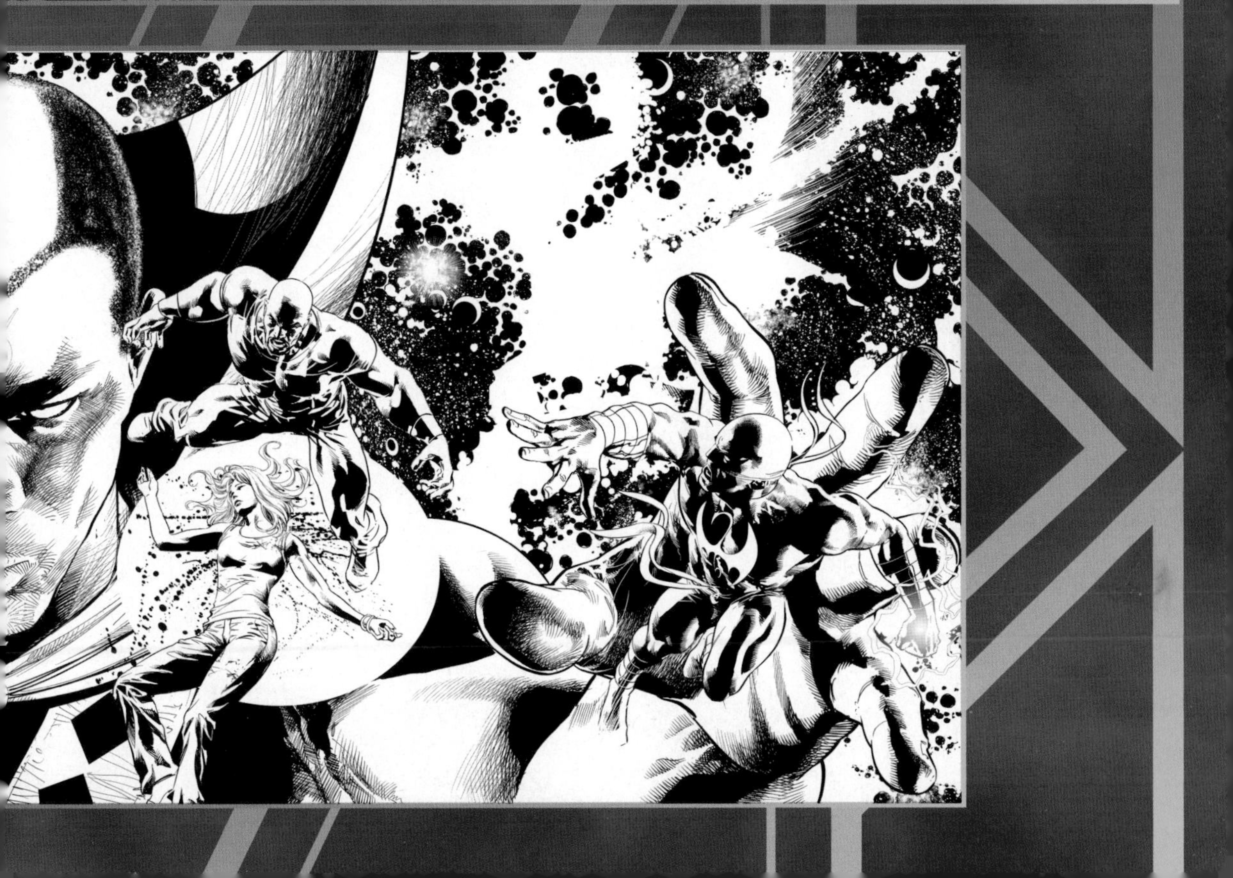

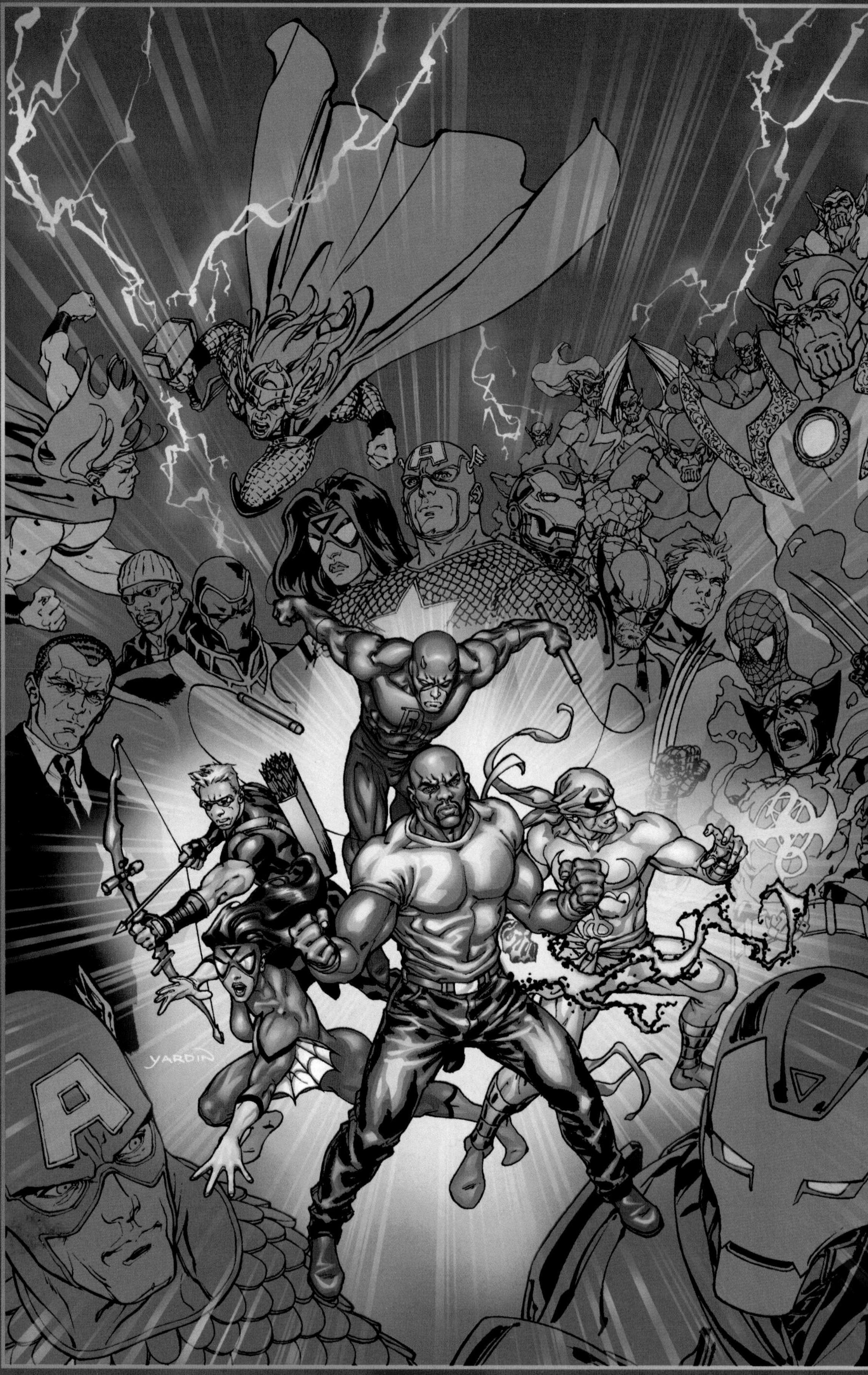
YARDIN

#34 FINALE VARIANT
BY DAVID YARDIN

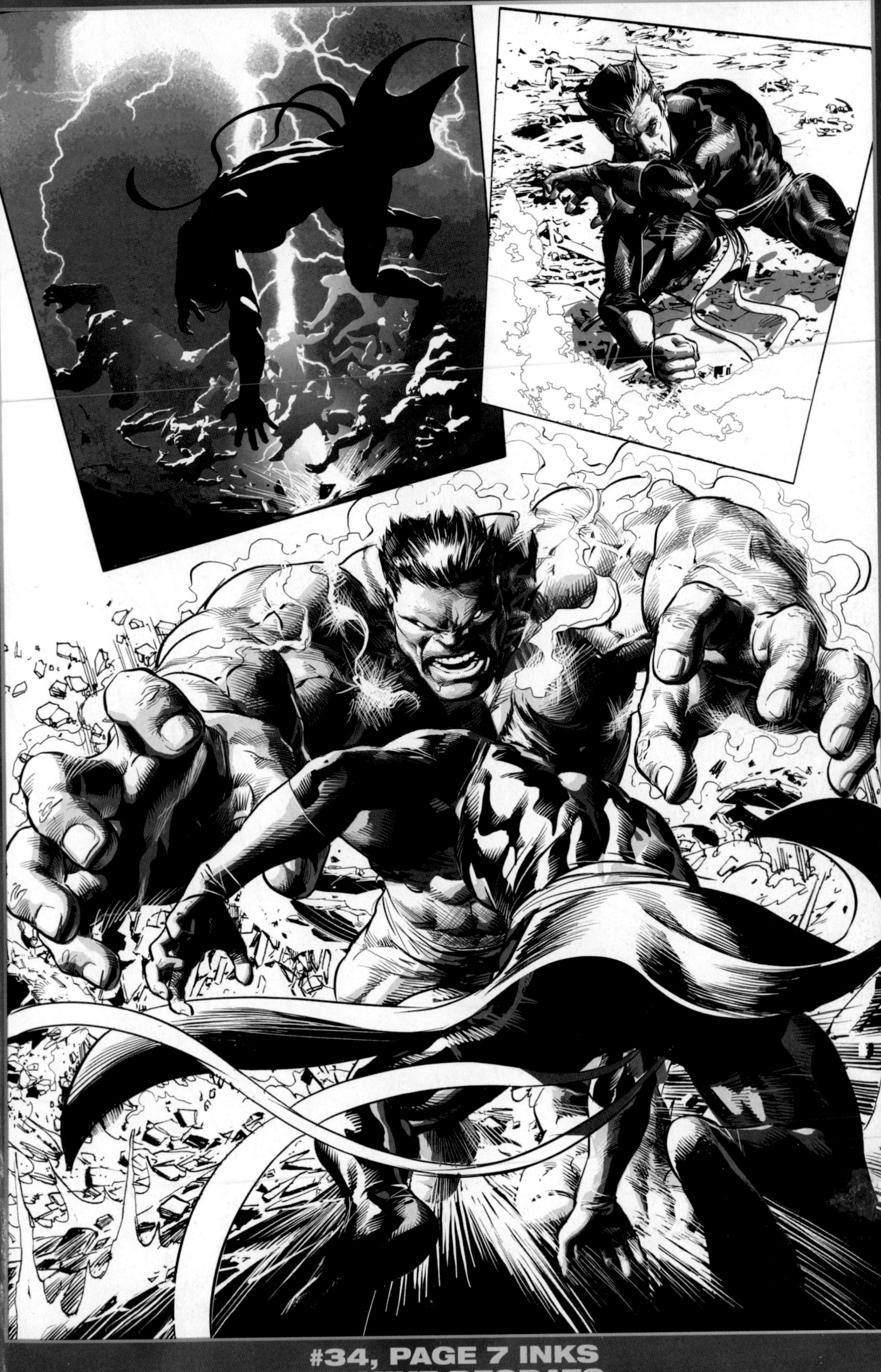

#34, PAGE 7 INKS
BY MIKE DEODATO

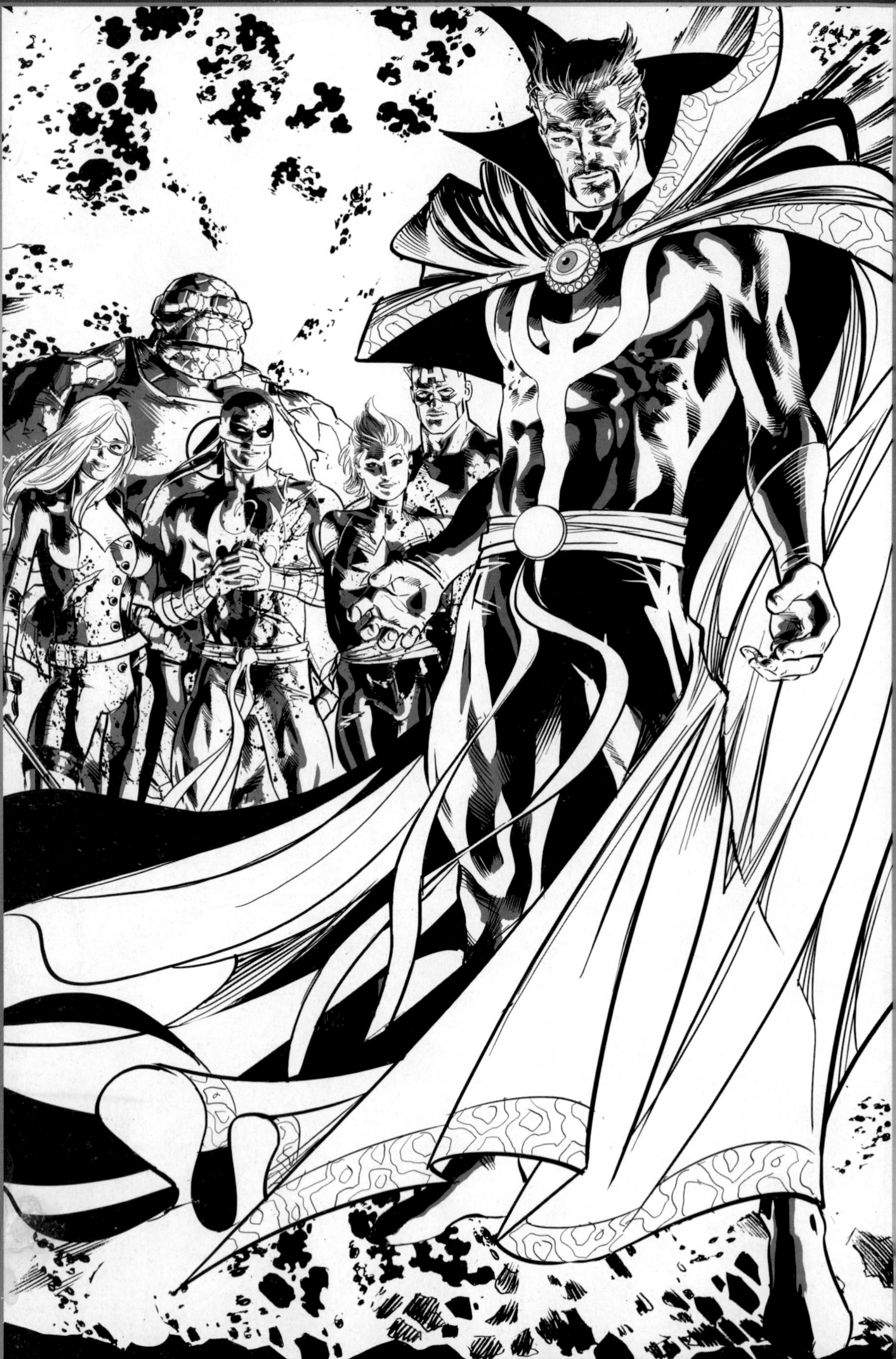

#34, PAGE 24 INKS
BY MIKE DEODATO